YOUR SEXUAL HEALTH

by Dr Jenny McCloskey
edited by Dr Barbara M Seagle

illustrations by Dr Stephen Fenner

HALO BOOKS

All practical care has been taken in the writing of this book, to make it as accurate and up-to-date as possible. The author, Dr. McCloskey, is a respected AIDS and STD clinician. Sections of the book have been extensively verified by other specialists. However, no amount of work and expertise can yet produce a guide to STDs which can be guaranteed to be totally accurate. There is too much which simply isn't known, or is still subject to some informed guesswork. Research is proceeding apace, and theories and treatments will change. **You are advised to check with your doctor.**

Suggestions for improvements to this book in future editions are very welcome. It is intended to be a practical, working guide which can grow through user input. Please write to the Publisher, at the address below. If we use your suggestions we'll send you a copy of that edition free.

Library of Congress Cataloging-in-Publication Data

McCloskey, Jenny
        Your sexual health / Jenny McCloskey
        336p.   cm.
    Summary: Discusses various kinds of sexually transmitted diseases, their symptoms, methods of transmission, and ways of guarding against them.
        ISBN 1-879904-08-X : $15.95
        1. Hygiene, Sexual–Juvenile literature. 2. Sexually transmitted diseases–Prevention–Juvenile literature. [1. Sexually transmitted diseases.] I. Title.
RA788.M34   1993
613.9'51–dc20

                      92-35228
                        CIP
                          AC

Original edition: Elephas Books, Australia, 1992
American edition: Halo Books, 1993
Copyright 1992 Jenny McCloskey Illustrations © Elephas Books

Halo Books
P.O. Box 2529
San Francisco, CA 94126
Fax: (415) 434-3441

Sexually transmittable disease, STD. Just the name strikes fear, the same deep seated fear earlier generations reserved for bubonic plague and leprosy. One day medical breakthroughs will reduce the threat of STDs to a nasty memory, but that day is not going to be in this century. The range of known STDs and the numbers of people afflicted by them is increasing, not decreasing.

If you were born sometime in the last 35 years, the chances are high that at least once in your life you will suffer from some genital related disease which could be sexually transmitted. Some STDs do not even require that you be sexually active.

Your best defence is knowledge: knowledge of the STDs and their transmission, and most importantly knowledge of what you can do to reduce the risks and take control of your own sexual health.

This book offers knowledge. It is a practical, easily understood, up-to-date and very comprehensive guide to sexually transmittable diseases. Some chapters, like *Your Sexual Health and Attitude, Keeping Yourself Safe* and *Building Good Health* are designed to be read right through. Some chapters may be of particular interest to you, and you will want to read all of them. Others you might skim over the detail, knowing you can return to it should you ever need to understand more about a particular STD.

Every home should have a copy — especially every home with a teenager.

This book is dedicated to the late Dr Jack Schneider, one of my fathers in medicine, who believed in me more than I did. Thank-you, Jack, for your trust and for opening for me the doors to a career in genito-urinary medicine.

Jenny

ACKNOWLEDGEMENTS

A special thank-you is due to the following colleagues who helped me with the preparation of this book: Jacqueline Anstead, Dr David Blackledge, Dr Donald Clarke, Dr Mick Connaughton, Dr Derek Evans, Dr Louise Farrell, Dr Anne Freiberg, Dr Martyn French, Dr Ian Hammond, Dr Alex Henderson, Professor Dick Joske, Dr Gwen Leavesley, Dr Jan Machin, Dr Brian McGregor, Dr Ken Mitchell, Dr Keith Ott, Dr Ellis Pixley, Dr Kevin Sesnan, Dr Allan Shafer, Dr David Smith, Dr Margaret Smith, Dr Judith Straton, Dr Martin Stuckey, and Dr Charles Watson all in Perth; Dr John Carnie and Dr Ian Denham in Melbourne; Dr Ross Philpott and Dr Gavin Hart in Adelaide; Dr David Plummer in Gosford, NSW; Dr Basil Donovan in Sydney; Dr Gordon White in Canberra; and Associate Professor Geo von Krogh in Sweden. An extra special thank-you goes to Dr Morris Gollow (Perth) and Dr David Bradford (Melbourne) for their immense help. It was greatly appreciated. In addition I would like to thank my friends Julie Travis, Laila Mills, Merva Andrews and my psychologist friend Helen Costello, for their support and positive encouragement. A special thank-you also goes to the editor Michael Woodhouse for his constructive advice and help.

CONTENTS

Chapter 3
Normal Anatomy & STD Examinations 56

Section Three

Chapter 8

FOREWORD

Sans meno in sans corporis
(A healthy mind in a healthy body)

We live in an age of technological marvels, and nowhere is this more apparent than in medicine. Organ transplants, micro-surgery, in-vitro fertilization — it seems there is nothing mankind cannot do, if we put our minds to it. Ultimately that may be true, but for the present there remain a good number of medical problems which cannot be easily remedied by a visit to the doctor.

There is an epidemic of sexually transmittable diseases (STDs) sweeping our planet, aided by social disruption, ethical changes and rapid transport. For many of these diseases there is good treatment, but for some the prospects include life-long infection, serious illness and even death.

If the doctors can't make it right, what are you to do? Put your head in the sand and abandon control of your body to the blows of chance?

Fortunately you can make a difference to your chances of catching an STD. The attitudes and behaviors you choose will largely determine the risks to your health. You can take responsibility for your own sexual health, if you care enough about yourself, and if you know how. That is what this book is about.

Here we learn of the diseases that have plagued mankind since Biblical times and of the many new diseases that have become world wide pandemics. We learn what these diseases are and what they can do, how they are spread and how to recognise them from the signs and symptoms they present. In it is detailed the curative therapy available for all except the viral diseases, and even the supportive and suppressive treatment for these.

Most importantly, we learn what each of us can do to reduce the risks of catching an STD. Throughout this book behavioral factors are constantly stressed as instigators of the problems, and that we are all ultimately responsible for our personal behavior. This emphasis culminates in the final chapter with Dr McCloskey's holistic approach to a healthy lifestyle.

Who is at risk of catching a genital disease? Experience suggests people are most likely to catch a sexual disease when they are in the age range 15 to 30. The bottom end of this age range is probably much lower than parents would like to think, but the facts are that many students are sexually active before they leave school. And just one sexual contact, even if it does not involve intercourse, can be enough to pass on a life threatening STD.

The high incidence of sexual disease amongst teenagers indicates that lack of knowledge is a major factor in becoming infected. With better information, many teenagers could have avoided a lot of pain, trauma and sometimes tragedy.

The information contained in this book is comprehensive and detailed. It is presented clearly and simply, in words easily understood by all, especially teenagers.

It is said that 'knowledge is power', the power to make informed decisions. This book provides the knowledge you need so you can make informed decisions about your sexual health, the sexual health of your family and of the community we all must live in.

It will help fill an important gap in the knowledge of both the general public and of health care workers concerning the epidemic of STDs that plagues our modern world. I commend it to all teenagers, parents and medical practitioners who deal with STDs.

I am doubly pleased to be writing this foreword. This is the first book on sexual health (venereology) written by a female physician, and the author, Dr Jenny McCloskey, was a particularly noteworthy student of mine.

Jenny completed her medical degree at the University of Melbourne in 1976, where she shared the Australian Medical Association Prize in Public Health. As a medical registrar at the Sir Charles Gairdner Hospital in Western Australia she gained extensive experience in various medical specialities including hematology and oncology.

She was introduced to me by the late Dr J Schneider, an old friend of mine, to whom this book is dedicated. He recommended her as a doctor interested in pursuing a career in the management of sexually transmittable diseases (STDs). I was then Director of the Venereal Disease Control Branch of the Health Department of Western Australia and thus responsible for the training of the doctors who would manage all aspects of STDs in the future.

After an interview I was pleased to accept Jenny for training. My judgement of her was verified as she went from strength to strength, displaying a bright intelligence and mature understanding of a difficult and demanding medical discipline. Eventually she travelled to England to undertake the postgraduate course in venereology at the University of London, gaining her Diploma of Venereology (London) as the leading student in her class. Finally it was my privilege as President of the Australasian College of Venereologists to install her as an elected fellow of the college (F A C Ven).

Jenny's work has involved travel throughout Western Australia, lecturing and teaching health professionals, community groups and aboriginal communities. She practices in Perth as a Venereologist.

While Jenny's technical knowledge and skills are a matter of record, I think her patients value her most for her empathy, positive encouragement and compassion in what can only be a difficult time for a patient. These qualities shine through in her writing. They give this book a feeling of caring that can be more powerful than any medicine.

Dr M M Gollow
Member of the Order of Australia
Inaugural President and Fellow of the
Australasian College of Venereologists

Preface to the
AMERICAN EDITION

This is a book about power: the power to know about your body and your sexuality, and the power to make responsible decisions about emotional and sexual health for you and your partner.

Decisions about sexuality have become increasingly complex. For young people who may not be ready for a life-long commitment to a sexual partner, issues of safety and health have become crucial to these decisions. Alarming reports about the rising incidence of AIDS and other sexually transmitted diseases fill newspapers and television news hours, but education, which could substitute knowledge for fear, has been comparatively lacking. Power to control the spread of sexually transmitted diseases demands an understanding of disease process. And that understanding, in turn, demands a knowledge of the causes, risk increasing behaviors, symptoms, and available effective treatments for each sexually transmitted infection. That knowledge is what this book offers its readers.

Any book about sex is sure to stimulate moral debate. Debate is the healthy result of increasing knowledge and should be welcomed. However, as Dr. McCloskey says in her Author's Note, this book is not about morality. Nor is it about how to prevent pregnancy. This is a book about how to protect yourself from sexually transmitted diseases. These diseases have affected humankind from earliest history. Kings Henry II and Henry VIII of England, Charles V of France, Frederick the Great of Austria, author Gustave Flaubert, composers Beethoven and Schumann, painter Paul Gaugin, and explorer Captain James Cook were all affected by sexually transmitted disease. The cause of their illnesses was, in large part, ignorance. And ignorance continues to promote the spread of these infections today.

It has been a pleasure for me to review and edit Dr McCloskey's thorough and readable book for an American audience. It is my hope that it will find a place in health and sexuality courses in

American schools as well as in personal libraries. I have tried to Americanize the text and update or revise information which may differ between Australia and the United States.

In her chapter on HIV, the virus that causes AIDS, Dr. McCloskey states: "There is only one person who can effectively take responsibility for your sexual health and that is you. No-one else can look after your body for you. You were born with it, it's yours for life, so look after it." I share Dr. McCloskey's faith in the power of knowledge to promote sexual health and responsible sexual decision making.

Barbara M. Seagle, M.D.
Brookline, 1993

Barbara M. Seagle, M.D., cares for children from birth through young adulthood in her pediatric practice in Brookline, Massachusetts. She received her medical degree cum laude from Boston University School of Medicine and completed her internship and residency in Pediatrics at The Children's Hospital in Boston, Massachusetts. She actively enjoys teaching medical students and residents and is a Clinical Instructor in Pediatrics at Harvard Medical School.

Author's Note
SEX AND YOU

For some people the act of sex is sacred, a blessing conferred by God as part of the sacrament of marriage. For others, it is a source of physical pleasure to be indulged in at whim, with whoever is available. For some people, sex means vaginal penetration of one woman by one man, lying face to face. For others it can mean a variety of activities and positions, with people not necessarily of the opposite sex, and not necessarily one at a time. Sex can be a vital part of a deep and richly rewarding emotional relationship; it can also be a casual act of physical gratification.

What we do with our bodies sexually is a question of morality. It's an important question, one that everyone has to make decisions on, even if they decide by default. I hope that this book will stimulate people to think about moral questions, to make choices and control their own moral and sexual lives.

This book however is not about morality, it's about sex. My aim is to provide the information people need to make their own decisions and to protect themselves as far as possible from sexual disease. I have therefore covered all types of sexual activities. I have presented the facts as simply and clearly as possible, without moral judgement. I have argued strongly that self respect is vital to sexual health, but I consider this a fact of disease control, independent of its moral connotations.

Sexual behavior cannot be divorced from moral judgements, but the facts about sexual disease can be. That is what I have tried to do.

I have taken this approach because much of what has been said and written about sexual disease, for the general reader, has been biased by particular moral viewpoints it is intended to serve. Some people have overplayed the dangers, trying to use fear as an added coercion to their viewpoint. Others have tried to make light of the risks, in order to dispel criticism.

Regardless of the moral standpoint argued from, I believe that distortion of the facts can only lead people to mistaken judgements. People have a right to make their own decisions. They have a right to sound information, to help them make those decisions. Presenting that information is my task.

If you are a parent or teacher using this book as an educational tool, then you will be aware that information needs to be accompanied by a moral framework from which it can be analysed and made sense of. Providing that framework is your task, and I have tried not to interfere with it.

Jenny McCloskey

Section One

Sex, Attitude,

Risk and You

1

YOUR SEXUAL HEALTH & ATTITUDE

> Our self image is the blueprint which determines exactly how we will behave, who we will mix with, what we will try and what we will avoid; our every thought and every action stem from the way we see ourselves.
>
> Andrew Matthews, *Being Happy*, 1988

Your sexual health and attitude are determined by multiple influences — your parents, friends, teachers and your environment and culture — but the most important influence is you.

Most of the time we do not question the way we behave. Our actions reflect habits of thought and established beliefs about ourselves and others. We should critically examine our thoughts and behaviors. Sometimes we will need to adapt our beliefs to new realities. The capacity for positive change is vital to success in life.

A Bill of Human Rights

I believe every person has the right to:

1. Respect
2. Honesty
3. Express your own feelings
4. Be listened to
5. Be taken seriously
6. Be different
7. Make mistakes
8. Be perfect
9. Be detached
10. Be loved
11. Love yourself

Author Stuart Wilde proclaimed the first nine of t
rights at a talk I attended in 1990. The last two (the
loved and the right to love yourself) I have added.

I believe the key to sexual health (and to happiness in
the last one: the right to love yourself. Only through lea
love yourself you will find happiness, peace and bliss. I
talking here about sexual love but about agape (pronoun c
garp-ee). Agape is probably best defined as a tremendous lo
life and is akin to altruistic love or having regard for the wellb
of others.

What does loving yourself mean when our society says we shou
do things for others? Loving yourself is a feeling of being centre
and calm within. When we can find this within ourselves we can
help others to be like this too. We bring love in abundance to our
lives.

To learn to do this you need to be able to discipline yourself.
You need to be able to say, 'No'. You need the discipline of being
able to make yourself do things that are good for you and not do
the things that are bad for you. Discipline is not a really popular
concept in our self-indulgent society. Often we find it very difficult
to say 'No' to things we know are bad for us. We say 'just this
one more time' and think it will not make any difference. But it
does. Things add up little by little. Instead we might learn that
saying 'No' just one more time strengthens our character, helps us
to respect ourselves, and is the path to making our lives just that
little bit happier.

Respect yourself and assert your rights

People often think that if they say 'No' it means they don't like
or love the person who is asking. How wrong this is! Responsible
parents often say 'No' to their loved children. They will say 'No'
when the child wants to play on the road or with a knife, precisely
because they love their child. It is the same in adult life except
we've forgotten that saying 'No', because we care about ourselves
and the other person, can be positive.

Learn to be assertive. In our society we think that to be assertive
is to be aggressive. It is not. It is just that you respect yourself,
and the more you learn to respect yourself the more you will learn
to respect others. You have a right to say, 'I want . . .' and 'I
insist . . . ' and to be heard by your partner. If your partner does

not hear or listen to you this is telling you something very fundamental about your relationship: that your basic rights of being a person are not being respected. Please allow yourself to have these rights.

OK, I say what I want and my partner says what they want, and they are different. Where do I go from here? You have got past the first major hurdle. You are both talking about what you want. That is the basis of a relationship: to discuss what you both want then to talk about a solution where you will both be happy because you respect each other's feelings and right to be different.

In looking after your sexual health you have a right to want to remain healthy and free of disease. You must take these responsibilities on your own shoulders and not assume your partner will be responsible for you. In good relationships your partner will want to share the responsibility with you and they will talk about it. There will be no assumptions.

Talk talk talk

In a relationship we often act as though the other person is clairvoyant — that they know what we are thinking or what our feelings are, without being told. This idea may strike you as romantic, but most partners are not clairvoyant — you need to get used to explaining yourself so that they understand you. Often you need to repeat yourself so the message gets through. Perhaps one of the hardest things for a human being to do is to really recognise and accept as valid another person's point of view, when it is different from their own.

Practice saying explicitly what you mean and checking that you have been clearly understood. *'Are you sure?' 'Is that all?' 'Do you really mean . . . ?' 'What is it that you are trying to say?'* Help your partner to say exactly what they mean, especially when they are embarrassed or frightened. Remember in any discussion do not devalue yourself. Stick to your Bill of Rights. If there is a disagreement, respect the other person's opinion and acknowledge that you have heard it but stick to what you *feel* is right for you. *'I appreciate your opinion but I do not accept that it is right for me.'*

Communication, respect and STDs

What's all this got to do with sexual diseases? So far in this chapter I've been talking about your rights as a person and about communication and respect in a relationship. That might be fine in a marriage guidance book, but what's it got to do with sexual disease? Quite a lot.

Examine your current sexual relationships. Is there any risk that you could catch a sexually transmittable disease? Do you have just one partner? How often do you change partners? Is your partner being faithful to you? If you are not being faithful to your partner, what makes you think they are being faithful to you? Remember it can take only one fleeting sexual contact to catch a disease. What is your partner's sexual history? What of your own sexual past, are you sure you are not carrying hidden infection? Only if you can fully answer all these questions can you really know what your risk of sexual disease is. Only then can you know if you are taking all the precautions necessary to maintain your sexual health.

I think you'll see that only relationships based on open and trusting communication can allow you to assess your risk and act to control it.

Sex just happens — or does it?

There is a myth in our society that sex is something that 'just happens'. There is also a myth that men in particular have uncontrollable sexual urges. Many people act out these myths, using them as an excuse not to take responsibility for themselves. This is where the practice of discipline and saying 'No' is essential.

The more you say 'No' the stronger you become as a person. When people do not own responsibility for their own sexual urges they often deny the fact that there are diseases circulating which they can catch. They expect other people to make the world safe for them. But when there are lots of other people like them, also denying their responsibilities, the world is not safe at all.

In real life the people involved actually think about sex before it happens: that it might happen and that they would like it to happen. You can plan ahead. The hardest thing to do is to make a change and maintain the change, but when you are sure you are making a correct decision stick to your guns. Remember your Bill of Rights.

Are you saying I shouldn't have sex?

No. Sex is a normal part of a happy and fulfilled life. When the situation is right for you, I see no reason to say 'No'. The reason we have such a high level of sexual disease today is that many people have sex when the situation is not right for them: when there are uncontrolled risks of infection, for example. If they respected themselves, they wouldn't expose themselves to risks. They would say 'No', and work at building safer sexual relationships. The value of saying 'No' is not in abstinence, it is in choosing good (and safe) relationships over dangerous contacts. It is an act of self love.

I don't like being different from my friends

Most people feel like this. We don't like being the odd one out. Remember though that we are all different. Each one of us is made differently, looks different, thinks differently and has their own feelings. Sometimes there can be similarities, but we have to acknowledge that we have a right to be different. Just because your friends do it one way doesn't mean that you have to do it that way. Often it takes someone to do whatever it is a different way, for the friends to actually feel OK about doing it differently. If one member of the group is strong enough to show that difference is OK, the group attitude can change.

Often the people in a group who keep doing things the same old way actually feel that what is happening is wrong, but they are too frightened of being that little bit different to do anything about it.

Changing for the better does not happen quickly and easily. People are always wary and a little afraid of change. To understand this just consider our news media. Every time something new happens it's the fights, anger and resistance that are the focus of attention, ahead of any positive aspects of the change.

Our society resists change and so do most of us. It is normal to feel afraid and worried about new things. It can seem too frightening to try new ways when we don't know what is going to happen. But it is not healthy if our fear stops us trying to change to improve ourselves and our lives.

Make your own decisions

Usually when people start becoming sexually active they get into a certain pattern of sexual behavior. That pattern tends to remain with them for the rest of their lives. Often they do not choose that pattern, it is simply the norm of the day for their peer group, but they go on repeating it year after year, without thinking about change. Unless we stop and think about ourselves and evaluate who we are and what we want we don't even consider there could be other ways of living our lives.

When you are going to try something new it is often helpful for you to have talked it over with a good friend so that you feel stronger about trying.

I like taking risks

Having been a motor bike rider, mountaineer and rock climber and lover of 'off piste skiing' I have a good idea of what risk taking is all about. The thrill lies in facing a risk and overcoming it through your own skill. Naturally you take safety precautions. You wear a helmet on a bike. Mountaineering, you use a helmet, ice axe, crampons and ropes. Most important, you practise your skill to be sure you can manage the dangers, before you expose yourself to greater risk. You'll tackle a lot of smaller mountains before you take on Mt Everest.

Risk taking in the sexual arena is not the same thing. When you jump into bed with someone whose sexual history you don't know, when you engage in an unsafe sexual practice, you are entering a lottery. You are not testing some disease-avoidance skill you have practised, you are simply taking a chance, like driving through a red light with your eyes closed. You might enjoy the sex, but the risk is more terrifying than thrilling.

Maybe you do regard sex as a sport. That's your choice. My recommendation (to you and to everyone who takes the risk of sexual contact) is to prepare yourself with the best safety equipment and protection you can. You wouldn't risk your life on a mountain without the right equipment and knowledge, you wouldn't go parachuting without a parachute, so why risk your life in bed? Arm yourself with knowledge, take precautions, and learn to say no when your sexual health is threatened.

I like drinking alcohol or getting high on drugs

Drugs of all kinds are popular in our society. People see them as providing escape, relief and pleasure. Unfortunately many drugs including the legal drug alcohol have some less desirable consequences, one of which can be a reduction in self-caring. Under the influence, things can happen on the spur of the moment, because they feel good, without much thought for the consequences.

If you enjoy 'getting wasted' this way then at least prepare yourself in advance either by making sure you have the right safety equipment or by going with friends you know you can rely on to keep you out of trouble.

It seems unbelievable, but I've talked with many patients who had one wild night out then woke up to find they had been to bed with someone who was HIV antibody positive. Their pain and suffering has far outweighed their few hours or minutes of pleasure.

Some people will choose to change their sexual behavior on moral or religious grounds, but these are not the only reasons. Simple common sense in reducing your risk of disease, because you care about yourself, is enough of a reason.

Self respect

You've probably realized that what I've been talking about in this chapter is self respect and self love. I'm arguing for a recognition of the individual importance and worth of every person, most importantly by themselves.

Too often we under-rate the value of a little more self discipline and a little more caring. We tend to accept situations that are not as good as they could be. I'm asking you to swing your pendulum of self respect and value more to the positive side. Each one of us plays a part in creating the society we live in. If individuals choose to be stronger and healthier, we will all benefit. We do have a choice.

What changes should I make?

Chapter 2 *Keeping Yourself Safe* will tell you a lot more about safe sexual behavior, including what you should know about a potential partner, the risks of different sexual practices, and what you can do to reduce the risks. With this information, you can decide if you want to make any changes to your sex life, or how you want your sex life to be. Chapter 2 also talks some more about self respect and its relationship to sexual health.

I want to change, but how do I go about it?

The first thing is to be clear about the changes you want to make. Talk to your friends or a person you can trust, or see a counsellor. All the STD clinic s now have counsellors who are able to help you and their services are free. When you are clear about the changes you want, write them down. This helps your unconscious mind become aware that you are serious and helps it prepare for change. Re-read the Bill of Rights to yourself. Practice saying 'No'. Try a week where you say 'No' to different things at least once a day. This helps you become more disciplined and grow stronger inside.

Learn to enjoy saying 'No' because you are aware that it is making your life healthier.

Remember that change often takes a while. When you decide to do something important, life usually turns up some whopper of a test, as if to say, 'Do you really mean it?' Know that you will be tested and decide to go through with it. When you're on the other side of the problem you are successful, you have made the change! You can say, 'Well done self!'

Read Chapter 2 *Keeping Yourself Safe* for more advice on how to make the changes you want.

2

KEEPING YOURSELF SAFE

This chapter is about making sex safer. Knowing that you are protected, cared for and safe is a good premise on which to commence sexual activity. Certainly you can enjoy yourself more if you aren't constantly worried that you might be catching some terrible disease.

Safer sex requires some thought and forward planning on your part. As I've written in Chapter 1, sex doesn't just happen. The thought that it might happen or that you would like it to happen goes through your mind first. You can make time to prepare yourself, so that you take the minimum risk.

There's sex and sex

People can have sex in a great many different and very varied ways. Societies tend to accept just a few (or even just one) of these options, and often to condemn the rest. Practices which are accepted in one culture can be condemned in another.

Some of the things you can do sexually with another person are more dangerous than others. The pleasure and satisfaction they bring is often not related to how dangerous they are: pleasure and satisfaction are more likely to reflect the relationship between the people, and the work they've put into building that relationship.

Following are some of the sexual options you can choose from.

Abstinence

In today's high-risk world, increasing numbers of people are choosing abstinence from sexual activity, if not as a permanent state then at least for the time when they don't have a long-term partner. Abstinence is not popular in our indulgent society, but I highly recommend it, at least until you are sure of your partner.

Abstinence is certainly the safest sexual state. Beware though, some people who choose abstinence find that when they take drugs like alcohol they have been so sex starved that for a while they forget about being abstinent, only to have very deep and sincere regrets later.

To prevent this happening (and for your well-being) it is important to realize that the human body adores being touched, hugged and caressed. If you choose abstinence you still need to respect your body's needs for nurturing, touching and warmth. Seek out friends you can hug or have touch you, or book yourself in for a regular massage from a reputable health masseur. Ask around through alternative health circles to find one of these reputable masseurs who work to release the body's ills and tension without stimulating sexual activity during the massage.

Abstinence means avoidance of sexual intercourse. There are quite a few activities that are compatible with abstinence. They include hugging, kissing, squeezing, fondling, caressing, rubbing, tickling, patting and holding. These are all completely safe.

Some people may also be interested in activities such as spanking, fantasy games, slapping, dressing up and bathing or showering together.

Any activity which causes cuts or abrasions is not recommended, because of the risk of transferring body fluids.

Masturbation

This is a completely safe activity if you do it by yourself. If you masturbate with someone else or masturbate each other, the safety rule   is: do not let their body secretions get inside your body, including your mouth. By secretions I mean vaginal juices (pussy juice), pre-cum and ejaculate (sprog, cum), pus or seepage from any sores, or blood.

If you do come in contact with these secretions wash them off immediately with soap and water, or spit them out and wash your mouth out.

Sex with partners

The more sexual partners you have, the greater your risk of catching a sexual disease. If you have multiple partners, your risk is greatly increased. Multiple does not mean you go to bed with more than one person at the same time (though it can include that). Multiple means that you regularly change your partner. Each new partner involves some risk, and the risks add up. Suppose there is a one in ten chance that a new partner will be carrying some disease. If you have two partners, your chances are doubled. Five partners, five times. Enough partners and you can be virtually assured of catching something. The partners of people with multiple partners are themselves more likely to have multiple partners, and this further increases the risk.

So, the fewer partners you have, the less risk you face. The safest thing is to have one partner for a long time (years), both of you remaining sexually faithful to each other. For some this may mean the one partner for life. This is not always possible; relationships end for a variety of reasons, and some people do not want to stay with one partner.

Talking with a new partner

However many partners you have (just one is enough to pass on an infection) you can act to reduce your risk. Instead of jumping into bed with them, you should first talk.

What you need to know is something about your potential partner's sexual past. Top of your list is to find out if they have engaged in any high risk activity for Human Immunodeficiency Virus or HIV infection. This is the virus which causes the disease AIDS (Acquired Immune Deficiency Syndrome). Here are the questions you should ask.

Have they ever used intravenous drugs or shared equipment? Have they ever had sex with a prostitute: if so when and where? Was a condom worn? Did the condom break?

Have they ever had a blood transfusion? What was it for and when was it given? Was it at home or overseas? Have they been tested for the HIV infection since then? The risky times were between 1980 and 1985, before HIV antibody testing was introduced. The risk from blood transfusion at home is now quite low. If the transfusion was received overseas between 1975 and 1985 there is some risk and an HIV test is advisable. Some underdeveloped countries still do not test blood for HIV or other infections. This is a useful fact to remember if you are travelling and are in an accident. You may wish to go home for treatment rather than be treated in that country.

Has your potential partner had sex with someone from overseas? Was it in a country with a lot of HIV, such as some parts of Africa, South America and South-east Asia? Did they wear a condom? How long ago was it and have they had an HIV test since? Did they get sick afterwards? What sort of illness was it?

If it's a male, have they ever had sex with another male? When was the last time? What sort of sex did they do? Was it high risk sex or was there no contact with body secretions?

Finally, and hardest of all, have any of their sex partners had any of the above risks? In many cases, the honest answer will be, they don't know. And that means that without more information (a full STD checkup) you cannot know how big a risk you will be taking by getting into bed with them.

You'll notice that some of these risk factors (like blood transfusions) may have been beyond the person's control. There's not much to be gained in recriminations over any of the above behaviors, after the event. All that remains to do is assess the risk and take appropriate action.

If your potential partner has engaged in any of the above activities, they should at least have an HIV antibody test and preferably a complete set of STD checks before you have sex with them. HIV is only one of the risks, though it is the most deadly. If they have engaged in any of the above activities in the last three months, then you should wait another three months and then have the test.

If there is any uncertainty about previous partners, then a full STD checkup is called for. If you are not sure about any of the answers you've received, it is your right to insist on a full checkup.

You also need to know that your partner is generally well with no symptoms of disease. You should ask if they have previously had any sexually transmitted disease. If they have, what was it and were they checked to make sure it had gone away? If your partner has had a sexually transmitted disease, have a look at the relevant chapter in this book to see if there is still a chance that you could get the same infection. This is possible for people with genital herpes and genital wart infection. After you have read the relevant chapter you may still have some questions you want answered, so go and see your local doctor or call an STD clinic.

Time for a change

In the past people didn't ask their partners about their sexual history. The subject was largely taboo, people didn't know much about STDs, they were embarrassed and would probably have felt insulted. This silence was not OK. The consequence was that many people suffered needlessly.

Today the risks are far greater than they were for your parents. The incidence of sexually transmitted disease is rising, in some cases to epidemic proportions. Old diseases that seemed to be declining are now increasing, and there are serious new diseases.

It's time we changed our attitudes and habits. Today, it should be normal behavior for new partners to question each other, to take precautions and to have tests. Change is always awkward and difficult at first, but this change is long overdue.

How to ask your partner about their sexual history

Talking to your partner about their sexual history may seem to be very hard to do, and at first it will be, but these days more and more people are doing it because they want to feel safe and because they want to feel OK about having children. Some of the STDs can interfere with your later ability to have healthy children, whether you are a male or a female, so the anxiety and embarrassment that you may go through is all worthwhile.

Probably your partner wants to talk to you about the same things but is just as embarrassed and afraid as you are. If you go ahead and start talking to them there will be somewhere along the line this incredible sigh of relief that it's all getting out in the open and over and done with. Everyone has the same feelings of insecurity, fear and anxiety as you, but people learn to cope with these feelings in all sorts of different ways. The healthiest way is to be open about them.

Some people will deny the fears are there, especially if they have a past they would rather forget (and maybe an infection that won't let them forget). In the long run it is much harder for these people to be open and to change than it may be for you.

No matter how hard it is to talk to a potential partner about their sexual history, it is easier than coping with HIV or herpes or syphilis or any of the other infections. Remember, it's your life and your body. If you respect yourself, you'll take responsibility for yourself.

Finally, some partners will refuse to talk about their sexual past. You should refuse to have sex with them — find yourself someone else.

We've talked, and it seems all clear

If both your sexual histories are free of any risk activities, past infections or partners who might have been at risk or previously infected, then you are fairly safe to commence a sexual relationship.

You might both still prefer to have a general STD check (including the HIV antibody test) and even have a look at your partner's genitals before you start having sex, just so you can relax and enjoy yourselves in confidence.

I still recommend you use condoms for the first six months. Using condoms at first allows both of you time to really get to know each other. My observations suggest it often takes up to six months in a relationship for people to feel safe with each other and let the other person know about the parts of themselves which are not so nice.

Often people have things in their past (and sometimes things in their present) which they are afraid to let their new partner know about. Perhaps they are worried this would end the relationship. It is extremely common in relationships for such things to be kept secret, at least for a while. At the time, the most important thing is the excitement of romance — reality cannot be allowed to spoil a fairy tale beginning.

Using condoms at the start provides a safety barrier in case the relationship doesn't work out or you later find out things about your partner that they didn't tell you. Enjoy your fairy tale with your Prince or Princess Charming, but stay safe and true to yourself. Remember always that you are the only person who can be responsible for looking after you.

STD checks

Unless you are absolutely sure about your new partner and their sexual history (including the sexual history of all their previous partners), you should insist on a full STD checkup before you start having sex. If you both have the tests, you can think of it as a demonstration to your partner of the honesty with which you are approaching the relationship. It's something you give them. You shouldn't think of it as a trial in which someone has to prove their innocence.

If both your tests come back negative, you are safe to start a sexual relationship – unless one of you has engaged in risk behavior for HIV (AIDS) during the past six months. See Chapter 7 for details.

The usual HIV test does not look for the human immunodeficiency virus, which is very hard to detect, but for the antibodies your body develops to fight the virus. It may take up to six months from the time of HIV infection until the antibodies appear. During this time the person will be highly contagious, but they may test negative. You can only be sure by having a second test six months after ceasing all HIV risk behavior.

Again, my recommendation is that you use condoms for the first six months of a new relationship, even if you are sure neither of you is at risk for HIV.

Sex without penetration

You've decided to have sex with a partner. There are still choices you can make which affect your risk of sexual disease. Our culture tends to portray sex as being the penetration of a vagina by a penis, as though other types of sexual activity don't exist. Other cultures have emphasised different ways of having sex and some have even made a study of the variety of types of sexual contact. You may not want to practice the whole Kama Sutra, but you should be aware that there are options.

The safest forms of sex with a partner do not involve penetration, either of the vagina, mouth or anus, by a penis. Hugging, kissing and touching can become much more important and sensuous. Massage can become part of love-making. Touching and rubbing the genitals provides more direct stimulation. Partners can masturbate each other, or themselves. Non-penetration doesn't mean not having orgasms: in fact, after a while some people (especially women) can become more relaxed about sex without penetration, and achieve orgasm more easily.

Penetration of the vagina using your fingers is fairly safe, providing your hands are clean and do not have any open sores. Germs can however be transferred from one site to another this way so some people like to wash their fingers before they transfer them to another place.

Use of the tongue for sexual stimulation is covered further on, in the section *Oral Sex.*

Sex without penetration by the penis is more common with younger couples (sometimes it's called heavy petting). It used to be more common in the male homosexual community, and has become more popular again as a result of the HIV risk. It remains steadfastly popular in the female homosexual community.

Sex without penetration does not have to be a second rate substitute for 'the real thing'. If you work at it – just as you have to work at any kind of sexual relationship – it can be as sensual, exciting and satisfying as other forms of sex.

Sex toys

Some people like to use various 'sex toys' as part of lovemaking, others find the idea repulsive. Sex toys include dildos, vibrators and Accu-Jacs. Sex toys are generally safe as long as they are kept clean and are used in such a way that they do not break the skin. They can be covered with a condom to make things even safer. The toys can be cleaned with hot soapy water and then wiped with alcohol or a solution of bleach: one part bleach to nine parts water. Wash off the bleach before the toy is used or you may find it more stimulating than you intended!

Many sex toys involve penetration of the vagina and sometimes the anus. If you are practising sex without penetration by the penis, you can still safely use these toys. They are not made out of flesh and blood and so cannot catch diseases. Infectious germs can live on the surface of sex toys, at least for a while, that is why they must be kept clean and not used in any way that could break the skin.

If you are using a sex toy to insert in both partners, be sure to clean it thoroughly (or change its condom) in between each insertion. Also, if you use a sex toy in the anus, it must be cleaned before using it in the vagina or mouth. This is to prevent the transfer of germs from person to person (or anus to vagina or mouth) on the surface of the sex toy. If you use sex toys this way, it's much better to have one toy for each person and separate toys for the anus and vagina.

Oral Sex

Oral sex means using the tongue and lips to stimulate the penis (blow job, giving head), vagina (cunnilingus or eating pussy) or anus (rimming). More research needs to be done to fully quantify the risks of oral sex.

Often people who wisely use condoms for intercourse involving penetration then don't worry about getting secretions in their mouths during oral sex. Yet oral sex involves a transfer of genital secretion – vaginal juices (pussy juice), pre-cum and semen (sprog, cum) – from one person to another.

Use of the mouth on the penis involves some risk: hepatitis, genital herpes, warts, gonorrhea, syphilis and chlamydia can be passed on this way. It is thought HIV can also be passed on this way. If there are cuts or sores in your mouth, or you have just brushed your teeth, the chance of catching an infection may be higher.

You can use a condom to protect against these risks, and some manufacturers are now offering condoms which don't taste so bad. Other possibilities include using a rubber square used by dentists called a dental dam, or using several layers of plastic such as Gladwrap (remember to remove the sandwiches first)! Putting honey or raspberry jam on the rubber or plastic makes it taste a lot better.

Most commonly the penis is put in the mouth head on, but it can be approached from the side and stimulated by playing it like an harmonica. This technique, called humming, avoids getting secretions in the mouth and so reduces the risks.

Use of the mouth and tongue on the vagina can also be risky. Genital herpes, hepatitis, genital warts, syphilis, gonorrhea and chlamydia can be transferred this way. It's possible that HIV can be caught this way.

Use of the tongue on the anus involves particular risk of hepatitis A and some infections that cause diarrhea.

It is wise to avoid oral sex when you have infected gums or ulcers in your mouth. Similarly oral sex should be avoided if there are sores on the penis, vagina or anus. It is recommended that men do not ejaculate into someone's mouth, and that you do not let someone come in your mouth. If they do, spit it out and rinse your mouth if possible. Similarly vaginal juices should not enter the mouth. Be careful with your teeth when performing oral sex: do not bite too hard so that blood is drawn.

'Normal' or vaginal sex

The most common form of sex involves penetration of a vagina by a penis. This system is designed by nature to ensure that sperm deposited by the male is lodged securely, deep inside the female, in a warm moist environment where it has the maximum chance of surviving to fertilise an egg. The environment which is best for sperm is also best for a whole range of sex diseases: once they get there, they have a good chance of surviving and growing.

During sex, much of the skin area of the penis is in close physical contact with the mucous membranes inside the vagina. That's quite a lot of contact area. The movement of the penis inside the vagina means that skin rubs against mucous membranes. Infections living on the skin surface can get spread around and transferred. Minute cracks or tears often open up in the skin. These can be too small to see, but they allow blood and other body fluids to pass out – and in. There is also skin contact outside the vagina, where the genitals touch. Infections which live around the genitals can be transferred.

In summary then, if one partner has a sex disease, having sex by putting a penis inside a vagina is a very efficient way of transferring that infection to the other partner, and ensuring that it survives and grows in its new host.

Although many people seem to think instinctively of a man passing a disease on to a woman, this transfer also works the other way round. Vaginal secretions may carry HIV or hepatitis B or other diseases, just as readily as ejaculate.

Anal sex

Anal intercourse is common among some gay men, but it is also practised by heterosexual couples. Sometimes it is used to prevent pregnancy, though this is less common now that contraceptives are widely available.

Anal intercourse is the highest risk activity for catching or passing on HIV and hepatitis B infection. The risk of acquiring HIV infection through anal sex is nearly as high for the giver as for the receiver.

The mucous membranes in the anal canal are easily broken

during sexual intercourse. This means the HIV infection can readily get into the blood stream. In addition, infection with HIV can occur even without breaks in the lining skin.

Other bugs that live in the intestines can also be passed on. The names of some of these other bugs are *Giardia lamblia,* shigella, and salmonella. All of these can cause diarrhea and other symptoms.

If you do have anal sex, then I recommend that you always wear a condom, or that your partner always wears one, that it is put on correctly and that you use plenty of water based lubricant.

How safe are condoms?

Using a condom every time will significantly reduce your risk of catching a sexual disease, but it will not eliminate it.

Condoms only protect the part of the body they cover. They are particularly good for protecting against sexually transmitted diseases that involve the urinary opening, such as chlamydia and gonorrhea and probably HIV and hepatitis B.

Sex however usually involves contact of areas not protected by the condom. The base of the penis and the scrotum (balls) can be in close contact with the labium (the lips on the outside of the vagina). Pelvic movement during sex means that exterior pubic areas are rubbed together. Consequently, condoms are not so good for preventing infections which can live on the skin and hair near the genitals, such as herpes, crabs, scabies, syphilis and warts. These are all highly infectious and can be caught just by touching the skin.

Don't think because of this that you may as well give up on condoms. The diseases that can be caught despite using a condom are mostly less serious than those a condom will protect against, and the risk of catching them is still reduced by wearing a condom. Condoms remain the best protection against sexually transmittable diseases if you are going to have sex involving penetration.

Improving condom effectiveness

You can improve the protection offered by condoms by taking care in the way you use them.

Genital secretions − vaginal juices (pussy juice), pre-cum and semen (sprog, cum) − can contain the hepatitis and human immunodeficiency virus. It's not enough just to prevent semen entering the vagina, which a condom does − to be really safe, you should not allow any of these body secretions to get in your body.

That includes dribbles and spills.

The penis must be removed as soon as ejaculation occurs otherwise the ejaculate will spill out the side or the condom may break. Condoms seem more likely to break during prolonged sexual activity, so if you are going on for a long time, change the condom.

Many women whose partners use condoms, experience mild soreness at their vaginal opening, and think this is normal. Often it is due to friction from the condom — it's even possible to get rubber burns.

I recommend use of a water based lubricant such as Lubafax, even if the condom is lubricated. As well as preventing rubber burns, a lubricant may reduce the chance of the condom breaking. Very importantly, many people find that a lubricant makes the use of condoms far less intrusive. The condom feels more like normal skin, and you'll be less aware of wearing it. Use a dollop about the size of a ten cent piece, placed either at the opening of the vagina or smeared on the outside of the condom. Make sure it is a water based lubricant, as other lubricant bases may weaken the condom. See the instructions at the end of this chapter.

Douches are not generally recommended as they can cause inflammation and may reduce the body's natural defenses.

Nonoxynol 9 is a spermicide that kills HIV. If there is a lot of HIV present there may not be enough spermicide to kill all the virus. The potency of nonoxynol 9 may be diluted by sexual secretions. It should be used as well as a condom, not instead of a condom, to provide an extra margin of safety. You can buy condoms already treated with nonoxynol 9. It tastes awful (try it) and certainly puts people off oral sex.

In summary, if condoms are put on correctly (a fun way to put them on is with four hands but please be careful with the fingernails) then they offer good but not complete protection against sexually transmitted diseases. Just as they offer good but not complete protection against pregnancy.

What about withdrawal?

Withdrawal of the penis from the vagina before the man reaches orgasm or comes is sometimes used as a method of contraception. Some people think it reduces the risk of catching a sexual disease, because no sperm is deposited. This is false. Pre-cum (fluid emitted from the penis before orgasm) can carry infections including HIV, so withdrawal is no protection.

None of the other risks of unprotected sex are reduced by withdrawal either. You can still get herpes, crabs, warts and hepatitis. You can still get pregnant too.

What about the pill and other contraceptives?

The oral contraceptive pill provides little protection against catching or spreading STDs. Other forms of protection need to be used if you are on the pill. It is extremely effective however in preventing pregnancy.

The same applies for intrauterine contraceptive devices (IUDs), removal of the uterus (hysterectomy) and tubal ligation (having the tubes tied). You won't get pregnant, but you need to take other precautions to avoid acquiring STDs.

The diaphragm or cervical cap may reduce the risk of some infections that involve the cervix, but will not stop infections that involve other parts of the genitals. Additional precautions are needed to avoid infection.

Douching may actually increase your chance of catching an STD because it can cause inflammation. It's not much good as a contraceptive either.

Risky partners

A risky partner is one who also has sex with other people, uses injected drugs, or has an unknown sexual past and hasn't been fully tested for STDs. The chance of them having or catching an STD is high. If you have a risky partner you should take precautions to make sure you don't get infected through sex with them.

Condoms are the safest way of stopping most STDs being passed on. You should encourage your partner to have regular tests and to try and avoid circumstances where they might pick up infection from someone else. Sometimes this means that you are the one who has to buy the condoms or provide the clean needles. Some women I know always make sure there is a supply of condoms in their husband's drawer when they know their husband is having sex with other women. From what I've heard, it's probably a good idea to make sure there is also a supply in the car (replace them regularly as they may perish in the heat). Always make sure he wears a condom when he has sex with you. I endorse the saying "If it's not on, it's not on."

Such precautions will reduce your risk, but if you are having sex with a risky partner there is nothing you can do to absolutely guarantee you will not catch some STD. The longer the relationship goes on, the greater your risk.

Sex and travel

If you travel you should be aware that some communities have more sexually transmitted disease than others. In some areas STDs are rampant. HIV infection tends to be present wherever there is sexually transmitted disease and is becoming more common, especially in the underdeveloped countries. Even in places where there is a lot of sexually transmittable disease about, the locals may be unaware of it or even try to tell you it is not true or that it is nothing to worry about. Don't believe them. Take precautions anyway.

When you travel it is often a good idea to take an adequate supply of condoms and lubricant if you think there is a possibility that you will have sex. Condom standards and fit vary.

If you are in a relationship and your partner is travelling, talk to them about their sexual activity while away. If you think they might be going to have sex, insist they wear condoms every time. It might even help if you pack the condoms and lubricant in their luggage. You might not enjoy the situation or the conversation, but it's better to face up to reality than to catch an STD.

If you do catch an STD it is a good idea to have a complete STD check up. STDs seem to like each other's company, so it's quite common to catch more than one at a time. A complete checkup will involve tests for syphilis, gonorrhea, chlamydia and HIV infection, if you agree to them. Often these potentially very harmful infections cause no symptoms, so if you are not tested you will not know that you have them. They can be treated, so you should find out.

Assess your own risk

Well, I've told you what I can about the different types of sexual activity and the risks they carry. What you do sexually is up to you. You may decide to stick to minimum risk activities, or you may not. Whatever you choose, you owe it to yourself to keep the risks to the minimum by taking all possible precautions.

Remember:

- Abstinence and masturbation by yourself are the only totally safe options.
- Sex not involving penetration is the safest form of sex with a partner.
- Sex toys can be safe if treated properly.
- Multiple partners or changing your partners often significantly increases your risk.
- If you regularly change your partners, then have regular STD checks too, before you have sex with any new partner.
- Condoms provide good protection against the worst sexual diseases, but their protection is not 100%. Use them whenever there is any doubt!
- Condoms work better with a lubricant – make sure it is water based.
- Genital secretions including vaginal juices (pussy juice), pre-cum and semen (sprog, cum) can carry disease. Avoid getting these in your body.
- Talk to your partner before you start having sex, so you can each assess the risk.
- If there is any doubt, both of you should have full tests before you have sex.
- It's best to use condoms for the first six months of a relationship, just to be sure.
- Be sensitive for the feeling deep inside you that lets you know if you're not respecting yourself and your body.

How to use a condom

Condoms come in different shapes and sizes. Try a selection to find out which best suit you. Condoms also come in varying thicknesses. If you find condoms sometimes break when you use them, change to a thicker type. There are special reinforced condoms you should use if you do anal sex.

Condoms are tested to make sure they meet certain safety standards. Other countries you may visit do not have the same standards, so if you are travelling take a supply with you. Keep them out of the sun. Condoms kept in the glove compartment of a car should be replaced regularly.

Condoms should be put on at the start of any sexual foreplay, before the penis comes in contact with the other person's genitals.

Squeeze the air out of the tip of the condom. Place the condom over the head of the erect penis, then using the fingers roll it down right to the base of the penis. Be careful not to tear the condom with your fingernails.

Condoms are usually pre-lubricated but it helps to use extra lubricant. Make sure the lubricant is water based (other lubricants may weaken the condom). You can spread lubricant on the outside of the condom so it feels more like skin, or put a dollop at the opening of the vagina (or the anus for anal sex).

If intercourse is prolonged it's a good idea to change the condom half way through. This reduces the chance of it breaking.

Withdraw the penis as soon as ejaculation has occurred. This reduces the risk of the condom breaking or of ejaculate spilling down the side of the condom.

To withdraw, hold on to the condom at the base of the penis and pull gently. Carefully remove the condom and dispose of it in a bag in a rubbish bin. (Never flush a condom down a septic tank system.) If possible, wash your hands.

If condoms are being used for oral sex you can make them taste better by putting jam or honey on the outside.

Figure 2.1 How to use a condom

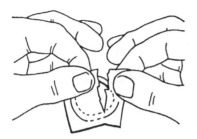

Carefully open the packet.

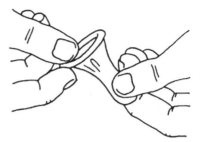

Squeeze the air out of the tip and place the condom on the head of the penis.

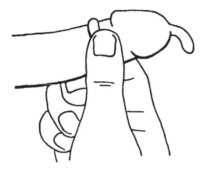

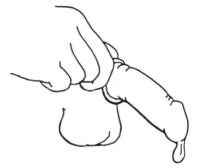

Roll the condom down to the base of the penis. Be careful not to tear the condom with your fingernails. Now is a good time to rub some water based lubricant over the condom.

The assistance of Ansell International in the preparation of this figure is gratefully acknowledged.

3

NORMAL ANATOMY
& STD EXAMINATIONS

KEY CONCEPTS

Bacteria A microscopic organism which can cause infection. It is usually round or cigar shaped. On average 500 would stretch across a pinhead. Bacteria are living cells which can divide to reproduce themselves. Whether or not they actually cause infection depends on the type of organism, where in the body they are living, and the immune defense system of the person.

Columnar epithelium Tall cells which line many of the internal surfaces of the body.

Genital anatomy The sex organs of the male or female that are used for sexual activity.

STD Sexually transmittable Disease.

STD examination The examination and tests done by a health worker to see if you have a sexually transmittable disease.

Stratified squamous epithelium Flat cells occurring in many layers.

Viruses The smallest of the disease causing organisms, viruses live inside the cells of a person's body. They cannot live outside of cells.

The body

We've all got one and we're all totally dependent on it. Surprisingly though a lot of people don't know much about their body or how it works, or how to take care of it. This chapter covers the basics of normal human genital anatomy, as far as it is relevant to sexual intercourse.

Normal Female Anatomy

If you are not quite sure of your own female anatomy, take this book into a quiet room with a locked door, a mirror and a good light. Even if you think you know where the various parts are it won't hurt to become more familiar with them. When you have a good awareness of yourself it is easy to know if you have a problem and need to see a doctor. You'll know if that bump was there before or if that freckle has moved.

On the outside

The top part of the area between the legs that is covered with hair is called the vulva. The very top of this which covers the pubic bone is called the mons pubis. Slang names for the vulva abound and new ones are always being made up. Common are black forest, crotch, crutch, cunt, down under, gash, muff, private parts, pubes, pussy, twat and twot.

The vulva covers the urinary and vaginal openings. It is very sensitive to touch. If you look carefully you will see there are two lips which make up the vulva. These are called the labia majora (also known as the flaps or lips). At puberty they become covered with hair.

On the labia are sebaceous glands. Occasionally these become infected and form pimples.

Where the labia majora join at the top is a lump which is extremely sensitive, called the clitoris (Big C, button, clit). This is the female equivalent of the penis. Stimulation of the clitoris leads to sexual arousal, when it becomes stiff. Where the labia majora join at the bottom is called the fourchette.

Figure 3.1 The female body

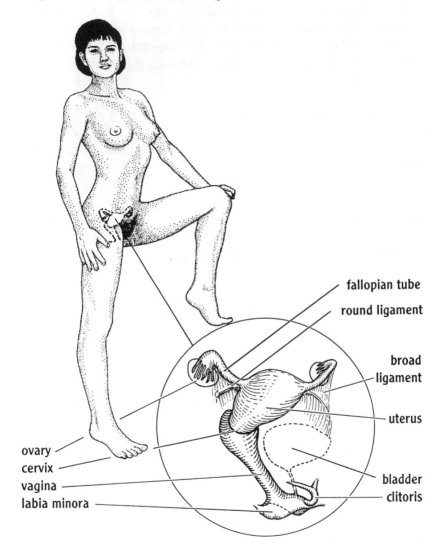

Looking inside

The inner surface of the labia majora is smooth. If you part them you will be able to see two small inner lips called the labia minora. These join the clitoris at the top and fourchette at the bottom.

Figure 3.2 Female sexual anatomy

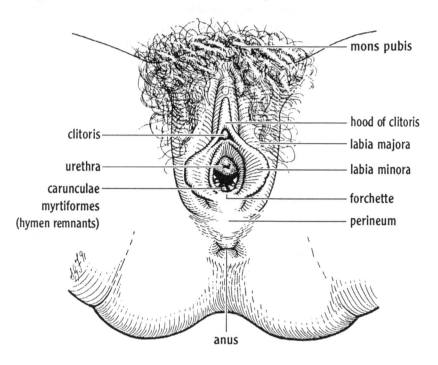

mons pubis

hood of clitoris

clitoris

labia majora

urethra

labia minora

carunculae
myrtiformes
(hymen remnants)

forchette

perineum

anus

The area between the labia minora is called the vestibule. In this area are (from the top down): the urinary opening, the opening of some special glands called Bartholin's glands and the opening of the vagina. Bartholin's glands make a lubricant for sexual intercourse. They are found on each side with the opening about two thirds of the way down the labium majora on the inside. The opening is small and you will probably not be able to see it. Sometimes these glands can become blocked or infected and swell up.

It is worth spending some time to look at these inner areas in the mirror. Identify the clitoris and notice its sensitivity. Gently part the outer and inner lips to find the urinary opening. This is often difficult to recognise at first but lies below the clitoris on the inside of the lips. It is quite pink and fleshy. Sometimes you will need to really stretch the skin to find it, but be gentle when you do this. Samples for tests for STDs are often taken from this opening.

Lower down still you will find the opening of your vagina (slang names include box, cunt, front passage, gash, hole). At the opening of the vagina is the hymen or the remains of it. The hymen is a piece of skin which blocks off a lot of the opening of the vagina. It is present at birth but can be broken or stretched by vigorous exercise, inserting tampons and sexual intercourse. In some women the hymen is quite tough and difficult to break down, in others it is thinner and easily stretched. Once the hymen is broken it leaves behind some wavy pieces of skin called carunculae myrtiformes. These can be seen in some women and are occasionally mistaken for warts. Gently put a finger into your vagina and feel around inside. It has lots of folds and if you squeeze your pelvic muscles you will be able to feel them tightening around your finger.

The vagina is lined by flat cells in up to eight layers. The cells are called stratified squamous cells. It is because they are in layers and the vagina has lots of folds that the vagina can be stretched without the skin surface breaking.

The cells in the vagina contain glycogen. The secretions which the vagina normally makes include a fluid which is acidic. This fluid contains some of the flat cells and various bacteria, the main one of which is the Bacillus of Döderlein. This bacteria acts on the glycogen in the cells to produce an acid inside the vagina called lactic acid.

Before puberty the vaginal wall is thin and the cells do not contain much glycogen. After menopause (when the menstrual periods stop) the vaginal walls again become thin, the glycogen disappears from the cells and the Döderlein bacteria disappear.

Vulvas and vaginas are different

Different people and different races have more hair than others. The vulva may be large and pronounced, or smaller and flatter.

The labia in women are all different in size, shape and color. Some are big and fat, some are thin and wrinkly, and there are many variations in between. All of them are normal and no two women look exactly the same.

Some women have large vaginas and others are smaller. Some vaginas are tight, some are stretched. The size can depend not only on the way you are made but also on whether you have had children or not and your ability to relax the muscles of the pelvis.

Some women can change the muscle tone in their vaginas. No two women are the same.

The vulva and the vagina change as girls grow up to become women. Vaginas often change after childbirth due to the stretching. They can change at menopause too, when a woman's menstrual periods stop and she stops becoming fertile: the vagina may become smaller and can dry out unless hormone treatment is taken. Vulvas become thinner and more wrinkly after menopause.

Deep inside

The vagina goes upwards and backwards 100mm to 150mm (four to six inches) to the cervix or 'neck of the womb' which is at the top of the vagina. If you insert your finger even higher you may be able to feel your cervix. It is round and firm with a small dimple in the centre called the cervical os.

The cervix is actually the lower third of the uterus or womb. The uterus opens into the cervix at the cervical os.

The uterus is a muscular bag shaped like an upside down pear which lies in the pelvis. When you become pregnant a fertilised egg implants into the wall of the uterus and grows there, causing the uterus to swell. Usually it is only about 50mm wide by 75mm long (two inches by three inches) but it is often smaller than this in women who are taking the oral contraceptive pill.

The uterus is held in place by two slings from the pelvic bones called the broad ligaments. In a large number of women the uterus faces forward and lies on the surface of the bladder. This is called anteverted. In other women it faces backwards and is called retroverted. Either position is normal.

The cells which line the lower and upper parts of the cervix are of different types. Some complex changes take place at the area where the cell types meet. This is the area where cancer of the cervix is thought to start.. You can read more about it (including how to avoid cancer of the cervix) in Chapter 19.

The fallopian tubes join the uterus at the top on either side. They lie in the top part of the broad ligaments. Eggs travel along the fallopian tubes on their journey to the uterus or womb. These tubes are sometimes tied or cut to stop the passage of the eggs and so prevent pregnancy. The operation to do this is called tubal ligation.

Figure 3.3 The female urogenital tract

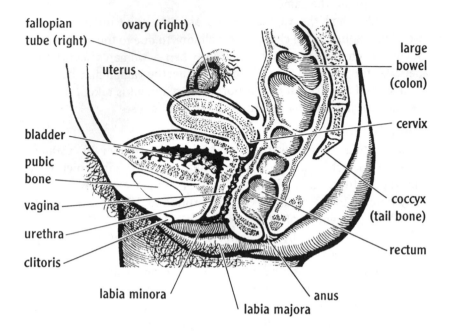

Half of the cells lining the fallopian tubes secrete mucus. The other half have fine hair like projections on them called cilia which move the secretions and egg along the tube. Eggs on their way to the uterus ride along with the mucous.

The cilia or hairs of the fallopian tubes can be damaged by pelvic infection so that the egg cannot be moved into the womb. Infection with gonorrhea or chlamydia are the most common infections that damage the cilia of the tubes.

Close by where the tubes open into the abdomen are the ovaries where eggs are produced. There are two ovaries, one on each side. They are oval shaped, each about 40mm (one and a half inches) in length. They attach to the back side of the broad ligament. One part of the end of the fallopian tube is attached to the ovary.

Normal Male Anatomy

Just as for women, the easiest way for you to learn about your anatomy is to lock yourself in a well lit room with a mirror and have a look at yourself.

Circumcision

Some men are circumcised and others not. Circumcision is an operation which removes the fold of skin (called the foreskin) around the head of the penis. (Slang names for penis include cock, dick, doodle, hanger, jimmy, love-pump, meat, one-eyed-trouser-snake, prick, rod, the-old-fella, slug, willie, wolloper or even blue-veined-junket-pumper.)

Sometimes circumcision is done because of infection or birth abnormalities, sometimes it is performed as a religious custom, but mostly parents have their sons circumcised because the father is circumcised, or it is a tradition in their family. Many people think that circumcision is more hygienic however fewer circumcisions are being performed in western societies than used to be. If you are not circumcised you should be sure to wash regularly under the foreskin using water not soap (soap can cause a rash). Providing you keep yourself clean, not being circumcised does not increase your risk of infection. Figure 3.6 shows a penis which has been circumcised and one which hasn't.

Some men are not able to pull their foreskin back completely. If this is the situation for you, do not force the foreskin back. Visit your doctor and tell them about it. They will have a look and will discuss with you whether anything needs to be done.

Penises are different

A foreskin or the lack of it is not the only difference in appearance between penises. Penises can be short or long, thick or thin, with big heads or small heads, pointy or tapered or an even thickness. Some penises have very prominent veins. When erect, penises can change dramatically. Some become greatly enlarged, others swell only a little. Some erect penises have pronounced bends in them.

Penises and testicles (balls) shrink when they are cold. This is because the body takes blood away from them, in order to keep the blood warm. Sometimes one or both testicles can even disappear back inside the body, descending again when conditions are more comfortable.

Figure 3.4 The male body

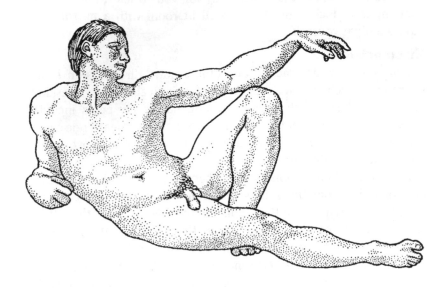

Studies have reported the average size of the penis when flaccid (not erect) from 65mm to 100mm (2.5 inches to 4 inches) in length and 25mm (1 inch) in diameter. The average when erect is from 140mm to 165mm (5.5 inches to 6.5 inches) in length and 40mm (1.5 inches) in diameter. It can vary from 50mm to 250mm (2 inches to 10 inches) in length.

Men can get upset about the relative size of their penis and a lot of jokes are made about penis size, but it is mainly how they are used that makes the difference.

The structure of the penis

At the very end of the penis is the urinary opening (eye). This is in the centre of part of the penis called the head or glans penis. Sometimes the opening is on the lower part of the glans, this is a common variant and nothing to worry about. There are two tiny glands called Tyson's glands that open next to the eye, and secrete a white substance. Where the glans or head joins onto the shaft of the penis there are often tiny lumps called the papillae of the coronal sulcus which are commonly mistaken for warts.

Figure 3.5 Male sexual anatomy

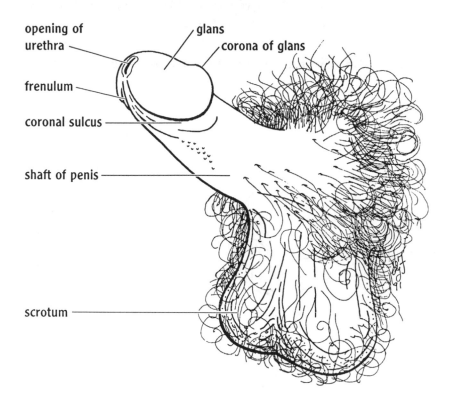

opening of
urethra

glans

corona of glans

frenulum

coronal sulcus

shaft of penis

scrotum

Between the glans penis and shaft of the penis is a slight groove called the coronal sulcus. On the bottom side of this groove is a ridge of skin called the frenulum. On either side of the frenulum are small glands which are symmetrical and white. Sometimes you can't see them at all, other times there are up to six of them, three on each side. These are also commonly mistaken for warts.

Just below the coronal sulcus there may be small white lumps under the skin called Fordyce's spots. Sometimes these can be quite small and look like grains of sand. There are other glands in this area which secrete a white cheesy substance named smegma. This needs to be washed away each day in men who are not circumcised, otherwise it becomes smelly and infected.

There are many sebaceous glands on the penis. These often become more noticeable as you grow older. They look like tiny pimples. Sometimes they become infected.

Figure 3.6 Circumcised and uncircumcised penises

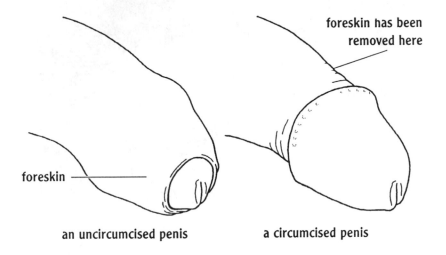

foreskin has been removed here

foreskin

an uncircumcised penis   a circumcised penis

The urethra which carries urine from the bladder to the end of the penis travels down the middle of the penis, slightly closer to the underside.

Above and to either side of the urethra is spongy tissue called corpora cavernosa which fills up with blood during an erection (boner, hard-on, fat, stiff).

Using two hands feel the scrotum, the skin sack which contains the two testicles or testes (balls). The testicles are egg shaped and soft. They correspond to the ovaries in a woman. They manufacture male hormone and sperm. Roll them between your fingers and thumbs. If it hurts you are squeezing too hard. Often it is best to feel them between both hands. In a normal testicle there should not be any lumps: if you find one you should go and see your doctor within the week.

At the back of each testicle you will be able to feel an epididymis. It is a coiled tube shaped like a sausage and runs from the top of each testicle downwards about 40mm (one and a half inches). It's a little larger at the top than the bottom. About five metres (16 feet) of tube are coiled in each epididymis. Sperm from the testicles travels along this tube.

Figure 3.7 The male urogenital tract

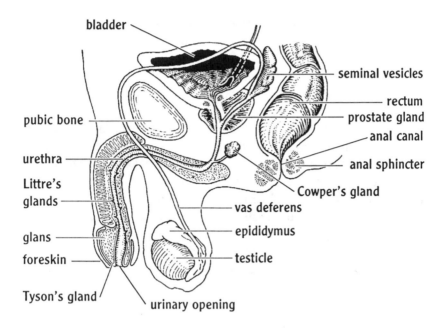

bladder
seminal vesicles
rectum
pubic bone
prostate gland
anal canal
urethra
anal sphincter
Littre's glands
Cowper's gland
vas deferens
glans
epididymus
foreskin
testicle
Tyson's gland
urinary opening

At its base each epididymis is connected to the ductus deferens, a tube which carries the sperm back up through the scrotal sac and into the abdomen. It passes through the prostate gland and empties into the seminal vesicles, two soft tubes which are just behind the bladder.

The total journey is more than six metres and takes a sperm about 12 days. This is essential because the sperm when produced by the testicles are immature and incapable of causing pregnancy. By the time they get to the seminal vesicles they are ready.

The prostate

The prostate gland is found at the opening of the bladder where it becomes the urethra: the tube that carries urine and ejaculate to the opening at the end of the penis. The prostate has the size and shape of a chestnut except in older men where it is larger. It encircles the urethra near the bladder. The prostate is made of glands that make secretions that form approximately 30% of the ejaculate volume. The outside part of the prostate can be felt by the doctor feeling inside the anal canal with a finger. This examination does not hurt unless there is inflammation present.

Ejaculation

When ejaculation occurs the sperm passes back through the prostate via a tube called the ejaculatory duct, which joins onto the urethra. The urethra starts at the base of the bladder. Mostly it carries urine from the bladder down through the penis, but when ejaculation occurs it shuts down its connection to the bladder and carries sperm instead.

What is ejaculated is not all sperm. Glands associated with the epididymis contribute some fluid to help the sperm move along. The sperm and epididymal fluid together make up 10% of the ejaculate (cum, love juice, pearl necklace, sprog).

Fluid from the seminal vesicles makes up about 60% to 70% of the ejaculate. This fluid is alkaline and slightly yellowish.

The prostate gland provides the final 20% to 30% of the ejaculate. Prostatic fluid normally is neither acid nor alkaline, but when the prostate is inflamed the secretion is often alkaline. The ejaculate from the prostate is rich in zinc and magnesium.

Common Anatomy

The lymphatic system

All parts of the body are supplied by blood vessels. There is also another system of vessels called lymphatic vessels which carry a fluid called lymph from all areas of the body to regional lymph nodes. Lymph nodes are bean shaped lumps, found at intervals on the lymphatic vessels. They contain special blood cells called lymphocytes. They filter the lymph, cleaning out infection and dead cells. Lymph nodes often occur in groups. They are commonly found in the neck when you have a cold, in the armpit if you have an infection on your arm or hand and in the groin if you have an infection on your legs or a sexually transmittable disease.

Fluid from the lymph nodes is carried on to deeper lymphatic channels which eventually empty into one of the great veins of the body.

The rectum

The rectum is the fairly straight final section of the intestine, about 150mm (six inches) long, which ends at the anus. Slang names for the rectum include ass, bum, asshole and back-passage.

The anus is the name given to the outside opening of the rectum, where feces (shit) are expelled from the body. A slang name for the anus is ring.

The rectum is kept closed by a muscle called the anal sphincter.

The anal canal is the final part of the rectum where it joins the anus. It is lined with flat stratified squamous cells, the same sort of cells which lie on the outside skin. Higher up the rectum is lined with tall columnar cells. At an area called the transformation zone the squamous cells change over to tall columnar cells which line the rectum. The transformation zone is the area where cancer of the anus is thought to start. The situation is similar to the cell change-over point in the cervix in women. Tests are now being devised to check the cells of the anal transformation zone for pre-cancer, just like the PAP smear test of the cervix.

The mouth

The tonsils are found at the back of the mouth, which is called the pharynx. Tonsils are lined by cells called squamous cells. Infection with gonorrhea or chlamydia can occur at the back of the mouth if you have oral sex with an infected person. Even if you have had your tonsils removed there are still areas which remain that can be a site of infection.

The body's protection against STDs

The skin linings of the surface of the body (epithelium) and inside the body (mucosal surfaces) protect the body against invasion by germs. They do this in several ways. Most germs need a break in the skin to enter the body, so intact skin is a good protection. Some infections need to attach to cells to cause an infection. Healthy skin cells inhibit attachment of foreign cells by processes called mucous washing and mucociliary action. These are a little like washing and sweeping. Normal mucosal cell secretion can also contain substances that block the effect of germs and prevent infection.

With all these defenses, the skin provides a pretty good barrier against the entry of foreign organisms – when it is all in one piece. Sexual intercourse commonly causes tiny breaks in the skin, so infection can bypass its defences. If warts or other infections are present breaks in the skin are more common, increasing the risk of further infection.

Figure 3.8 The rectum

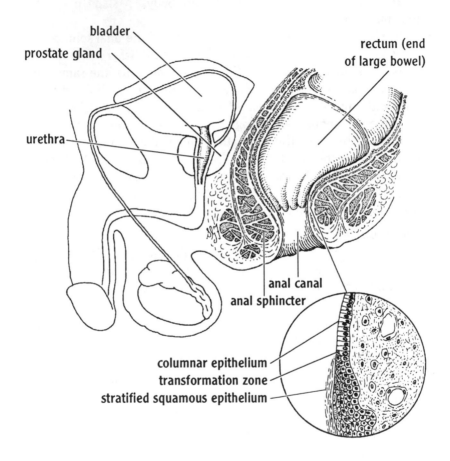

bladder

prostate gland

rectum (end of large bowel)

urethra

anal canal

anal sphincter

columnar epithelium

transformation zone

stratified squamous epithelium

The importance of STD examinations

The human body is an amazingly complex organism. It appears to be very finely balanced, yet in many ways it has a great tolerance for dysfunction. Often it can overcome infection and heal itself. It can shake off flu, recover from measles and attack foreign bodies in the blood stream.

Many sexually transmittable diseases however seem to have the upper hand. Infections like syphilis and chlamydia once established can only be eradicated by drugs. Some diseases like herpes and HIV (AIDS) cannot currently be eradicated, but for most sexually transmittable diseases there are now good treatments available. Even for herpes and HIV (AIDS) there are treatments which help manage the infection and permit an improved lifestyle.

Successful treatment however depends on early diagnosis. In most cases if you allow the disease to go on before you get treatment, it will do much more damage and be much harder to get rid of. Many STDs can cause loss of fertility if left untreated, some can cause other permanent disability and even death.

Also, going untreated may mean you are spreading your diseases to other people, who in turn may unknowingly spread them to more people, increasing the general level of infection in the community.

It is important *to you* to be tested if ever you have any suspicion that you might be infected and to be treated right away.

You should always get a full STD checkup, if any infection is found. If you have one type of sex disease it is quite likely that you will also have another. Sexually transmittable bugs seem to enjoy each other's company. Often catching one type of sexual disease weakens your body's resistance to other kinds, making multiple infection more likely. It is therefore in your best interests to have as thorough an examination as possible.

What is an STD examination like for women?

When a doctor examines you for sexually transmittable diseases they will look at your vulva, the opening to your vagina and pubic hair region.

Tests will be made of any sores that may be present. Samples will be taken from the urinary opening and from the secretions of the vagina, the walls of the vagina and from the cervical os (the hole in the cervix). The tests (except for a PAP smear) can all be done at any time in your monthly cycle, even if you are having your period. The common infections looked for are genital warts, molluscum contagiosum, genital herpes, gonorrhea, chlamydia, candida, bacterial vaginosis and trichomoniasis. Blood tests are usually taken for syphilis, sometimes hepatitis B and HIV (AIDS) infection if you consent to the test.

Figure 3.9 STD examinations

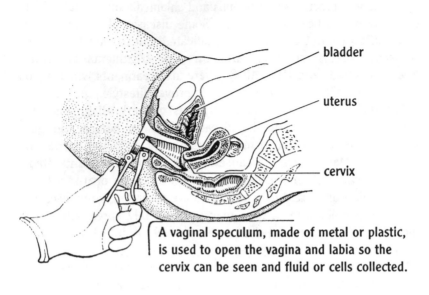

bladder

uterus

cervix

A vaginal speculum, made of metal or plastic, is used to open the vagina and labia so the cervix can be seen and fluid or cells collected.

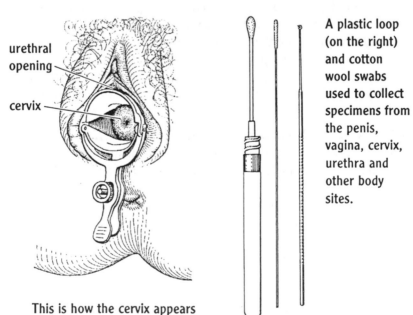

urethral opening

cervix

This is how the cervix appears looking through a speculum.

A plastic loop (on the right) and cotton wool swabs used to collect specimens from the penis, vagina, cervix, urethra and other body sites.

Samples for the PAP smear test are taken from the bottom side of the cervix, the surface of the cervix and from the cervical os. See Chapter 19 *The Abnormal PAP Smear and Cancer Of The Cervix* for more information.

The doctor will insert one or two fingers into your vagina, with the other hand just above the front of your pubic bone, so they can feel your cervix, womb and fallopian tubes. This is to see if there are any abnormal lumps or any tenderness that may suggest serious infection. Sometimes this may feel uncomfortable if your bladder is full, but if there are no problems this part of the examination does not hurt.

The doctor may insert an instrument called a speculum into your vagina so they can see the cervix and walls of the vagina. The speculum slips in easily especially if it is warmed and you are very relaxed.

Some women tense up when they have a vaginal examination and the muscles at the opening of the vagina become very tight. This makes it hard for both of you. Practice allowing these muscles to be relaxed. One way to help this happen is to breathe in slowly and deeply then as you slowly breathe out imagine you are breathing out all tension and feel all the tension leaving your body. This breathing exercise is in fact a useful one for any situation in which you feel uptight or angry. The trick is to breathe slowly. Try counting from one to ten as you breathe. If you are doing this to release anger, when you breathe out imagine the anger leaving your body, and *feel* it leaving your body.

In addition to examining your genital areas including looking at your anus, the doctor will of course ask you questions and may examine other parts of your body.

What is an STD examination like for men?

The doctor will look at the pubic region and feel the groin to see if any of the glands are swollen. They will feel the scrotal sac and its contents to see if there are any lumps or areas of tenderness. The doctor will also look at the eye of the penis to see if there is any discharge or maybe a wart. If there is a discharge present, a little will be scooped onto a swab and smeared on a glass slide so it can be looked at under a microscope. The doctor will pull back the foreskin if you are uncircumcised and check the skin underneath to see if there are any rashes, warts, other lumps or sores. The rest of the penis is also checked just to make sure there are no other signs of infection or disease. Often warts and other lumps can hide down at the bottom of the penis amongst the hairs where they are hard to see.

In a routine check up the usual tests from the eye of the penis are for gonorrhea and chlamydia. To do these tests the doctor inserts two small swabs, one at a time, into the eye of the penis so that the cotton tip is covered. Usually the swabs are lubricated before they are inserted, so as to reduce the discomfort.

The test for chlamydia requires the doctor to make sure that some tall columnar cells have been collected. Most men and women find this test a little uncomfortable and in both sexes some burning is experienced on passing urine the next one or two times. This is because if the test is done properly, a tiny scratch on the surface lining of the urethra occurs. A blood test for syphilis, hepatitis B and HIV (AIDS) may also be taken provided you consent to this being done.

As well as examining your genital area including looking at your anus, the doctor will of course ask you questions and may examine other parts of your body.

Section Two

The Viral STDs

4

GENITAL HERPES

KEY CONCEPTS

Acyclovir A drug which stops multiplication of the herpes simplex virus and which is used to treat some people with herpes simplex infection.

Auto-inoculation Spreading an infection further on yourself. This happens when you touch or rub the infected area then touch another part of your body.

Herpes virus A family of viruses.

Lesion An abnormality of the body such as an infection, area of injury or a growth such as cancer.

Primary herpes infection Infection with the herpes simplex virus for the first time.

Recurrent infection More outbreaks of the infection after it has first occurred.

Type I Infection with one of the herpes family viruses called herpes simplex type I.

Type II Infection with one of the herpes family viruses called herpes simplex type II.

Virus The smallest of disease causing organisms, a virus contains genetic material (RNA or DNA). A virus can only live inside a cell.

The herpes family

Genital herpes is caused by a virus called herpes simplex. There are two types of this virus: type I and type II. Type I mainly causes cold sores of the lips. It is a very common infection that affects many people in childhood. Sometimes they do not even know they have it.

The second type of herpes virus mainly infects the genital region, but can sometimes spread to the mouth during oral sex with someone who is infectious.

These two herpes viruses belong to a family of viruses called herpes viruses. In the same family of viruses are chicken pox virus (Varicella-zoster virus) and the virus that causes glandular fever (Epstein-Barr virus, also known as kissing disease or infectious mononucleosis. Cytomegalovirus, which is the most common viral cause of birth defects in babies also belongs to this family group. A newly discovered member of this family is the human herpes virus 6, and again research is showing it to be quite a common infection, especially in childhood. It is not thought to cause genital infection.

All the viruses in the herpes family have in common that once they infect a person, the infection stays in the cells of that person's body for the rest of their life. The viruses can become active again later in their life, possibly making them sick and infectious again.

Are all types of genital herpes the same?

No. There are different strains. Some apparently never cause repeated outbreaks, others are more severe. In addition each person reacts differently to a herpes infection, some people having many recurrences, others with the same strain having few or no recurrences. If you have genital herpes and you meet someone else with genital herpes you should still make sure that you take steps to avoid catching their type.

How do you catch the herpes virus?

Type I herpes is usually caught in early childhood from other children, but it can be caught at any time in your life from someone who is infectious. This virus is usually caught by kissing or by droplet spread, from sneezing or coughing. It can also be caught by oral sex. Someone with the sores on their mouth or lips can spread it to the genitals of a partner, who can then pass it back to their genitals during sexual intercourse. Type I herpes which is transferred to the genitals does not change into type II herpes. It is usually only a problem for the first outbreak in the genitals.

Type II herpes is usually caught by sexual intercourse with someone else who has it and is infectious. It can also be caught in the mouth via oral sex.

New studies are showing that genital herpes infection is far more common than it was first thought. Many people with the infection do not even know they have had it. Some people who know they have had it cannot tell if they are having a recurrence and therefore are infectious.

If I've had sex with someone with herpes will I get it?

Probably not. It depends how infectious they were and how good your own immunity is. If you were unfortunate enough to catch it, the symptoms will usually appear within two to 14 days, although it has been known to take as little as 24 hours or as long as years. Some people catch it but never develop symptoms. Most often people with herpes cannot be sure who they caught it from.

What is it like to have herpes?

In the first outbreak (primary infection) most people feel generally miserable and unwell. Often they have a temperature and mild headache. There is soreness and itching where the infection is and there may be some discomfort passing urine. The local lymph glands are usually quite swollen and sore. In women there is often a vaginal discharge, and there may be an associated yeast infection. Small blisters may be seen on the skin of the penis and the vulva or sometimes other areas of skin close to the genitals. These are full of infectious herpes simplex virus. Usually they burst after a few days, leaving a small sore that heals over with a scab and falls off leaving no scar. The first infection can last up to three weeks without treatment.

If you think you are having an outbreak of genital herpes infection for the first time, go and see your local doctor or a doctor at an STD clinic. There is very good treatment to make you feel better within 24 hours and stop the infection spreading further than it already has. It is important for the doctor to do tests to find out what sort of infection it is you have, in particular whether it is type I or type II herpes simplex infection. You should also be checked to make sure you do not have any other infection as well.

Another good reason for being checked is that the symptoms or signs you are experiencing may not be herpes. I see many people who think they are having herpes recurrences when in fact it is not that at all.

Figure 4.1 Herpes blisters and sores

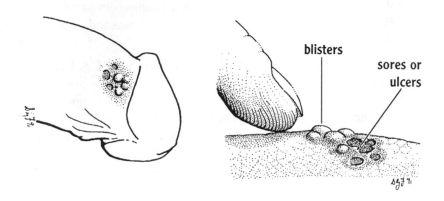

blisters

sores or ulcers

How is herpes diagnosed?

The usual test for genital herpes is to take some fluid from the blister or ulcer and grow the virus. The virus can grow in 48 hours but sometimes it grows quite slowly, taking up to a week. If the test is negative it does not prove absolutely that you don't have herpes, as there is a chance the virus wasn't picked up in the test. If you're not sure and the symptoms recur, have the test repeated within 24 hours of the recurrence.

Blood tests are not usually accurate enough to diagnose the type of herpes infection which has occurred.

What happens after the first outbreak of herpes?

If you catch type I herpes in the genital area it is probable that you will never again have another outbreak of that infection there. This is why it is a good idea if you think you might have an infection with genital herpes to see your doctor and have tests to find out what sort of infection it is. You will certainly feel much better if you find out that it is only herpes type I.

If you have just had your first infection with type II herpes don't be dismayed, the news is not as bad as it seems. You have a better than 50% chance of never suffering another outbreak! Be optimistic and hope that you will be one of the lucky majority.

Recurrences

Recurrences are milder than the first outbreak, and usually they become less severe and less frequent with time.

Recurrences occur because the virus, once it gets into the body, stays in the nerve cells. For various reasons the virus travels down to the skin surface where it may be associated with an outbreak.

Sometimes just prior to a recurrence people get a funny feeling or an itch, and then blisters appear. (Putting ice on the spot when it becomes itchy may stop the outbreak, but this does not work for everyone.) Others have slightly stronger feelings and yet others may have no symptoms at all, even if there is a small blister or sore.

People with a recurrence are infectious from the prodrome, which is the first abnormal feeling in the area, until all the scabs have fallen off, or the skin has healed over.

How should I look after myself if I have a primary herpes infection?

If this is your first outbreak of herpes, you can be reassured it will get better soon. Even if you are one of the unfortunate minority who go on to further infections, you can be confident that future infections will not be as bad as the first time. Recurrences become less frequent and become less severe over time. The first episode is always the worst.

Unfortunately for women, their first infection is often worse than it is for men, because a much larger area of skin is involved. The vagina and cervix are usually infected.

When you are infected you are sick. You may have a slight headache and feel feverish. You should give yourself as much rest and sleep as you possibly can. You should definitely be resting in bed with someone helping to look after you. Washing the sore area with a salt and water solution is the cheapest and most effective way of relieving pain and keeping the area clean. One quarter of a teaspoon of cooking salt to one cup of water is the recipe. Of course you can use warm water if you like.

Bathe the sore area every three to four hours, or more often if it gives relief. Some people have to bathe themselves every one or two hours for a while. For women who really are having a severe outbreak and are having difficulty urinating, it is sometimes useful to urinate into a tub of water or bath of water. This eases the stinging and burning.

Very occasionally women having their first outbreak find it is so bad that they can't pass water, and they need to be admitted to the hospital. Even if this happens to you, don't be discouraged. How bad the first outbreak is has nothing to do with whether you are going to get any recurrence, and please remember that the majority don't.

If you think you are having your first herpes outbreak, for your own sake see a doctor. If tests confirm a primary herpes infection, you can be prescribed acyclovir tablets. Acyclovir stops the virus from multiplying, so the infection gets better more quickly, the pain goes more quickly and you are not as infectious for as long. Unfortunately the tablets do not eradicate the infection from your body and do not reduce your chances of having a recurrence.

If you are female and having your first outbreak, and you are on the oral contraceptive pill, it is sometimes wise to continue taking the active pill tablets so that you miss having your menstrual period during the time when the infection is bad. To do this you go straight on to the next packet of pill tablets instead of missing tablets for a week or taking a week of sugar tablets. Discuss this with your doctor first.

Don't wear tight clothing, or clothes that rub the infected area.

The lesions or sores which appear with an outbreak of herpes are highly infectious. If you touch the spot where there is a sore and then touch yourself on another part of your body, the infection can be spread there. If you touch someone else, they can be infected.

Always wash your hands immediately if you touch a herpes sore. Do not share your bath towel with any one else when you have a herpes outbreak. However, herpes cannot be spread on the bathroom soap or toilet seat.

It always surprises me to have to say this but when you are sore below it is best to avoid sex. Definitely sex should be avoided whilst you or your partner has an active herpes infection, to stop the infection spreading to other places and to allow the infected area time to heal.

You or your partner are infectious until all the lesions have healed over and the scabs have fallen off. People with their first infection are infectious for longer than those who are having a recurrence. Oral sex (placing the mouth to the genitals), manual stimulation (touching the genitals with your hands) and actual sexual intercourse should be avoided until all the area has healed.

Avoiding sex does not mean you can't touch each other or kiss and hug. Only the infected area is infectious.

Taking care of yourself after the first outbreak

If you have herpes recurrences, don't say that you are 'suffering from an attack'. Using words like this puts the virus in control of you. It is much better to use the terms herpes outbreak or herpes recurrence. If you suffer from frequent recurrences this choice of terminology is extremely important in your regaining control over your health. How you think about yourself seems to have a lot to do with how your body reacts to disease.

Some people find that recurrences are triggered by stress, over-work, overuse of alcohol or other drugs, repressed anger, smoking too much, menstruation, other illness, hard physical exertion, and eating poorly.

If you do have recurrences it is important to keep yourself healthy. You might find it helpful to read Chapter 22 *Building Good Health*. Lots of rest and relaxation is important, some people find that playing golf, fishing, or doing yoga is helpful. Others find benefit in attending a herpes support group. Your doctor or local clinic should be able to give you information about this. It's wise to check with your doctor to confirm that the symptoms you have really are herpes. Many times people think they are having a herpes recurrence when really it is something else.

Many people find benefit in psychological counselling, and for some only a few visits are all that is needed before they stop having recurrences. For others it may take longer.

Occasionally people suffering repeated recurrences need to take acyclovir tablets. Acyclovir is very useful to give a person a break from frequent recurrences so they can feel what it's like to be well again.

Each person needs their own individual treatment program. It depends on what you and your doctor feel is best for you.

Long term use of acyclovir

So far I've said some good things about the benefits of acyclovir, but as you may have guessed there are cautions about its use.

Doctors are concerned over-use of acyclovir will encourage the emergence of new and resistant strains of herpes, just as past over-use of antibiotics has been associated with the development of bugs that are not killed by the antibiotic. There are already reports that some types of herpes may be resistant or partially resistant to the action of acyclovir.

The long term side-effects of acyclovir are not known. Acyclovir has not been available for very long. Studies of people taking it for up to four or five years are available and so far so good, but that is all that can be said.

Generally I am reluctant to encourage young, fit, otherwise healthy people of childbearing age, to go onto tablets without some effort on their part to change their lifestyle or other factors that can be causing the recurrences.

There is an exception however. Anyone who is infected with HIV (the human immunodeficiency virus which causes AIDS) should have treatment with acyclovir if they have recurrent herpes. This is because frequent herpes outbreaks have been associated with a speeding up of the progression of the HIV infection to AIDS.

People who are given long term acyclovir should make sure they avoid becoming pregnant and should also have their liver and kidney function tested regularly to make sure the drugs are not causing harm.

Herpes, pregnancy and babies

Contrary to popular myth, people with genital herpes find it as easy to get pregnant as other people, so be careful!

For details on herpes and pregnancy, see Chapter 20.

Will herpes affect my baby?

People with genital herpes infection should tell their obstetrician (doctor who looks after pregnant women and delivers babies). Pregnant women who have had the infection should tell their obstetrician, no matter how long ago the infection was, and even if they have never had a recurrence. Male parents-to-be who have genital herpes infection should let their partner's obstetrician know, even if their partner hasn't had any signs of the infection.

The obstetrician is then warned to look out for signs of the infection in the last month or so of pregnancy. Most women with herpes infection do not have an outbreak at this time, but if they do, the obstetrician is likely to perform a caesarean delivery (operation to deliver the baby out of the abdomen) to avoid the possibility of the baby becoming infected when passing through the birth canal.

The problem these days seems not to be the people who know they have herpes but the people who don't know, especially if it's their first infection.

For more details on herpes and babies, see Chapter 21.

How can I avoid passing on herpes to my partner?

It is important to talk to your partner and let them know that you have the infection. If you are having an outbreak you are infectious from the time you first develop symptoms until the last scab has fallen off. You must avoid sexual intercourse including foreplay and touching the infected area during all this time. Having sex using condoms during this time is not advised as there is a risk of contact with infectious secretions.

When the infection is not active the risk of it being passed on is low. In long term relationships where condoms are not being used it is probable that at some stage the partner will also catch the herpes infection, even when all precautions are taken. Luckily though for most couples the infection in the partner is not too troublesome except for the first outbreak. Infection can sometimes occur in the partner without them even knowing about it.

Acyclovir will not stop the virus being passed on although there is some evidence that it may reduce the risk. Talk to your doctor about this.

Sometimes in long term relationships herpes can appear seemingly out of the blue, even though neither partner has been unfaithful. This can happen because the original infection may not have been noticed and so no precautions have been taken.

How can I avoid catching herpes?

Talk to your partner and ask them whether they or their previous partners have had herpes. If you are entering a new sexual relationship it is a good idea to both go and have a general STD (Sexually transmittable Disease) checkup prior to starting to have sex.

Even if you are both cleared it is a good idea to use condom s until you both know the relationship is a good one and that you are going to be with each other for a long time (many years).

Condoms are not a 100% safeguard against catching genital herpes. Condoms only protect the area of skin they cover. For example if there is a herpes outbreak on the scrotum or vulva, condom s will not stop the infection from being passed on. Condoms do however greatly reduce the risk, so they are a good common sense thing to use in early relationships until you can be certain your partner has nothing to hide from you.

Relationships often take up to six to nine months before uncomfortable aspects about yourself and your partner are discussed. When people fall in love it is like a fairy tale they have dreamed about and they do not want to do or say anything which may possibly destroy the relationship by frightening the other person away. Later they may feel more secure and able to risk revealing hidden truths. Remember the Bill of Rights and your right to protect yourself.

Finally, don't forget, people can be infected with herpes without even knowing it. Some people can pass herpes on without themselves having any signs or symptoms. People who have herpes and are on acyclovir can still be infectious. It's your right and your responsibility to protect yourself.

5

GENITAL WARTS & HUMAN PAPILLOMAVIRUS INFECTION (HPV)

KEY CONCEPTS

Genital wart A wart that likes to grow on the genitals.

Incubation period The length of time it takes to develop illness after infection first occurs.

Macroscopic infection An infection you can see with the naked eye or feel.

Pap smear A test performed on the cervix to examine the cells on the cervix.

Podophyllin A drug used to treat genital warts.

Pre-cancer The changes in cells that occur before cancer occurs. These changes are not cancer.

Subclinical infection An infection you can't see with the naked eye.

Wart An overgrowth of skin cells, caused by the human papillomavirus, resulting in a lump that can be seen with the naked eye or felt.

What are warts?

A wart is an overgrowth of skin cells forming a lump. This lump can be so tiny it's almost invisible, or it can be quite noticeable.

Warts are caused by the human papillomavirus (HPV). There are over 60 different types of HPV. So far only 14 of these have been found to cause warts in the genital area.

Types 6 and 11, for example, tend to live in the genital area and not on other parts of the body. They are the most common type of HPV that causes genital warts you can see with the naked eye or feel.

HPV types 16 and 18 are more likely to be found in association with changes on the cervix. These changes need to be monitored closely, though thankfully the latest research indicates that most people with these types of HPV do not develop long term problems.

You cannot catch genital warts from warts growing on someone's hands, knees or other non-genital skin.

Figure 5.1 Types of HPV and associated diseases

TYPE	DISEASE
HPV 1a,b,c	Warts of the soles of the feet
HPV 2a-e	Common warts
HPV 3a,b	Flat warts/warts of childhood
HPV 4	Warts of the soles of the feet or palms of the hand
HPV 5a,b	Flat spots in patients with an unusual form of skin disease called epidermodysplasia verruciformis (EV)
HPV 6a-f	Genital warts/cervical pre-cancer/vulvar pre-cancer/giant warts/a wart cancer type called Buschke-Lowenstein tumour/laryngeal warts
HPV 7	'Butchers' warts
HPV 8	Flat spots in EV patients
HPV 9	Warts and flat spots in EV patients
HPV 10a,b	Flat warts
HPV 11a,b	Genital warts/cervical pre-cancer/vulvar pre-cancer/giant warts/a wart cancer type called Buschke-Lowenstein's tumour/laryngeal warts
HPV 12	Warts and flat spots in EV patients
HPV 13	A type of mouth lesion called Heck lesions
HPV 14a,b	Skin lesions of EV patients
HPV 15	Skin lesions of EV patients

HPV 16	Flat genital growths not usually seen as a wart/cervical pre-cancer/vulvar pre-cancer/Bowenoid papulosis* and forerunners of this/Bowen's disease/cancer of the cervix, vulva, penis and larynx
HPV 17a,b	Skin lesions from EV patients
HPV 18	Cancer of the cervix and penis
HPV 19-29	Various warty and overgrowth lesions on the skin of EV patients
HPV 30	Cancer of the larynx
HPV 31	Cancer of the cervix
HPV 32	A type of mouth lesion called Heck lesions
HPV 33	Bowenoid papulosis*/cancer of the cervix
HPV 34	Bowenoid papulosis*
HPV 35	Cervical pre-cancer/cancer of the cervix
HPV 36	Actinic keratosis (a skin growth)
HPV 37	Keratoacanthoma (a special type of skin growth)
HPV 39	Cervical pre-cancer and cancer of the cervix
HPV 38	Malignant melanoma (one case)
HPV 40	Cancer of the larynx
HPV 41	Multiple flat warts on skin from a young girl
HPV 42	Cervical and vulvar pre-cancer
HPV 43	Cervical pre-cancer
HPV 44	Cervical pre-cancer
HPV 45	Cervical pre-cancer and cancer of the cervix
HPV 51	Cervical pre-cancer and cancer of the cervix
HPV 52	Cervical pre-cancer and cancer of the cervix
HPV 54	Cancer of the penis/cervical pre-cancer and cancer of the cervix
HPV 55	Bowenoid papulosis*
HPV 56	Cervical pre-cancer
HPV 57	Pre-cancer of the cervix and mouth

*A special type of warty growth called Bowenoid papulosis. This occurs only in men and is on the penis.

Warts on the hands and knees and other non-genital areas cannot turn into genital warts. You cannot catch genital warts from someone's hand, knee or skin warts.

The human papillomavirus (HPV) belongs to a family of viruses called papovaviruses. It is a DNA virus. DNA is the part of the virus that stores instructions on how to behave, rather like a computer program. Many DNA viruses remain in the body forever, once they are caught. Examples are herpes, hepatitis B, pox, Epstein-Barr, cytomegalovirus and varicella-zoster viruses.

The number of people with genital warts seems to be increasing. The whole subject of genital warts and genital HPV has become very complex and confusing. Just about every month something new is learnt about HPVs, but so far as we learn more we discover just how much more remains to be learned.

Much more research is needed to fully understand the nature of HPV and to discover satisfactory treatments and cures. In the meantime doctors are forced to work with incomplete knowledge, and there are some questions you might like to ask which can't be answered.

Stages of HPV

There are several stages of human papillomavirus (HPV) development. Latent or subclinical HPV can't be seen with the naked eye and can't be felt. It may not even be picked up by the usual tests. More advanced HPV may lie close to the surface of the skin but still be detected only by sophisticated tests such as colposcopy (a type of microscope) or a PAP smear. In other HPV infections the warts can be felt and often seen with the naked eye.

Basically however there are two broad groups of human papillomavirus manifestation, latent or subclinical and clinical or macroscopic infection.

Latent or Subclinical HPV manifestation

Human papillomavirus you can't see with the naked eye or feel, may be called subclinical or latent. Some subclinical warts may look like baby macroscopic warts, if you look at them with the aid of acetic acid and magnification. Others have a completely different appearance. When HPV is latent the skin looks normal.

There is no way yet of telling whether the HPV you can't see or feel is active and infectious, or asleep (dormant) and non infectious. It may be that HPV which is hidden away is being kept in check by a good body immune system, which stops the virus from growing up to the surface of the skin.

Latent and subclinical HPV manifestation are at least 100 times more common than the ones you can see or feel. Studies are now suggesting that HPV may be extremely widespread. Possibly it is acquired at birth or during early childhood. Some researchers consider that to have HPV may even be normal. Scientists are still debating. If it is normal for the majority of people to have genital human papillomavirus, then it is not yet understood why some people develop macroscopic infection (warts you can see with the naked eye or feel) and others do not. Possibilities include contact with someone who has a lot of active HPV, and factors involving the body's own defence mechanisms.

Clinical warts (macroscopic infection)

Warts you can see with the naked eye or feel, are called clinical or macroscopic infections. The medical name is condylomata.

In developed countries these warts are the most common sexually transmitted viral disease, three times more common than genital herpes. Most people who get them are aged sixteen to 25 years.

Clinical warts are piled up heaps of skin cells filled with genital human papillomavirus. They range in size from smaller than a pinhead to several centimetres in diameter. Most are less than one centimetre, unless they are left untreated. Usually there is a range of sizes.

They occur in many different shapes. They can be shaped like a cauliflower (this is called acuminate), like a pimple (this is called papular), or flat.

Someone who has warts can have just one type, but most commonly they have a mixture of flat ones, pimply ones and sometimes cauliflower ones. Warts typically occur in groups or crops, most often several crops at a time, in different places.

The cauliflower type prefer moist areas which get slightly damaged during intercourse. Most people don't realize slight damage occurs to the skin each time you have sex. There are usually tiny breaks in the skin, so small you can't see them without a microscope. These breaks occur in places such as the opening of the vagina, the vulva, and under the foreskin and at the base of the penis.

In the drier areas warts tend to be more rounded and pimply than cauliflower like, and also tend to have a thicker layer of skin covering them. Sometimes this thicker layer of covering skin makes the treatment a little bit more difficult.

Figure 5.2 Types of wart growth

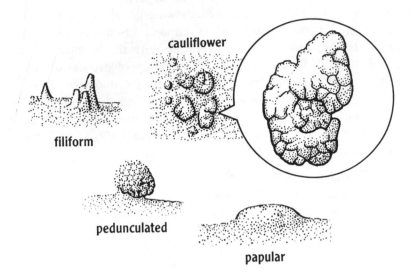

cauliflower

filiform

pedunculated

papular

Up to 25% of men with warts you can see on the penis have warts in the eye of the penis. Sometimes when the warts occur in the eye of the penis and you can't see how far down they go, you have to see a water-works specialist, called a urologist.

Up to one in three females and one in ten males with warts also have warts in the anal area or on the skin between the anus and genitals, even if they have not had anal sex. HPV may be transferred to these areas by secretions during sexual intercourse. If receptive anal sex has been practised the doctor will have to check in the anus. These days most doctors try to discourage men and women from having unprotected anal sex because of the risk of infection, especially with the human immunodeficiency virus (HIV), which causes AIDS.

In women warts are occasionally found on the inside walls of the vagina, on the cervix and sometimes at the urethral opening. When they are found inside, the woman needs to be referred to a specialist for laser, diathermy, cryotherapy or occasionally ointment treatment.

Women who have warts you can see or feel on the inside (the cervix or vagina) almost always have them on the outside as well. The reverse however is not true: most women who have warts on the outside do not also have warts in their vagina or cervix that require treatment.

When you have any warts which can be seen, usually you also have subclinical warts, the kind which can't be seen except with special techniques.

Figure 5.3 Wart virus activation

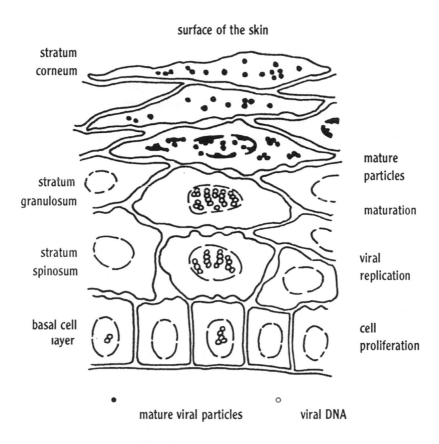

surface of the skin

stratum corneum

stratum granulosum

mature particles

maturation

stratum spinosum

viral replication

basal cell layer

cell proliferation

● mature viral particles   ○ viral DNA

Where in the skin is the human papillomavirus?

The skin is made up of several layers which are supported by a layer called the dermis. See Figure 5.3. The bottom layer is called the basal cell layer, the next layer is called the stratum spinosum, the next layer the stratum granulosum and the top layer the stratum corneum.

Human papillomavirus is found in the bottom layer of cells of the skin called the basal cell layer. It is generally assumed that the virus leads to changes in some of the bottom layer of cells, which may cause increased cell growth and thus some of the manifestations of human papillomavirus. Studies have shown that extensive multiplication of the human papillomavirus first occurs in the stratum spinosum (second bottom layer). In experiments on animals human papillomavirus virus causes overgrowth of cells in this layer. The medical name for this overgrowth of cells is acanthosis.

If the human papillomavirus continues to be active, mature or adult virus particles are first found in the nucleoli (a part of the DNA centre of the cell) of the stratum spinosum, and in the stratum granulosum (third and second layers from the top). Where the cells form the stratum corneum (outside or top layer of skin) there are a lot of mature wart virus particles present. These are highly infectious.

Cells in the top skin layer produce a protein called keratin which makes the skin tough and waterproof. The human papillomavirus makes the cells produce more keratin. This is called keratosis. Normally cells in the top layer of skin have no nuclei in them, but some cells which have been keratinised may have nuclei: this is called parakeratosis.

Human papillomavirus has been found in normal skin up to two centimetres from a genital wart as well as being found in the skin of people without genital warts, including virgins.

How common is HPV?

Early estimates of HPV ranged from as low as 1% or 2% of people. Better tests raised the figure to 20% to 40%. Just becoming available is new testing equipment so sensitive it can pick up small numbers of human papillomavirus inside a cell. Some studies with this equipment indicate that a carrier state for human papillomavirus exists in most adolescents. Indications from some studies are that up to 90% of adults have one type of genital HPV (type 16), at least in latent form. See Chapter 19 *The Abnormal PAP Smear and Cancer of the Cervix* for more details.

Figure 5.4 The structure of warts

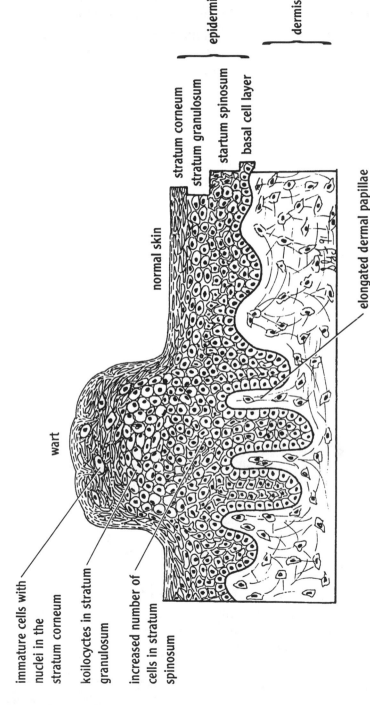

Figure 5.4 The structure of warts

Figure 5.5 Skin cell changes in HPV

Skin Layer	Microscopic appearance
Stratum corneum (top layer)	Hyperkeratosis (increased keratin)/ parakeratosis nuclei in otherwise mature cells)
Stratum granulosum	Koilocytes These are unusual cells caused by HPV. They can only be seen under a microscope. These cells have a clear area next to the cell nucleus which sometimes pushes the nucleus to the side of the cell.
Stratum spinosum	Increased number of cells (acanthosis)
Basal cells (Bottom layer)	Normal
Dermis	Papillae (folds of skin) elongated but underlying dermis is normal. This is the layer which supports the above layers of skin.

Testing for HPV

Clinical warts can usually be seen with the naked eye or felt, but testing for latent human papillomavirus infection in the lower layers of the skin can be difficult. Methods used include the PAP smear, colposcopy, and specialized tests on biopsies of skin. New methods of testing are being developed, and it seems sometimes that every more powerful method of detecting HPV reveals more HPV!

Are warts really a serious problem?

If so many people have genital HPV, and it is so often subclinical or latent and apparently no problem, it's reasonable to ask if warts are worth worrying about at all.

Most wart infections seem not to be harmful apart from the fact they can spread on you or your partner. Warts may go away by themselves.

Some types of genital warts however have a strong association with cancer, in both men and women, and that's a very good first reason for having treatment for any genital warts you can see or feel.

Genital warts are often associated with other infections, for example chlamydia, which can occur with no symptoms in either men or women. A checkup will confirm whether or not what you have is warts, and whether it is associated with anything else.

If you have warts there is a high chance you will pass them on to your partner. The risk of passing them on can be as high as 66% if they have only recently developed on you. Your partner may get them in places where they need an operation to remove them, such as the opening of the urethra or on the surface of the cervix. Warts can also be spread to the mouth by oral sex, although this is very rare.

Human papillomavirus can be transmitted to your baby. See Chapter 21 *STDs and Your Baby.*

Sometimes warts can be painful during sex. Other problems include itchiness and bleeding that results from small breaks in the skin underneath or between crowded warts. Infection puts a strain on the body's immune system, increasing susceptibility to other infections. It is difficult to keep the skin clean where warts are present.

Your warts might not bother you now, but if you leave them untreated you can spread the infection on your own body and the problem may become more serious.

When you have warts which can be seen, I recommend you do not have sex. Having sex will increase the spread of infection on yourself and your partner. It's easier for your body to fight a limited rather than widely spread infection. Getting rid of the warts means you can start having sex again.

Most people want to get rid of warts quickly because the infection makes them feel dirty or ugly.

In summary, there are many good reasons for having warts treated, even if they do not appear to be causing any immediate harm. The length of time it takes to get rid of warts varies from person to person and the type of treatment that is used.

HPV and cancer

Several HPV types have been detected in cervical cancers and are regarded as high risk. HPV type 16 is most common, followed by HPV type 18. Less common high risk HPV types are 31, 33, 35, 39, 45, 51, 52, 54 and 56. See Figure 5.1.

HPV types 6 and 11 have been detected in more than 90% of common genital wart infections. HPV types 42, 43, 44 and 55 have been detected in either flat or subclinical lesions (the ones you can't see). Their cancer causing potential is considered low.

Smoking is believed to be an important cofactor in warts and cervical cancer. Nicotine has been found in cervical mucus at ten times the concentration in the blood of the same person. Research has shown that nicotine alters the human papillomavirus to a form in which it combines with the DNA of the cell nucleus. This may be a way in which cancer is started.

The development of cancer of the cervix may occur over a five to 15 year period. For the vulva, penis, anus and rectum the cancer risk is low and the process very slow. HIV infection can accelerate the progression of cervical and anal cell abnormality to cancer.

It is extremely important for all women to have regular PAP smears so that any areas which may become cancerous are treated early. A lot of women I have talked to have been quite frightened of the treatment, but really if the areas that need treatment are small, it can be done as an outpatient and does not seem to interfere with the ability to get pregnant and have children. See Chapter 19 *The Abnormal PAP Smear and Cancer Of The Cervix* for more information.

How do you catch warts?

In this chapter we are talking only about warts that occur in the genital region. The warts you can see or feel are caught mainly by having sexual intercourse with someone who has them.

You can also spread warts on yourself by touching or scratching them, then touching yourself somewhere else on the genitals. This form of spread is called auto-inoculation. It can happen once the warts are big enough to see or just before they get to this stage.

The possibility of transmission by things like towels or doctors' instruments is currently being explored. Doctors call this transmission by fomites.

If I have sex with someone with warts will I get it?

Currently there is no way to measure exactly how infective or contagious warts are. This is because the human papillomavirus cannot be grown in laboratories, so infectivity experiments cannot be done. When infection of cells does occur it takes a long time to develop macroscopic infection — anything from three weeks to nine months and occasionally longer. The reason for this is uncertain.

We do know that if someone has genital warts that you can see, the chance of a person they have sex with catching warts is very high, about a two out of three chance of catching the disease.

This means that if you have warts you can see, you should see your doctor to get them treated. If you don't get warts treated you run the risk of spreading them more on yourself, as well as giving them to your partner. Your partner should be treated too.

People who have been treated for the warts you can see with the naked eye or feel should regard themselves as infectious and continue to take precautions for at six months after treatment, even though there are no visible warts remaining, because there is a possibility of the warts coming back during that time.

How infectious are the warts you can't see or feel?

If you have been told you have genital HPV but you have never had warts you can see or feel, and you have been checked by a doctor practised at looking for warts, then this question applies to you. Unfortunately, there is not yet any medical evidence that answers it. That's not the news people want to hear, but research should soon provide an answer. I don't usually recommend any precautionary measures except to make sure that you do not catch some other sex disease.

How long does it take for warts to appear?

If you catch warts, it can be as short as three weeks or up to eight months or longer before they appear. Most commonly it's from six to eight weeks. Changes due to human papillomavirus on the cervix however, may take up to six months or longer to show. For this reason women with genital wart infection should always have another PAP smear within 12 months of having macroscopic genital warts.

Where to look for warts in women

If you have warts and you want to check where they are or make sure they are all treated, it is best to examine yourself systematically with a mirror.

Start by looking and feeling with your fingers in the pubic hairs along the pubic bone. Feel and look on the labia majora (the big flaps), then the skin between the vagina and anus and the anal skin. It is quite common for warts to be missed in the anal skin and the mons pubis (the hair at the top of the pubic bone). You may want to wash your hands before you go further, then spread the flaps out so you can see the moist, smaller inner flaps, called the labia minora.

Carefully run your fingers over the skin. The warts if you can't see them feel harder than the rest of the skin. For women it's usually easier to feel the warts than to see them.

Quite often warts hide at the urinary opening (urethra) or in the folds of the vagina at the entrance. The skin has to be really stretched here to see the warts.

Warts in the mouth can occur under the tongue, on the roof of the mouth or on the insides of the cheek. It is extremely uncommon for warts to occur on the surface of the tongue, and those big pink lumps on the tongue at the back of your mouth are normal lumps called papillae. If you feel a new lump in your mouth that you think might be a wart, get your doctor to check it for you. Luckily it is not common for warts to occur in the mouth.

If you have had anal sex and you have perianal warts (warts near the anus) there is a 50% chance they will extend inside your anal canal.

Women with warts should visit a doctor to see if the warts extend inside the walls of the vagina or onto the cervix.

Where to look for warts in men

In men it is a little easier to see warts than it is for women. Start by looking into the eye of the penis. To do this you need to open the lips of the eye as the warts can hide just inside the opening. If there are no warts at the opening it is exceedingly rare to have warts you can see in the tube further down. If you can see the bottom of any wart it is again unlikely there are any further down the tube.

Sometimes doctors will look inside the opening of the tube after a wart has been treated. This can be done with an instrument called a cystoscope, or a smaller and shorter instrument which is similar to the instrument used for looking in ears.

The next area to inspect is the head of the penis or glans penis. If you are not circumcised you have to retract the foreskin. Be careful not to mistake the frilly bits around the edge as warts. Some men have bigger frills than others. Uncircumcised men tend to have worse wart infection than circumcised men and the warts tend to hide under the foreskin where it is quite moist.

Now move on to the coronal sulcus, the area just under the head of the penis. Be careful not to mistake the normal glands close to the frenulum as warts. Mostly they are small but they can be large and there can be as many as six. They are commonly mistaken for warts. Unlike warts they are usually exactly symmetrical, one mirroring the other on each side of the frenulum. See Figure 5.6.

Next look at the shaft of the penis, then the bottom of the penis among the pubic hairs and then the scrotum. Check the anal area. Up to 10% of men with warts have anal warts. Very rarely warts occur in the mouth. See the end of the section on women (above) for more information.

If you have perianal warts (warts near the anus) and have had anal sex, there is a 50% chance the warts will extend inside your anal canal.

I've heard about the vinegar test

Sometimes it is useful for a doctor to use 3% to 5% acetic acid to look for wart infection. Normal vinegar contains at least 4% acetic acid.

When acetic acid is applied to skin in the genital area it is taken up by cells containing the human papillomavirus, which go white. However not all things that go white are warts. It is quite common for people with skin fungal infections to have white patches and areas that have been recently treated often go white. The times when this test is most useful are when a doctor is treating troublesome warts and wants to mark the area of skin that needs treatment.

In men the acetic acid is applied all over the penis. In women it is painted onto the cervix and the result examined with the aid of a colposcope (a type of magnifying glass).

Things which can be mistaken for warts

It is extremely awkward to get a good view of your genital area, especially for women. You can get into all sorts of contortions, but an appropriately placed mirror is the best approach. Anal warts are almost impossible for you to inspect yourself.

Figure 5.6 Normal features sometimes mistaken for warts

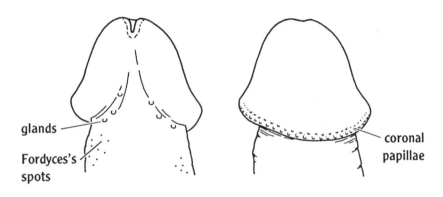

glands

Fordyces's spots

coronal papillae

It can be very difficult to tell if a lump on the skin of your genitals is a wart. When a lump appears in this region you should see a doctor, to be sure.

The most common mistake people make is when they have a pimple and they think it is a wart. Pimples in the genital region are very common in both men and women.

Another common mistake is made by young men who often notice an enlargement of glands in the skin of the penis as they grow older, and they mistake these normal little white lumps for warts.

In women prominent papillae (normal skin growths called vestibular papillae) on the inner surface of the labia and vaginal opening can be mistaken for warts, even by experienced doctors.

Sometimes warts are mistaken for another disease called

molluscum contagiosum. This is caused by a virus, it is contagious and it can be spread during sex. Children often catch it from other children, however in children it is spread by casual contact, not by sex. It causes lumps that grow full of white stuff. These lumps have a dimple in the centre. In people with HIV infection these lumps can grow quite large and do not always have the umbilicated centre.

Molluscum contagiosum is not thought to be particularly serious, but it should be treated. Molluscum lesions are highly infectious. Like warts they can be itchy, but (also like warts) if you scratch them you will spread them further on your body.

If you are at all suspicious or uncertain, don't be embarrassed to see your doctor. Ask them to check you to make sure there is no infection, especially one of the other sex diseases like chlamydia that can occur with no signs or symptoms. It is quite common for more than one sex disease to be caught at the same time.

Syphilis can also cause skin growths that look like warts, but syphilis is easily distinguished from other infections by a blood test.

What treatment is available for warts?

The first sort of treatment I want to tell you about I call the 'Picasso' treatment. It is to apply podophyllin paint (usually a 25% concentration in alcohol) to the infected areas. Picasso may well be turning in his grave!

Unfortunately with this treatment and other forms of treatment the warts often recur. Podophyllotoxin is an alternative reported to have lower recurrence rates, but it is still not 100% effective.

Part of the reason for recurrences of genital wart infection is that only the warts on the surface which are seen are treated. Others under the skin can only be treated when they reach the surface.

Podophyllin is still the best first treatment because it is cheap, easily applied and can produce dramatic success in some patients, even when they have extensive infection. Podophyllotoxin, a purer drug than podophyllin, will soon be available in Australia and will become the drug of first choice.

The treatment is not painful although sometimes burning is felt for a minute or two. You can apply it yourself once you have been shown what to do. A doctor's prescription is required. The solution is placed on the wart and a little around the wart using a match stick and allowed to dry. This process is repeated two more times. The paint is then washed off after four hours, sooner if sensitivity such as burning or pain persists after administration. The paint is applied like this every two to seven days until the warts disappear. Some doctors will give you slightly different instructions and some doctors are so concerned about the possible side effects they will not give you the treatment to do yourself. Be careful to follow your doctor's instructions because the podophyllin is not always put in a special methylated spirit, and when this happens the base that is used may stick to the skin and not wash off like the above solution. If the warts are still present after three weeks an alternative treatment should be used.

You should not use podophyllin if there is a skin infection or a sore on the skin, because it may give you severe burns. If the doctor gives you the podophyllin treatment to apply at home you must use the paint only on yourself. The paint cannot be used after the date on the bottle has expired.

Don't drink alcohol until the paint is washed off, as alcohol can enhance the toxic effects of podophyllin inside the body. Podophyllin is a very toxic chemical which is absorbed through the skin. It must only be used in tiny amounts.

The paint cannot be used inside the vagina or urethra because it goes directly into the bloodstream and can cause serious harm such as paralysis or a severe depression of the body's blood cells. Some of the other side effects are kidney and liver problems if it is used in too large quantities and absorbed inside the body. People have died from using this treatment the wrong way, so always follow your doctor's instructions. If you are not sure about your doctor's instructions don't be afraid to call back to clarify or ask another physician or clinic.

Pregnant women should not use this treatment as it can harm the baby and cause growth abnormalities.

Reading all this you may think you will try an over the counter treatment for general warts instead! Well, the news is worse than for podophyllin. The over the counter treatments are designed for ordinary skin, which is tougher than genital skin. These treatments invariably cause severe burning and ulcers and resultant scarring of the genital skin: don't try using them.

Another treatment that is quite good is one I call the 'Eskimo treatment. For this treatment the doctor freezes the wart. This is done with liquid nitrogen or a freezing instrument called a cryoprobe.

Other treatments are with chemicals such as trichloroacetic acid (TCA), silver nitrate (if you don't mind getting black spots where you have been treated, until the wart falls off), surgical scissor excision, diathermy or hyfrecation, laser and 5% flurouracil cream.

Trichloroacetic acid (TCA) 80% to 85% is an acid which burns through the skin. It should be put only on the wart and then washed off after four hours. It is extremely important that TCA is placed only on the wart or it will burn normal skin, causing soreness. It is used differently if supplied in a lower concentration. This treatment is only available through specialized STD centres and has not been found to be better than any of the commonly used treatments.

Lasers can be used to treat warts wherever they are. It works by evaporating water from the cells being 'zapped'. This kills the cells. Laser treatment is particularly good for people who have recurrent or widespread disease.

Diathermy is an electrical treatment that works by burning the skin by direct heat. Hyfrecation is also an electrical treatment which can burn like diathermy when high voltages are used, but at lower voltages it works just like a laser by evaporating water from the cells.

Surgical excision means the wart is cut off with a pair of scissors, either under local or general anaesthetic. This treatment is particularly good for anal and perianal warts, although some bleeding occurs for a few days after the treatment. With perianal warts treatment to waterproof the skin with zinc and castor oil may reduce the chance of warts recurring.

Treatment by diathermy, hyfrecation and surgical excision require a local anaesthetic or sometimes a general anaesthetic. Usually the local anaesthetic is by injection with a tiny, tiny needle but there is a new local anaesthetic which can be rubbed on. It's called EMLA and works in sixty minutes or sooner. It is quite expensive.

Interferon is another treatment that seems to work in difficult cases. It is also used to treat a special type of leukaemia called hairy cell leukaemia and is being used to treat people with hepatitis

C. Interferon can be given by injection into the wart – not for people who don't like needles. Sometimes it is given direct into the bloodstream. It can clear warts but it also causes side effects such as a high temperature and feeling like you have flu. Treatment needs to be given more than once and is expensive.

Recurrences

It is a problem with warts that they often come back again after they have been treated. Don't despair, they do eventually go away, providing you keep up the treatment and avoid re-infection.

How should I look after myself if I have warts?

A good body immune system should keep warts from growing up to the surface of the skin. Things which are thought to encourage growth of the warts are the same things which reduce your body's immune status, such as severe illness like AIDS or certain serious kidney diseases, some drugs that doctors may give you such as prednisolone, re-exposure to large amounts of the wart virus, other infections, or local trauma such as an injury.

Smoking impairs the body's immunity to wart virus because it reduces the number of cells in the skin that are responsible for detecting the presence of HPV. These cells called Langerhans cells are like guard cells. If a person stops smoking the number of Langerhans cells gradually returns to normal.

What sort of sex can I have if I have warts?

The advice given to people with warts keeps changing as new information comes to hand. I'm giving you the best advice I can at this point in time, but I'm aware that other doctors may give you quite different advice and that the recommendations will continue to change.

People seem to forget that when a doctor advises you not to have sex while you have warts this means no masturbation either: masturbation just rubs them more on yourself.

It is especially important for women not to have sex when they have warts that can be seen or felt. This is to stop the infection being pushed inside the vagina and up onto the cervix. It is much harder to treat the warts inside.

It used to be common for doctors to tell men to wear condoms when they had visible warts but this was before people had thought about spreading the infection more on themselves than on the other person.

As you can see, it's not much fun having warts. Don't be too despondent though. As soon as the warts are gone (you can't see them any more) it is OK to start having sex again provided a condom is worn. The condom is to reduce the chance of passing them on or catching them again when they are very tiny and you can't quite see them. Ideally a vaginal condom would do the job better, but these are not readily available yet.

How long should you use condom s for? That's a trick question. Every doctor will give you a different answer. I usually recommend six months after the warts you can see have gone.

Why such a long time? It's because warts can come back any time up to six months in some people, making the person infectious again. Starting new sexual relationships I encourage the use of condoms for the first six months anyway. If you are in a long term relationship I recommend avoiding intercourse until the warts have gone, then depending on how strongly you feel about using condoms you can decide whether to use them or not. Discuss this with your doctor.

Pregnancy and warts

Warts may reappear during pregnancy. If you get them for the first time during pregnancy they may grow quite large and spread if they are not treated. Podophyllin should not be used in pregnancy.

Babies and warts

Sometimes the warts you can see are passed onto the baby. It is common for babies to acquire HPV at birth. Doctors call this spread from the mother to the baby vertical spread. See Chapter 21 *STDs and Your Baby*.

6

HEPATITIS

KEY CONCEPTS

Antibody   Protein produced by the body in response to toxins or foreign organisms.

Cirrhosis   Scarred liver due to long term damage.

Hepatitis   Inflammation of the liver.

Hepatitis B carrier   Someone who has been infectious with hepatitis B for at least six months.

Hepatitis B vaccination   A series of injections to build your body's immunity to prevent you from becoming infected with hepatitis B.

Hepatoma   A cancer of the liver.

Hepatitis by the alphabet

Hepatitis comes in several forms, identified by the letters A, B, C, D, and E. Hepatitis B is the most common, and that's what I'll talk about first.

What is hepatitis B?

Hepatitis B is an illness that results in inflammation of the liver. It can be pretty serious, many people who get it are ill for several months, though sometimes the symptoms are not obvious. If hepatitis B is not properly treated it can cause permanent liver damage, cirrhosis, cancer and death.

People sometimes call hepatitis yellow jaundice because that is what happens to people who catch it — they turn yellow, unless the hepatitis is very mild. Sometimes people turn yellow for other reasons, one of them is eating a lot of carrots. Yes, these people turn orange-yellow the same color as the carrots they have been eating! Luckily this doesn't do them any harm.

There are many causes of hepatitis. Drinking too much alcohol is one of the most common. Others are infection (particularly with viruses such as hepatitis A, B, C, D and E viruses), use of some drugs and exposure to toxic chemicals.

Hepatitis B is a viral infection caused by the hepatitis B virus. It is also called the Australia antigen because it was first described in an Australian Aboriginal in 1962. This man had used intravenous drugs while in New York.

Hepatitis B is a DNA virus that belongs to a group of viruses called the hepadnavirus group. It has a central core containing the DNA and a surface coat which is called the hepatitis B surface antigen.

How is hepatitis B caught?

Hepatitis B is spread the same way as the human immunodeficiency virus (HIV − the AIDS virus): by sex, by blood and from an infected mother to her baby.

Hepatitis also spreads in one way that HIV does not, and that is through body secretions. People who live in the same house as someone who is infectious with hepatitis B might also get it. Cuts, sores and grazes are thought to be very important ways the hepatitis B virus is spread within households.

The hepatitis B virus is much more infectious than HIV, and in some cases it spreads in ways that are not obvious.

The hepatitis B virus is found in blood, vaginal secretions, ejaculate, feces, breast milk, fluid which oozes out of sores, saliva, sweat and tears.

Saliva however is not thought to be a cause of spread. Tests on gibbons showed that they did not get infected even when they had large amounts of saliva from hepatitis B infected people put into their mouths, and then had their teeth brushed!

Hepatitis B can be spread by contaminated instruments such as those used for ear-piercing, tattooing, acupuncture and tribal rituals. It can also be passed on by sharing razors or sharing needles. It is possible but unlikely that it is spread by mosquitoes and bed bugs in countries where there is a very high carrier rate.

In many countries blood transfusions are tested for hepatitis B and C, syphilis and HIV to make sure they don't pass on these infections.

Are some groups more at risk from hepatitis B?

Hepatitis B is found more often among certain groups of people. It is particularly common in South East Asia, tropical Africa and parts of China. In these countries and continents it is very common for people to be infected around the time of birth or in early childhood. Some studies show that 70% to 95% of the population has had the infection at some time and that eight to 20% of the population are carriers. In Eastern Europe, the Mediterranean region, the USSR, South-West Asia and Central and South America from 20% to 55% of the population has been infected at some stage and two to seven per cent of the population are carriers.

There are thought to be over 300 million people infected throughout the world. One in five of these will die of cirrhosis and one in 20 will die of cancer of the liver (hepatoma).

Hepatitis B is also commonly found in people who use intravenous drugs and share needles (these people can get infected either from the shared needle, or they can get it from having sex with a partner who has it). It is also commonly found amongst males who practice anal sex, and among people who have a lot of sexual partners, particularly if they have sex with someone who comes from a country with a lot of hepatitis B.

What are the symptoms of hepatitis B?

Sometimes people get no symptoms. Others may get sick within six weeks or up to six months after they have come into contact with the infection. Initially people may just feel more tired than usual, with generalised aches and pains, and think they have the flu. Sometimes there can be pain in the finger joints and a rash on the body. Often the person feels unwell and does not feel like eating. Sometimes they are even sick enough to vomit. Some people get pain in their abdomen.

After this the jaundice may start. The urine is darker than usual and the whites of the eyes become yellow. The yellowness can sometimes be noticed over the whole body.

Often people with hepatitis B infection lose weight but regain it after they clear the infection from their system. It may take three to six months before the person is well again.

Most people with hepatitis B can be looked after at home with plenty of rest in bed and eating a balanced diet with food that does not make them feel nauseated.

People with very severe illness can stop thinking properly and develop severe bruising and swelling of the body (edema). People who are this sick need to be admitted to hospital for special treatment.

Hepatitis B is diagnosed by blood tests that look for the virus and check how well the liver is functioning.

Who is likely to catch hepatitis B?

Health care workers who come in contact with blood or secretions from infected people, mentally handicapped people who live in institutions, intravenous drug users, males who practice anal sex, people who have multiple sexual partners and people who live in a country where there is a lot of hepatitis B are all subject to above average risk of catching the disease.

How do I know if I have hepatitis B or have had hepatitis B?

To know for sure if you have or have had hepatitis you need to take a blood test. The test looks for the surface coat of the virus (hepatitis B surface antigen) and for antibodies against the virus coat called hepatitis B surface antibodies.

If you have hepatitis B surface antigen (HBsAg), you are infectious. If you have hepatitis B surface antibody you have had the infection or have been vaccinated, though it may take up to six months after infection with the virus to develop surface antibodies.

Generally you can only catch hepatitis B once. Provided you have reasonable amounts of antibodies you should be able to fight off future infections. The tests that are done usually tell you if your antibody levels are all right.

I've been told I'm a hepatitis carrier

Five to ten per cent of people who catch hepatitis B remain infected. People who have hepatitis B in their blood for longer than six months are called carriers. Of these, half will become non-infectious over the next six months to two years. The rest will remain infected indefinitely and may go on to develop complications.

If you are a carrier you should make sure that all people you have intimate contact with are vaccinated. This means all your sexual partners and people who live in the same house as you should be vaccinated. If you are female then your obstetrician should know when you are pregnant so that the baby can be vaccinated at birth.

Figure 6.1 The growth of hepatitis antibodies

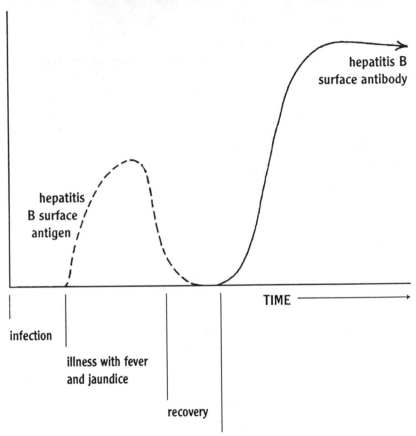

Carriers often have no symptoms and may not realize they are infectious unless they have a blood test.

Some doctors wanted to call homosexual carriers 'hepatitis Harolds' after the name of the patient in whom the carrier state was first fully established. This terminology did not catch on, but its basis was the similarity with 'typhoid Mary', an asymptomatic typhoid carrier in New York who infected many people through her work as a cook. In fact she was caught once but escaped to continue work as a cook, further spreading the infection.

Why is hepatitis B infection so serious?

Sometimes people who catch hepatitis B do not get better. They become carriers and mostly they remain continually infectious. They may get seriously ill and have to be admitted to hospital. Their liver can end up working so poorly that they can't make protein and they bleed badly. Some of these people die. Others go on to have chronic liver disease.

The medical names of these liver diseases are chronic persistent hepatitis, chronic lobular hepatitis, chronic active hepatitis and cirrhosis.

Others eventually develop cancer of the liver, called hepatoma. In special medical clinics hepatoma can sometimes be detected early and removed surgically before it causes any problems. It is one of the ten most common cancers in the world: there are approximately a quarter of a million new cases of liver cancer each year. In many countries liver cancer is the most common cancer in men.

Even that's not all: the results of persistent hepatitis B infection can also include kidney or blood vessel disease and other chronic medical conditions.

Hepatitis carriers should not donate semen, blood or body organs. They should inform their partners they are infectious and also let their doctor and dentist know.

People who have had hepatitis B infection in the past and become non infectious but then get HIV infection can have a recurrence of hepatitis. This can be checked for by blood testing. In addition, people who have HIV infection and then catch hepatitis B are more likely to become chronic carriers.

Hepatitis D

Hepatitis D is less common than hepatitis B, but it is also a very dangerous and sexually transmittable infection. It can be spread by blood and by sex.

Hepatitis D used to be called the delta virus. It is a tiny virus that can superinfect someone who already has hepatitis B infection.

It can also infect someone at the same time that they catch the hepatitis B virus.

If both the hepatitis B and delta virus infections occur at the same time there is often an extremely severe illness resulting in liver failure. Superinfection can sometimes cause an attack of acute hepatitis and subsequently the person may develop chronic liver disease.

There is no satisfactory treatment for delta hepatitis infection but as it can only infect people with the hepatitis B virus inside them, a vaccination against hepatitis B will also guard against hepatitis D.

Hepatitis D cannot infect someone who has cleared the hepatitis B infection out of their body and so developed an immunity.

Hepatitis A

Hepatitis A is a virus that lives in the feces and urine of infected people.

How is it caught?

Most commonly hepatitis A is spread by food or water which is contaminated with infected human feces and then eaten. It is quite a common infection in underdeveloped countries that do not have sewage systems and use their vegetable gardens as the toilet.

It is spread directly from person to person by contact with feces or urine. This can happen by sexual intercourse where the infected secretions are put in the mouth. Sometimes the virus may be on a used condom and if the hands are not washed after removal of the condom it may spread that way.

What happens if I catch hepatitis A?

If you catch the virus it can take anywhere from 10 to 50 days before you become ill, but not every one becomes ill. You may feel generally off-colour and nauseated, have a slight temperature, lose a little weight and become yellow. The yellow is most noticeable in the eyes. In addition you may feel sore just below the ribs on the right side where the liver is. Once you get over the illness you cannot catch it again, and there are no long term complications. You cannot become a carrier for hepatitis A.

How do I avoid catching hepatitis A?

If you are travelling to a country where hepatitis A is common you can be given an injection of immunoglobulin from your doctor just before you go. This gives your body protective antibodies to fight off the infection. In addition you should avoid food and water that might be contaminated with raw sewage. Always wash your hands after sexual intercourse. See Chapter 2 for more information on the safety of oral sex.

Hepatitis C

This is a virus which is spread through contaminated blood and in some circumstances by sexual intercourse with someone with the infection. It can take up to 50 days after infection before there are any symptoms and even longer for the blood test to show that you have the infection.

The blood test to detect this virus has only recently been developed and there are still problems with its use. It is not possible from the current blood test to differentiate between being a chronic hepatitis C carrier or having had the infection and cleared it from your system.

Up to half of the people who catch hepatitis C are thought to develop liver problems. If you are found to be positive for the hepatitis C test your doctor will probably repeat the test and perform liver function tests. If your liver function is abnormal you will probably be referred to a hospital for further investigation and treatment with alpha interferon .

Treatment for hepatitis

What should I do if I have been exposed to hepatitis?

If you come in contact with someone with hepatitis B (you have had sex with them, have shared needles with them, are living in the same house as them or have an accidental needlestick injury) then you should go and see your doctor straight away. Your doctor will probably take a blood sample from you and then start immediate treatment with hepatitis B vaccination. The vaccine given soon after exposure to the hepatitis B virus will stop you becoming a hepatitis carrier and it may stop you getting infected.

Your doctor may also give you hepatitis B immune globulin if it is within three days of coming in contact with the virus and you definitely know the person was sick with hepatitis B.

Some cases of chronic hepatitis B can be treated with frequent injections of alpha interferon given over several months.

What is hepatitis B vaccination?

The most commonly used vaccination these days is one genetically engineered in the laboratory. It contains a product that makes the body think it has been infected with hepatitis B, so that the body reacts against it and makes antibodies. Then when you come in contact with real hepatitis B your body can readily eradicate the infection before it has a chance to do any harm.

The currently used vaccine is made by growing only the hepatitis B surface antigen (without the rest of the inside of the virus) in bakers yeast. As it is not made from blood it cannot spread any other disease such as HIV infection. The vaccine is given in three doses, usually the first two injections being given one month apart and the third at six months. For the vaccine to work it needs to be given in the muscle of the arm. Occasionally people need a fourth dose to become immune. The immunity develops slowly but may be present after the second injection. There are hardly any side effects from this vaccine except an occasional soreness at the site of injection.

People with HIV infection may not respond properly to vaccination either by not developing an appropriate level of antibodies or by the antibody level falling off more quickly than it should. In other groups of people the vaccine has been shown to last for at least five years and possibly longer.

Who should be vaccinated?

People who use intravenous drugs, males who have sex with other males, people who have had multiple sex partners within the last six months or who are planning to have sex in a country where there is a lot of hepatitis B, people who are mentally handicapped and live in institutions, health workers who are exposed to secretions of people infected with hepatitis B, patients undergoing regular treatment with blood or blood products and sex industry workers should all be vaccinated. In addition the vaccination is being encouraged amongst those ethnic groups with a large amount of hepatitis B in their communities.

The hepatitis B vaccine has been shown to be extremely effective, so we can hope that in the future hepatitis B will be totally eradicated. However up to 10% of people vaccinated do not respond to the vaccine so it is important to have your antibody levels checked after you have completed the course of vaccinations. You may need an extra injection.

Hepatitis B and pregnancy

If you are a hepatitis B carrier, there is a 70% to 90% chance you will pass on the infection to your baby at the time of birth or afterwards. You should let your doctor know that you are a carrier so that your baby can be given treatment at birth to stop them becoming a chronic carrier and developing illness later on in life. See Chapter 20 *STDs and Pregnancy* for more information.

Hepatitis B and babies

Of those babies who catch hepatitis B from their mothers, 85% to 90% will become chronic carriers if they are not vaccinated at birth. See Chapter 21 *STDs and Your Baby* for more information.

7

HIV
(HUMAN IMMUNODEFICIENCY
VIRUS OR AIDS)

Editor's Note for American Edition

Teenagers and young adults are now considered to be a group at extreme risk for HIV infection in the United States. Recent studies have shown a sharp rise in the number of AIDS cases in patients aged 13 to 24 years. While, in the past, many in this age group had been infected by transfusion with contaminated blood products or during unprotected homosexual contacts, this is no longer true. One 1990 study has estimated that one in every five hundred American college students is HIV positive. By 1990, the majority of young women diagnosed with AIDS between ages 20 and 24 (and, therefore, most likely infected during their teen years), had acquired their infection during heterosexual contact.

All sexually active teens and young adults are at risk for HIV infection. All sex without a condom is unsafe sex for this age group. To protect yourself you must know about HIV and AIDS, but that knowledge is not enough. To protect yourself you must believe that you are at risk and take action to make sure you are safe.

Then somewhat unexpectedly, we found ourselves speaking in the language of human rights and dignity. For in what other health area, and at what other time, have we heard such talk of 'rights' and 'social justice'? In invoking the concepts of human rights, of non-discrimination, equity and justice, it is not only the content of policy and institutional action which has been challenged, but also the process through which policies and decisions have been reached.

Jonathan Mann, *AIDS,* 1990,4(suppl 1):S247-S250

KEY CONCEPTS

AIDS The final stages of infection with HIV where the body's immune system has been severely damaged.

HIV infection Infection with the human immunodeficiency virus.

Immune system The body's defences against infection which includes cells and proteins called antibodies.

Immunodeficiency A defect in the ability of the body to fight infection and disease.

Incubation time The length of time it takes for illness to appear after infection has occurred.

Opportunistic infection An infection by an organism that is normally within the body and causes no harm, but becomes a problem when the body's immune system is no longer working properly.

Risk Exposing oneself to danger that can result in harm.

Safer sex Sexual activity that reduces the risk of acquiring a sexually transmittable disease.

Seroconversion time The length of time it takes for antibodies to be made in the body once the infection has occurred.

Seropositive   Antibodies made by the body against HIV infection. They can be found by special blood tests.

T cell A type of white blood cell in the immune system.

Virus   The smallest of the disease causing organisms.

Zidovudine   A drug which stops the human immunodeficiency virus multiplying.

What is HIV?

The human immunodeficiency virus (HIV) is an infection that is most commonly caught through sex with an infected person. It can also be caught by sharing needles when injecting drugs. Infected mothers can transmit the virus to their infants in the womb or during the birth process.

HIV was first identified in the early 80s. Most people who had it then were male homosexuals and for a while it was thought that HIV might be an exclusively gay disease. This is not true. Many women are now infected and HIV can be caught through ordinary heterosexual contact.

Once a person is infected with HIV the virus stays in their body for the rest of their lives.

HIV reduces the body's ability to fight infection, and it leads to a wide range of illnesses. In many people HIV eventually develops into the disease called AIDS.

AIDS stands for Acquired Immune Deficiency Syndrome. This is an extremely serious and fatal disease, for which there is currently no cure.

A person who has HIV in their body is often said to be 'HIV antibody positive' or 'HIV positive'. This is because the standard test for HIV actually looks for the antibodies the body makes to defend itself, not the virus itself.

A person who has the HIV infection in their body does not necessarily have the disease AIDS, although they may go on to develop AIDS. Many people wrongly think that when you get infected with HIV you will die very soon or certainly within a few years. In fact HIV infection is mostly a very slowly developing infection and people are usually well for many years after they catch it.

The studies all quote different figures but in the well developed countries on average only 50% to 60% of the people infected get sick after 10 years. That's right, if you catch the infection today, there's a 40% to 50% chance you will still be well 10 years later, and who knows, by then doctors and scientists may have discovered a cure and/or a vaccine. Everyone however should take precautions to avoid becoming infected with HIV.

Even for people who get sick from the disease the treatment is getting better. People no longer have to be admitted to hospital as much as happened in the early days when the disease had just been discovered, and their life expectancy is much better. Some people with very severe HIV infection have lived for many years.

These are the positives that you should focus on if you do become infected. The fact remains however that HIV infection is a very dangerous infection, so far without cure. You should act to ensure you don't catch it.

I'm not homosexual and I don't use drugs, so I don't have to worry about catching AIDS

I hear all too many people saying this. It is not true. Anyone can catch HIV, including you if you place yourself at risk.

The major cause of spread of HIV infection throughout the world is by ordinary sex between men and women.

In one of the towns in Central Africa over 50% of the young women are now infected with HIV, with almost the same number of young men infected. This indicates how far HIV infection could spread throughout a community, if no action were taken to stop it. It is not just a disease of homosexual men.

In South East Asia up to 40% of the female prostitutes in some areas are infected. Up to 70% of the intravenous drug users there are also infected. This means that if someone has sex with a prostitute over there it's almost a one in two chance they will be having sex with someone with HIV infection. In Europe people often go to Africa for their holidays, and in the USA to Central or South America or the Caribbean, all areas with high levels of HIV infection.

You don't have to go on an overseas holiday to catch HIV,

someone else can do this for you. How many people do you know who go on an overseas holiday, have sex, then come home but don't tell their partners? These partners have other partners, they have other partners — and you could be one of them. Import by travellers is one of the major ways the virus is now likely to spread in countries that had efficient education campaigns before the infection had spread too widely.

Perhaps you are too afraid to ask your partner to have an HIV test in case they think you are implying previous unsafe behavior. Well, don't be. For your own sake, and for your partner's sake, ask. You don't have to imply anything about their sexual behavior, it's just that you don't know what their previous partners have been up to. Probably they don't either.

How do you get HIV?

HIV is concentrated inside the body in the blood, semen, vaginal fluids and breast milk. Consequently it is spread in three ways; by

- sex
- blood or blood products
- an infected mother to her baby, or by an infected baby to the mother (See Chapter 21 *STDs and Your Baby*).

Sexual intercourse with someone who is infected with HIV is the main way you could catch it.

HIV can also be caught by sharing needles and other equipment when taking drugs. Many STDs, including HIV, are caused by microbes that can get into the blood and stay there for a long time. Needles can carry traces of this infected blood. People who have sex with drug users who share needles are then at risk of infection, and people who have sex with them are at risk. Sharing needles is a way that sexual diseases such as HIV, syphilis and hepatitis B can jump from one social group to another, even if there is normally little contact between them.

It has happened that people have caught HIV from blood transfusions and other blood products. The dangers of transmission through blood products are now much better understood and new procedures and controls mean the risk of infection this way has been virtually eliminated. If you are a traveller you should be aware that some countries cannot afford to test blood that is transfused for HIV and other infections. You might be better off to fly home if you get sick.

The human immunodeficiency virus cannot jump from person to person like a flea, though some people have reacted with such panic you might think so. There is no risk in being near or touching someone with HIV infection. You cannot catch HIV by kissing, holding hands, hugging, drinking from the same glass or bottle or sharing kitchen utensils. Mosquitoes can't give you AIDS, nor can toilet seats.

What sort of sex gives you HIV?

You can catch HIV through vaginal sex, anal sex or oral sex, between a man and a woman, or between two men, or very rarely between two women. Pre-cum, semen and vaginal secretions from an infected person all contain enough HIV to infect you. This means that HIV can pass from a woman to a man as well as from a man to a woman.

Some sexual behaviors involve a higher risk of catching HIV than others. The riskiest is anal sex, whether between two men or a man and a woman. Also risky is sex with prostitutes (who are exposed to a greater risk of all kinds of STDs), sex with intravenous (injecting) drug users and sex with people from areas with high infection rates (South East Asia, Africa, South America, the Caribbean and an increasing number of other countries).

Almost as risky as doing these things yourself is to have sex with someone who has done any of them. This exposes you to all the risks they took.

Why is anal sex an easy way to catch the virus?

During anal sex, whether it is between men or between men and women, the back passage (rectum) gets torn because the lining does not stretch during sex like the vagina does. Tiny breaks appear in the lining. These may be too small to be noticed, but they make it easy for HIV to pass through into the body. Alternatively the blood from the breaks can contain HIV and be passed on. Direct infection of cells by HIV can also occur during anal sex, even if no tears occur.

HIV isn't the only infection that is very readily passed on by anal sex. All sorts of other bugs can enter the intestines and the blood stream this way. These infections may be less life threatening than HIV, but the body still has to mop them up.

Can a woman pass on HIV to a man?

Yes. HIV is present in vaginal secretions and in blood. If a man has sex with a woman who has the infection, she can pass it on to him. HIV can pass through small breaks in the skin of the penis which occur during sex (it is a rather rigorous exercise) or it may be possible for direct infection of the urethra (eye of the penis) to occur. Sometimes too, there is blood in the vaginal secretions, even though you can't see it. This happens for a few days before and after each menstrual period, and sometimes in the middle of the menstrual cycle. The presence of some other STD such as genital herpes, syphilis or genital chlamydia will make it easy for any HIV infection to be passed on.

If I have sex with someone with HIV, will I get it?

Maybe. If you have sex with an infected person, whether or not you catch HIV will depend on many factors involving you and the other person.

People who have poorly functioning immune systems may catch HIV more easily. Some things that make immune systems function badly are repeated infections and illnesses, poor hygiene, poor nutrition, stress, drug use (including alcohol and tobacco) and other sex diseases.

Also important is the number of times you have sex with the infected person. The more you have sex with them the more likely you are to pick up the infection.

Some HIV positive people are more infectious than others. People who have just caught HIV will be highly infectious until they develop antibodies. As time goes on they become more infectious. The virus they have may change to a nastier type which grows faster and causes illness sooner. If you have sex with a person where the virus has turned into a nastier type, or with a person who has large amounts of HIV inside them, the chance you will pick up the infection by having sex with them is increased.

HIV and other sex diseases

The presence of any other sort of sex disease increases the risk of catching HIV. gonorrhea, chlamydia, NSU, genital warts, syphilis, genital herpes, and chancroid have all been found to be associated with an increased risk of HIV infection.

Genital ulcers (sores) increase the chance of catching HIV infection by five to 10 times. This is because if the person with HIV infection has a sore, the cells in the sore are loaded with HIV which can be rubbed onto the other person during sex. The more cells there are with HIV the more likely it is the virus will be passed on. HIV infection often slows down the healing of these sores making the person highly infectious for longer.

If a person who doesn't have HIV has a sore and they have sex with someone who is infected with HIV it is very easy for the HIV to enter their body through the sore.

You can get sores for lots of reasons, one of which is other sex diseases. Syphilis, genital herpes, granuloma inguinale and chancroid (a sex disease found mainly in South East Asia and Africa) all cause sores. These sores are filled with the sort of cells the HIV likes to infect. Having one of these sex diseases greatly increases the risk of catching HIV.

I've heard about the HIV antibody test

When someone becomes infected with HIV the body starts fighting to eradicate the infection. One of the ways it tries to do this is by making antibodies against the virus.

This antibody reaction varies from person to person. Probably it changes depending on the way the person was exposed to HIV and the amount of HIV they were exposed to. The antibodies may show up as soon as two weeks after infection but may take as long as three months to show up. Very occasionally it takes even longer for the antibodies to show.

The common test for HIV infection is actually a test for the presence of these antibodies, which indicate exposure to HIV.

People who are HIV antibody positive are infectious and can pass the infection on by sex or sharing needles or other drug use equipment.

What does a negative HIV antibody test result mean?

If someone tells you they have had an HIV antibody test and they are clear, does this mean that you are safe? Not necessarily. A negative HIV antibody test might mean they do not have the infection. It may also be that they have recently caught the infection and are highly infectious but haven't developed the antibodies yet. To be sure, they must have gone at least six months before the test without engaging in any activities which might lead to infection.

Also, if they have had sex since the test they may have caught the infection then. The test result starts to go out of date from the day the blood is taken unless the person is not having any sex and is not using intravenous drugs.

You should talk to your potential partner about when they last had sex and whether they do anything else which might put them at risk of catching HIV. Even then, it's a good idea if you take some additional protective measures, such as waiting a bit longer before you have sex or using condom s. Remember that the danger of transmission comes from body fluids, so oral sex is also risky.

What happens if I get infected with HIV? (The stages of HIV infection)

When someone first becomes infected with HIV there is only a small amount of the virus present. Their body starts to produce antibodies to attack the virus. The person may have a flu-like illness with aches and pains, sore throat and a rash. This can last just a few days or several weeks and is worse in some people than in others. Often these people do not realize they have HIV infection (and are infectious).

Doctors talk about four stages of HIV infection. Sometimes these stages are referred to as groups. The mild illness just discussed is group I. The four groups are:

Group I	Seroconversion illness
Group II	Asymptomatic infection
Group III	Persistent generalised lymphadenopathy
Group IV	Acquired Immune Deficiency Syndrome (AIDS) or severe immunodeficiency

In group II the virus is established in cells inside the body, but appears almost to be asleep. People in group II usually have nothing wrong with them at all. They look perfectly healthy and can stay well at this stage longer than ten years. Unless they have an HIV test they may not know they are infected and infectious. Most of the people who are infected with HIV are currently in this group.

Over time the amount of HIV in the body increases. This is matched by a weakening of the body's immune system and eventually an increased susceptibility to diseases such as pneumonia.

Group III people have swollen lymph glands, a condition called persistent generalised lymphadenopathy. They can stay well for years yet, especially if they look after themselves, but eventually they are likely to go on to group IV infection.

Group IV people are really sick. In most cases they have severe damage to their immune system and are said to have immunodeficiency. Usually they are suffering from one or more other diseases.

Some experts class all people with group IV infection as having AIDS, others do not include those with certain illnesses such as Kaposi's sarcoma in the AIDS category unless they also have severe immunodeficiency.

Group IV infection (AIDS and severe immunodeficiency) is usually fatal, but can last up to many years. Usually death results from one or more of the illnesses the person's weakened immune system has succumbed to, rather than from HIV infection itself.

What illnesses do people with HIV get?

The common illnesses people with group IV HIV infection get are mouth infections, high temperatures, loss of weight, diarrhea, pneumonia, lumps on the skin, swollen lymph nodes, recurrent herpes infection, eye infections and brain infections. The medical names for these illnesses are *Pneumocystis carinii* pneumonia, Kaposi's sarcoma, candidiasis, toxoplasmosis, cryptococcosis, lymphoma, *Mycobacterium avium intracellulare*, herpes simplex, HIV encephalopathy, cytomegalovirus, HIV wasting disease, cryptosporidiosis and *Mycobacterium tuberculosis* (tuberculosis or TB).

There is treatment available for nearly all these illnesses, but as yet there is no cure which will restore the body's ability to deal with illness so it can do its share of the work in fighting infection and disease.

HIV infection and cancer of the cervix

Normally the development of cancer of the cervix is thought to occur over a five to 15 year period. People who are infected with HIV may have faster changes in the cells and if they are prone to develop cancer this can happen quickly. The changes on the cervix may be picked up by regular PAP smears. Similar changes may occur in the anal cells in men, and may progress to anal cancer. A test for anal pre-cancer (similar to the PAP smear test in women) is now being developed.

How HIV affects the immune system

To better understand how your immune system functions, imagine a tube of blood that has just been taken from you. If the blood is allowed to stand in the tube for a while it separates into three parts. The red blood cells settle at the bottom, in the middle is a very thin layer of white cells called the buffy coat and on top is a straw coloured liquid called serum. (See Figure 7.1.) The liquid top part is made of water, sugars, salts and proteins, some of which are antibody proteins. The white cells in the middle are made up of different types called: neutrophils, eosinophils, basophils, monocytes and lymphocytes. The lymphocytes can be divided into two types: B cells and T cells.

Figure 7.1 The components of blood

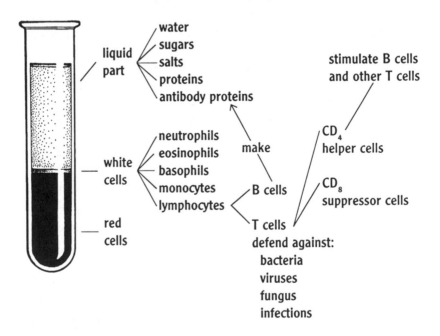

The T cells form a major part of the body's defence against bacterial, viral and fungal infections. There are several types of T cells including CD_4 cells called helper cells and CD_8 cells called suppressor cells. You can imagine the CD_4 cells being like 'pac men'. They work against certain infections and also stimulate other cells such as B cells and other T cells to become more active.

HIV particularly likes to attack CD_4 cells. The longer someone is infected with HIV and the more HIV they have inside their body the lower their CD_4 cell count becomes. Fewer CD_4 cells means the body is less able to recover from infection without outside assistance. In HIV infection other parts of the immune system are also affected resulting in a compounded inability for the body to successfully fight infection.

HIV also lives in special cells in the brain called microglial cells, macrophages (also found in blood and other parts of the body) and glands that produce sexual secretions.

Using the CD_4 count to guide treatment

A person's CD_4 count is a useful indicator of the progress of their HIV infection. So much research has been done on HIV infection that doctors are now able to predict when a person is likely to become ill. They do this by regularly seeing the people infected by HIV, checking them for illness and measuring the body's ability to fight infection. Different treatment centres will do different tests to assess this but all of them will do the CD_4 cell count. When it is found to be less than 200×10^6 cells/litre (200 cells/cmm) they will recommend antibiotics as a precaution against other diseases such as pneumonia.

The CD_4 count is a valuable tool, but some people take their CD_4 count as gospel each time they have it done. In fact many things make the CD_4 count variable. For example the reading is higher in the afternoon than in the morning, and vigorous exercise and other illness may also alter the reading. What the doctors go on is not just one reading but a series of readings done over a period of time. They watch for a trend in the CD_4 count in conjunction with other monitoring tests. If the CD_4 count is stable that is good news. If the CD_4 count is consistently getting lower and lower that means the amount of virus inside the person's body is growing and that in time they may become unwell.

The CD $_4$ count is not the only important test. Blood and skin tests and other special investigations depending on the individual's condition can be just as important.

Figure 7.2 Schematic diagram of the progression of HIV infection

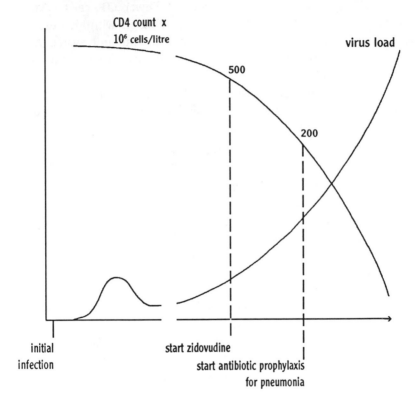

It is quite possible for the CD$_4$ count to increase, indicating an improvement in the body's immune system. Please have a look at Chapter 22 *Building Good Health.*

Treatment of HIV infection

Currently there is no cure for HIV. There is however a lot that can be done to manage the infection. Today people with HIV are living longer. They spend less time ill and in hospital. And there is always the hope that a cure will be found, soon.

The drug zidovudine has revolutionised treatment of HIV. It slows down the progression of the infection, particularly when it is used in the early stages. There are now many more drugs being used, some of them in combination with zidovudine, which are bringing about further advances in the management of HIV infection.

It is not known how long people can live with HIV infection. Certainly people can stay at group II infection for more than 10 years and perhaps indefinitely. While they stay in group II they can live full and fairly normal lives.

What triggers the move from group II to more advanced disease is not fully understood, but lifestyle factors like drug use (especially alcohol and tobacco), stress, diet, exercise, rest and mental attitude may have a lot to do with it. Really this is good news: it means that you can play a role in maintaining your own health, through your lifestyle choices. See Chapter 22 *Building Good Health.*

In summary, HIV infection is a very serious illness, but it is not the death sentence it was once thought to be. With proper treatment and by taking care of themselves, people infected with HIV can live comparatively normal lives for many years, and they can live in the hope that a cure will be found before they become seriously ill.

Zidovudine or AZT treatment

Researchers have found that the drug zidovudine (previously known as AZT) slows the growth of HIV inside the body. If people are started on this drug when their CD_4 count falls below 500 X $10^6/L$ the rate at which they become sick is slowed. Unfortunately zidovudine can have serious side effects, especially if it is taken over a long period of time or started too late in the disease when the immune system is very seriously impaired. Lower dosages seem to work as well as the higher doses that were used at first, and they have fewer side effects.

The importance of being tested

The treatments that are available, and the value of lifestyle modification, mean that it is a good idea to find out early if you are infected with HIV. Then your doctor can monitor your health and give you medication as you need it to slow down the growth of the virus. You will know to take better care of yourself and this will slow the growth of the infection. You will also be able to take precautions not to pass the infection on to anyone else.

Regardless of the result all people need to take precautions to avoid catching or passing on HIV infection, or catching a different strain of HIV. Often the hardest thing someone with HIV infection has to cope with, is guilt about the other people they may have infected.

If you have any reason to suspect you may have been exposed to HIV infection, or you just want to be sure, be brave and take the test from a sympathetic doctor or an STD clinic.

If you do find yourself to be infected I commend you for your bravery and for your responsibility, for taking the steps to find out. I hope that you will be cared for lovingly by all whom you come in contact with.

Steps to avoid HIV infection

There are things you can do to reduce the risk of catching HIV.

You can avoid high risk behavior such as anal sex, sharing needles, sex with prostitutes and sex with people from areas with high infection rates. You can avoid sexual partners who have anal sex, or sex with prostitutes, or sex with people from high risk areas, or share needles, or have sex with people who do any of these things. You can reduce your number of sexual partners, or how often you change partners. You can insist on both of you having full STD checks whenever you start a new sexual relationship, and continue to use condoms for the first six months.

Most important, if you do have a sexual contact where you are not absolutely sure of the other person's HIV status, make sure you use a condom and avoid getting sexual secretions such us cum, pre-cum or vaginal juices either inside your body or on your body if there are sores.

Do not put secretions which may contain HIV in your mouth either! That means no oral sex – or get used to the taste of condoms or some other barrier such as dental dams or plastic food wrap. You can put jam or honey on to change the taste and make it more interesting! If you do get secretions in your mouth spit them out and rinse your mouth out.

See Chapter 2 *Keeping Yourself Safe* for more details.

Living with people with HIV

You cannot catch HIV from normal social contact. Embracing, kissing and shaking hands are safe. Living in the same household as an HIV infected person is considered safe as long as you take care to avoid contact with their sexual secretions or blood. Sharing kitchen utensils including drinking glasses cannot transmit HIV. Sharing a toilet and using the same soap is also safe. You should not share razors or towels (this applies to people with almost any sexually transmittable disease).

If your partner is infected with HIV

If your partner is HIV positive and you choose to continue a sexual relationship with them, then you should consider ways of having sex that do not involve penetration. If you have sex with penetration, always use condoms, preferably with a water based lubricant (other lubricants may weaken the condom). You should take extreme care to avoid getting any of your partner's sexual secretions or blood in you. If either of you have any sores, avoid contact with these or cover them up. If you do get any secretions on you, wash them off as soon as you can with soap and water.

By taking these precautions you can reduce the risk of catching HIV yourself, but unfortunately you cannot have completely risk free sex with an HIV infected person. If you are in this situation you should seek advice from a doctor and perhaps a counsellor experienced in dealing with HIV patients. An STD clinic will be able to help you.

If I or my partner are infected, can we still have children?

See Chapter 20 *STDs and Pregnancy* and Chapter 21 *STDs and Your Baby.*

How many people are infected with HIV?

Nearly every country in the world now has reported cases of people dying from AIDS. Worldwide it is believed that six to 12 million people are infected with HIV. By the year 2000 it is expected at least 15 to 20 million people will be infected. In time a large number of these will go on to get sick from the disease.

In the US up to December 1992 there have been 253,448 reported cases of AIDS (group IV infection)

Figure 7.3 Cases of AIDS in the USA

Cumulative to December 1992

Men	Women	Children[1]	Total
221, 714	27,485	4,249	253,448

1 Children defined as aged under 13 years

Figure 7.4 Cases of HIV infection by Year

	1988	1989	1990	1991	1992[2]
Adults	33,480	38,578	40,298	41,871	39,000
Children[1]	588	674	730	601	600
Total	**34,068**	**39,252**	**41,028**	**42,472**	**39,600**

1 Children defined as aged under 13 years
2 Estimated

Remember that the above figures are only the known cases of infection. There are still a lot of people with HIV infection who have not been tested.

What does 'notifiable disease' mean?

HIV is a notifiable disease in many countries, which means that doctors treating patients with the HIV infection must notify a central health authority and give them certain details (some places require details but do not ask for name or address). It is important that the size of the epidemic is known so that appropriate health care can be budgeted and provided for as well as other steps being taken to control the disease.

There is a risk that infected people may avoid testing and treatment rather than have their partners notified. This reaction is often a misunderstanding of the reasons for notification, especially in countries where health care for HIV infected persons is provided free of charge by the government. To provide adequate funding for this health care the government needs to have accurate information on the number of people infected.

In addition, assessments of the extent of the problem have led to the funding of education programs for people at risk. These work to reduce the number of people becoming infected and so to protect the whole community.

A lot of people criticised the Grim Reaper campaign in Australia, but it certainly made most Australians aware that HIV infection is a problem. In some countries there hasn't been an education campaign and the people still do not know about HIV. Certainly the disease is present, but they do not know what precautions they should be taking and so they expose themselves to greater risk and encourage its spread.

In some countries information about HIV infection has been suppressed because governments are worried it will affect their tourist trade.

The spread of HIV infection

Many of the people with HIV don't even know they are infected because they feel perfectly well or are too frightened to have the test or are unaware that the infection exists. Some underdeveloped countries cannot afford the tests.

Often these people are continuing to spread the infection to their partners. Infection is spreading most rapidly in underdeveloped countries.

You don't even have to be promiscuous to catch HIV infection. One contact is enough.

To understand how HIV (and other STDs) spread, consider the following example. To keep the example simple we'll assume that having sex with an infected person always results in the infection being passed on, although this is not the case in the real world.

Suppose you live in a small town where your number of potential sexual partners is 100 and everyone on average changes their partner once a year. Now suppose that one unknown person out of this 100 has HIV infection. The first year your chance of infection is just one in a hundred. During that year however the infected person will infect someone else, so now there are two people out of 100 infected. The next year the infected two will infect two more people, the next year the infected four will infect four more and by the end of the sixth year 64 people out of 100 will be infected. If everyone changed partners that year, chances are they would all be infected.

Of course 100 potential sexual partners indicates a small total population. If the community offered say 30,000 potential partners it would take 15 years for everyone to become infected. Fifteen years is not much out of a lifetime. In 20 years of sexual activity a population of just over a million could be all infected. In 25 years a population of more than 33 million could be all infected – starting from just one single case.

This example is only hypothetical, but it makes clear that everyone must be responsible for controlling the spread of STDs.

There is only one person who can effectively take responsibility for your sexual health and that is you. No-one else can look after your body for you. You were born with it, it's yours for life, so look after it.

Some people only live for the moment and don't seem to care what happens to them. If they value themselves so little, that is perhaps their choice, but we should think about the future we are creating. Adults may choose to take risks, but children born already infected with HIV have not been given the opportunity of choosing. What sort of world does HIV offer today's children? In some parts of Africa AIDS is now called the 'grandparents' and children's disease' because they are the only ones left alive to care for their relatives and the land – the babies and parents have died from AIDS.

HIV and drug use

One of the most difficult problems health planners face is how to stop HIV infection spreading throughout the drug using population. Authorities now are being more open about drug use. The emphasis is shifting from punishment to treatment, at least for users. Studies have found drug use to be common in our society.

In some countries, though not in the United States, pharmacists have been extremely helpful in reducing the spread of HIV by providing cheap sterile needles and syringes to intravenous (or injecting) drug users. This has greatly reduced the number of drug users who are infected.

No-one knows the best way to control the spread of HIV amongst drug users: some radical new ways of looking after people with this problem may have to be tried. One thing we do know is that putting people in jail for using drugs does not work, as they even manage to get drugs smuggled into prison! Prison populations may be at particular risk of HIV infection, so putting people with high risk behavior in prison could actually increase the rate of HIV spread.

Whatever we try, our treatment of drug users should be compassionate and understanding: harsh treatment will only drive them underground. We won't be able to control the HIV epidemic if we can't reach the people who are infected or are at risk of being infected.

Section Three

The Non-viral STDs

8

BACTERIAL VAGINOSIS

KEY CONCEPTS

Bacteria   A disease causing organism, larger than a virus.

Clue cells   Vaginal wall cells coated with bacteria which give the cells a particular appearance under a microscope.

Gardnerella vaginalis   A normal organism in the vagina of many women.

Vaginal acidity   The vagina normally is acid with a pH of less than 4.5.

Vaginal ecosystem   The normal balance of organisms and pH that occurs in a healthy vagina.

What is bacterial vaginosis?

Bacterial vaginosis is a very common condition in women. It is caused by an overgrowth of normal bugs (bacteria) that live in the vagina. The bacteria are usually there anyway, but for some reason we don't yet know it sometimes grows out of its usual order. Maybe our body is a bit like the environment and if we don't look after it properly it gets out of balance: bacterial vaginosis could be a symptom of such poor functioning. We are only starting to find out how to look after the environment, perhaps we will have to go through something like the same learning process before we really understand our own bodies.

Thirty years ago it was thought that the bug which caused bacterial vaginosis was *Haemophilus vaginalis*, which was later renamed *Corynebacterium vaginalis* and then again (in 1978) renamed *Gardnerella vaginalis*. In the 1980s however researchers found that this condition is not the result solely of an overgrowth of *Gardnerella vaginalis* but is due to a disturbance of the entire normal bug system in the vagina. It involves an overgrowth of other bugs such as anaerobes, including two called *Mobiluncus curtisii* and *Mobiluncus mulierii*. These are called anaerobic, which means they can grow without oxygen. Under a microscope mobiluncus organisms look like curved rods, whereas gardnerella looks like a little round ball. The appearance of these mobiluncus bugs under a microscope suggests that there is also an increase in other anaerobic bugs. Many people I see with this condition get very upset because they think they have been given some terrible disease by their partner. In the case of bacterial vaginosis, that is not so. Believe it or not, up to 70% of women who don't have anything wrong with them can also have the bug *Gardnerella vaginalis* growing inside them.

More research is needed, but it seems that bacterial vaginosis is probably not even sexually transmittable. Usually the male partner of a woman being treated for bacterial vaginosis does not need any treatment. You don't even have to be sexually active to get bacterial vaginosis: this imbalance can happen to virgins.

Women with bacterial vaginosis have a thousand fold increase in the anaerobic bugs in their vagina, while the normal bugs called lactobacillus are so reduced in number that hardly any can be seen under a microscope. The excess of anaerobic bugs is often associated with the production of a smell.

Other names for bacterial vaginosis

Other names for this condition are nonspecific vaginitis, haemophilus associated vaginitis, or gardnerella associated vaginitis. The name vaginitis, though in common use, is not accurate. Vaginitis means inflammation of the vagina, but in bacterial vaginosis there is no inflammation, just an overgrowth of bugs that are normally present in the vagina.

The symptoms of bacterial vaginosis

Sometimes women can have this condition and not have any symptoms at all. In this situation there is no need for treatment because it is a condition which causes no harm.

The most common complaint from women with bacterial vaginosis is a smell from the vagina. It is often described as a fishy or musty smell which sometimes gets worse after sexual intercourse.

There may also be a vaginal discharge. The amount of discharge can vary from just a little to a lot. Usually the discharge is like white paste, but can be thin and watery, frothy or even yellow in color. A small number of women also have soreness of the vulva.

Other causes of similar symptoms can be from frequent vaginal douching, cosmetics and semen. Increased vaginal secretions can be due to an increase in the amount of sex you are having, or may be due to the menstrual cycle with increased secretion occurring around the time of ovulation. Pregnancy causes increased vaginal secretion in some women, as does the use of the oral contraceptive pill.

How is bacterial vaginosis diagnosed?

When a doctor looks inside your vagina with a speculum they may find a discharge which can be thin, watery, grey or white. This discharge tends to cling to the walls of the vagina.

The doctor may detect a smell or may add a chemical called potassium hydroxide to some of the discharge placed on a glass slide. If you have bacterial vaginosis the addition of the chemical to the slide makes a smell which is the same as the one you may have noticed. This test is called the 'whiff test'. The smell is due to substances called amines made by bacteria. The amines responsible for the smell have the quite uninviting names putrescine and cadaverine.

The doctor may then send a slide with the discharge on it to a laboratory, where it is examined under a microscope for 'clue cells'. These are vaginal wall cells covered with the bug *Gardnerella vaginalis*, which give the cell a characteristic appearance. Some laboratories try to grow *Gardnerella vaginalis* but in fact the presence of clue cells is usually a better indicator of the condition. As we have previously mentioned *Gardnerella vaginalis* is a normal organism in many women, so that if it is grown it does not mean an infection is present.

Clue cells

Medicine certainly has some funny names for things: 'clue cells' makes the whole thing sound like a Sherlock Holmes case. If you have had this problem for quite a while and it has finally been diagnosed, you might agree.

Don't jump to conclusions though: just because a doctor finds clue cells does not mean you have a condition which must be treated. The presence of these cells in some women is normal.

The doctor may also test the acidity of the vagina. Normally the vagina has a pH less than 4.5, but in bacterial vaginosis the vagina is not as acid as usual and the pH is higher than 4.5.

With all these tests it can happen that bacterial vaginosis is diagnosed in women who have no symptoms at all. It is important not to be treated if you have no symptoms because the condition causes you no harm.

If you are diagnosed as having bacterial vaginosis or if you have symptoms then the doctor will probably take more tests to make sure you do not have some other infection which might be causing or contributing to your symptoms.

Figure 8.1 A clue cell

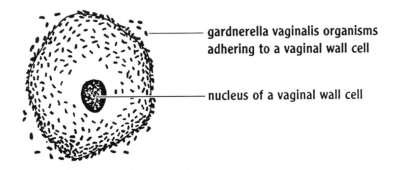

gardnerella vaginalis organisms adhering to a vaginal wall cell

nucleus of a vaginal wall cell

What can I do to make myself better?

If you are one of the women who has no symptoms then you are best off to not worry at all and have no treatment whatsoever. If you have symptoms and want to take medical treatment there are several options.

The most common treatment is with tablets called metronidazole or tinidazole. This is sometimes given as four tablets all at once and this is not at all a bad treatment if you have never had the problem before. However many women tend to get the condition more than once and in these circumstances a slightly longer course of treatment seems to produce better results. If you drink alcohol while you are taking metronidazole you will feel sick and want to vomit. You can get very ill even if you only drink a small amount. Sometimes people get a metallic taste in their mouth when they take these tablets.

If you decide reading this that you don't want to take metronidazole, there are not a lot of medical options.

Sometimes a course of amoxycillin, which is another kind of antibiotic, can help but, generally, it's the metronidazole treatment that seems to work best. Women who have repeated problems may benefit from a combination of the tablets (which treat the infection from inside the body) and a sulpha based vaginal cream, which treats the infection from the vagina. Sometimes two courses of this treatment are needed to clear up resistant cases.

Occasionally doctors may use another antibiotic called clindamycin. This drug can sometimes cause troublesome diarrhea, so doctors are not keen to try it unless they have tried everything else.

Not using tampons may help some women. I am not aware of any studies, but it is possible that tampons may alter the normal balance of vaginal bacteria. Changing the acidity of the vagina with aci-jel, or vinegar douches may help some women. See Chapter 9 *Candidiasis (Thrush)* for more information on this.

Should my partner be treated too?

There is no evidence that treatment of your male partner helps. This makes sense since the organism does not usually cause any problems in men. There are some rare situations where it is appropriate for the male partner to be treated.

Remember, the problem is simply that certain bugs which are normal in many women are appearing in too great a number. This is an imbalance rather than an infection.

9

CANDIDIASIS (THRUSH)

KEY CONCEPTS

Candida albicans The organism which causes candidiasis.

Predisposing conditions Conditions which make it more likely for a person to develop candidiasis.

What is candidiasis?

Candidiasis or candidosis, also known as thrush, is an overgrowth of a yeast fungus called *Candida albicans* in the vulva and vagina in women. In men overgrowth can occur on the penis. In people with HIV infection, overgrowth can occur in the mouth and spread down into the gullet. Occasionally it can spread into the blood stream. It can also occur on the skin. Babies can get thrush in their mouth or on their bottoms where it is called diaper rash.

Candida albicans is a normal organism which lives on your skin or inside you. It likes to live in warm places in the body such as the mouth, intestines, vagina and under the finger nails or on other places on the skin.

Some women have candida growing in their vaginas all the time without any problem. It is only when the candida overgrows that it causes a problem.

You can get thrush even if you are not sexually active.

How do women know when they have thrush?

When there is an overgrowth of candida in the vagina or on the vulva you may get itchy and develop a white vaginal discharge. This discharge can vary in consistency. It can be thick and lumpy or it can be mucous-like. It can also be yellow. The vulva and vagina may become hot, red, swollen and painful and you may experience a burning sensation. It may sting when you pass urine. Sometimes sexual intercourse may be uncomfortable or painful or soreness can develop after sexual intercourse, but I have known of women who said sex relieved their itch. The only sure way to know what the problem is, is to have tests done by your doctor.

How do men know when they have thrush?

If a male gets thrush redness or scaly skin develops on his penis and sometimes on his scrotum. Red patches or blotches or pink dots appear. These are often quite itchy. Under the foreskin the head of the penis may become ulcerated. Sometimes the ulcers are so small they cannot be seen without using a magnifying glass. Some men may have increased amounts of thrush growing on their skin without it troubling them. These men can be silent carriers, re-infecting their partners from time to time.

Figure 9.1 Candida albicans

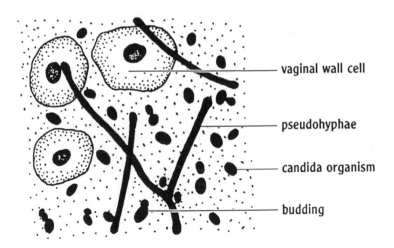

vaginal wall cell

pseudohyphae

candida organism

budding

How do you get thrush?

Men can get thrush from their female partners. Once they have thrush, it can spread from one part of their body to another.

For women, candida can enter the vagina from the anus or other parts of the skin, or come from an outside source such as the penis or hands of a sexual partner. Women can get candida from the applicator they are using to insert their thrush treatment. Most commonly though candida comes from the anus. Food is an important source of the organism.

What makes you more likely to get thrush?

Changes in the normal acidity of the vagina make it easier for candida to grow in larger amounts than it usually does. The normal vaginal acidity is a pH less than 4.5. This is maintained by special bacteria which live in the vagina called lactobacilli. A range of factors can alter the number of lactobacilli in the vagina, making the vaginal pH less acid and allowing candida to grow more easily. Here are some of these factors.

- Pregnancy.
- Being on the oral contraceptive pill.
- Certain times of the menstrual cycle, particularly the week before the period.
- Antibiotics which kill off the lactobacilli. (If you do get thrush when you are taking antibiotics, keep taking the antibiotics and get some thrush treatment. Some women who know they always get thrush when they have antibiotics can ask their doctor for thrush treatment at the same time and treat themselves so they do not get a bad outbreak. You need an understanding doctor and to know your own body to do this.)
- Wearing tight jeans, or nylon pants. This causes the area to stay warmer and more moist than usual, creating exactly the right conditions to encourage growth of yeast.
- Being run down and anaemic and not having enough sleep can make it easier for thrush to grow.
- Very occasionally your partner may have an overgrowth of candida and keep giving you an extra load for your body to deal with.
- Skin that is already inflamed or scratched or has sores on it will grow thrush much more readily.
- Diabetes.
- Being on immunosuppressive drugs.

What treatment is available?

If you think you have thrush it is advisable to go to your doctor to make sure there is not any other cause for your symptoms. Your doctor will probably give you an internal examination as well as looking at the genital area and will probably do laboratory tests to confirm that the problem is indeed thrush. There is no way to definitely say the problem is thrush and not something else without doing laboratory tests.

At the first sign of irritation stop using soap and use only water to clean yourself. Under no circumstances use a disinfectant, this just burns the skin and makes things worse.

Treatment for men with thrush is a cream rubbed onto the penis twice a day after showering. Soap should be avoided when there is a rash. Treatment should be continued for at least a week after the rash has gone to make sure the candida organisms are reduced in number.

The treatment for women is usually vaginal cream or suppositories. These are large tablets which you insert into the vagina. You may also be given some cream to rub on the outside to stop the itching. The length of the treatment you can be given varies. There are one, three, six, seven and fourteen day treatments available. Below is a list of the commonly prescribed treatments. The medical name has been used and is usually found in small print on the medication packet. The full course of treatment should be used even if you feel better. This is to make sure the amount of candida is reduced so that the chance of developing symptoms again is lessened.

Vaginal thrush (candidiasis) is effectively treated with clotrimazole or nystatin suppositories which are inserted into the vagina.

All the treatments work well but none seems to be better than the other at preventing recurrences. You need to discuss with your doctor which is the right treatment for you. Sometimes when you have had a problem with recurrent thrush a longer course of treatment seems to work better. Treatment should be continued during your menstrual period if that starts. Tampons are best avoided during treatment for thrush. Use sanitary napkins or pads instead.

Nystatin is the safest antifungal treatment to use during pregnancy. If you have had thrush before and have received treatment that worked then it is a good idea to stick to what you know works for you. Every person is different and what works well for one may not be as good in another, or may produce side effects in another person.

Should I have tablets to reduce the amount of candida in my intestines?

In severe cases you can take nystatin tablets by mouth, to reduce candida build up in your intestines. The combination of oral nystatin and nystatin cream has been shown to be effective, but oral nystatin added to the other antifungal treatments may not be as good.

There is another tablet called ketoconazole which can be taken by mouth, which is used to treat thrush. It is a highly effective treatment but has a rare and extremely dangerous problem of occasionally causing serious liver damage. In addition, treatment with ketoconazole does not stop thrush recurrences. If your doctor does put you on ketoconazole make sure you discuss all the potential side effects with them. Ketoconazole is however particularly good for treating extremely severe cases of infection, such as thrush in the gullet or in the bloodstream.

Another drug called fluconazole has just become available. It does not have the same side effects on the liver as ketoconazole.

Non prescription treatments

A variety of vaginal suppositories for the treatment of candidiasis are now available without prescription in the United States. Alternative practitioners have also suggested that dietary changes, vinegar and water douches and yoghurt applied to the vagina may help. If you have used a non-prescription medicine or alternative remedy without relief, you should be examined by your doctor to confirm your diagnosis.

Can I have sex while I'm on the treatment?

This should be discussed with your doctor, but in general there should be no reason why you can't have sex during the treatment provided it is enjoyable and doesn't hurt you. In fact some doctors say it is better if you do because intercourse rubs the treatment well in to all the nooks and crannies, makes the treatment fun and makes sure your partner gets treated at the same time.

Does my partner need treatment too?

Your partner should be treated if he or she has symptoms. If you are a woman and keep getting recurring thrush it is advisable to have your partner treated to reduce the amount of thrush that might be growing on his penis and exacerbating your condition, even if he doesn't have symptoms. Conversely if you are a male and keep getting a red, itchy sore penis it would be a good idea for your female partner to be examined and given treatment to reduce the amount of candida that is growing inside her vagina.

I keep getting it all the time. What should I do?

Make sure it is definitely thrush and thrush only which is the cause of your problems. I have seen a lot of women who have another cause for the discharge they attributed to thrush. Infection with chlamydia is just one example. Visit your doctor for laboratory tests. While you are there, make sure you get a sugar test to make sure you are not diabetic. Sometimes mild iron and vitamin deficiencies can cause thrush, so you may also need a blood test.

You should avoid wearing tights, nylon pants and tight trousers or jeans. The idea is to let lots of air in below!

When you have your period you may find that pads are better than tampons. Tampons tend to dry out the vagina and may even change the normal range of bacteria which live in the vagina, thus changing the normal vaginal acidity. Less acid in the vagina encourages the growth of candida.

Avoid perfumed soaps, vaginal deodorants and sprays or other chemicals. These just serve as irritants to prolong the infection.

When you go to the toilet you should always wipe from the front to the back to avoid contaminating the vulva with yeasts from the bowel. You should not have anal intercourse before you have vaginal intercourse.

If you are using applicators to insert pessaries throw them out. Applicators supplied with the medication can be a continued source of re-infection. If you have a fungal infection of your finger nail beds you should wear a disposable plastic glove to insert the pessary.

Changing underpants twice a day and changing your towel daily may help. Some people find that showering twice a day assists. A bath once a week with two cups of vinegar added to the water may help some people.

Shower as soon as you can after any exercise.

Prescribed treatment such as nystatin should be put on the affected area as well as the anus, the skin around the anus, and the skin between the anus and vulva.

If you are on the pill go and talk to your doctor about other possible methods of contraception or changing the brand you are on.

Avoid stress wherever possible, because stress can run down your immune system. Have a look at the Chapter 22 *Building Good Health*.

Make sure you partner is treated because if you keep having more thrush put inside your vagina or on your penis this may be more than your body can cope with. It is a good idea for your partner to use the treatment even if he or she has no symptoms, to reduce the amount of candida they may have.

Some medical conditions cause recurrent thrush, as do some treatments, particularly corticosteroids. If you have recurrent thrush problems and are on a drug which can make it more likely for you to develop thrush, discuss the problem with your doctor. It may be possible to have the dose adjusted, or to try a different treatment. Do not change any of your prescribed medication without discussing it first with your doctor.

10

CHLAMYDIA

KEY CONCEPTS

Asymptomatic infection Infection which causes no symptoms so that the person is unaware they have the infection. The disease is still there, it can still cause damage to them and they can pass it on to others.

Chlamydia infection sites Genital areas lined by columnar epithelium.

Chlamydia trachomatis The organism which causes genital chlamydia infection.

Pelvic inflammatory disease Inflammation of the fallopian tubes which may result in scarring of the tubes and sterility.

Sterility Inability to fertilise the ovum to cause pregnancy.

What is chlamydia?

The star of this chapter, *Chlamydia trachomatis*, is a bacteria which is passed on by sexual intercourse. It's a very old disease: some types of chlamydia infection were written about in ancient Egypt.

There are many types of chlamydia. *Chlamydia trachomatis* comes in several versions called serotypes, and labelled A, B, Ba, C, D, E, F, G, H, I, J, K, L1, L2 and L3. Types A to C cause trachoma, an infection of the eye. Types D through to K cause the genital infections discussed in this chapter. Types L1, L2 and L3 cause another sexually transmittable disease called lymphogranuloma venereum, which is discussed in Chapter 17 *The Other STDs*.

There is another sort of chlamydia called *Chlamydia psittaci* which you may have heard about. It is sexually transmitted in the Australian koala and causes infections which may make them infertile. It is also found in psittacine birds such as parrots and budgerigars, and in some other animals.

A new type of chlamydia called *Chlamydia pneumoniae* which causes pneumonia has recently been discovered.

Chlamydia trachomatis infection is among the most common sexually transmittable diseases in the developed countries, and at the moment is far more common than HIV infection. *Chlamydia trachomatis* infection is called the silent epidemic. There are thought to be about 100,000 people with this infection in Australia. In Sweden one third of the sexually active population is thought to catch chlamydia at least once during their lifetime.

Once it enters a cell inside the body chlamydia multiplies by splitting itself in half to form two, then four and so on. The collection of these organisms in the cell is called an inclusion body. Eventually the cell breaks and dies and the organism spreads to infect other cells.

The *Chlamydia trachomatis* infection usually only infects certain cells in the body called columnar cells. These are tall cells which line the inside surfaces of the body. chlamydia can only live inside cells and dies rapidly if there is no cell to attach itself to. This is because the chlamydia organism is unable to make its own energy and feeds off the energy made by the cell it is living in. It cannot live outside the body.

How is chlamydia caught?

Chlamydia is caught by having sexual intercourse with someone who has it. If you have sex with someone who has chlamydia it appears the chance of getting the infection is at least 60%.

You cannot catch chlamydia just by sleeping in the same bed or by sharing the same towels, and it is not caught from toilet seats.

Chlamydia can be caught in the cervix, urethra, throat and rectum, depending on whether these parts of the body have been used for sex. Occasionally it is spread from these parts of the body to the eye.

Chlamydia means cloak in Latin. Like its name, chlamydia is a hidden disease in many people. It can be present for many months or even years without the person knowing about it (this is called asymptomatic infection).

Often people will not know they have a problem until either they go and have tests, or change their partner. Having sex with a new partner sometimes starts symptoms in a person who has the infection but is unaware they have it.

The people most likely to catch chlamydia are people who are under the age of 25, people who have changed their sexual partner within the last two to three months, people who do not use condom s for sex, and people who have another sexually transmittable disease.

How common is chlamydia?

Chlamydia is much more common than you think. It is estimated that as many as one in 20 women could have the infection, and most of them don't realize it. Some studies show that in certain regions 20% of men and women and possibly even more are infected.

People who catch some other type of sexually transmittable disease are particularly at risk of catching chlamydia. Overall 50% of women who have gonorrhea also have chlamydia infection. In some countries such as Sweden 80% of women with gonorrhea also have chlamydia. In men with gonorrhea the chance that they will have chlamydia infection is at least 25%; higher in some countries.

Young women attending clinics for termination of pregnancy have also been found to be more likely to have chlamydia. This means their partners are more likely to have it too.

Remember, sexually transmittable diseases often travel together, if you catch one you should always be checked for others.

Chlamydia is unlikely to get better by itself, but it is only if someone develops symptoms or is tested for it that the infection is discovered.

What symptoms do men get?

At least 10% of men with chlamydia will have no symptoms at all. There is nothing that will give them the faintest inkling that they have an infection that may cause problems to their partner or to themselves. Nevertheless, their hidden infection may eventually leave them unable to have children.

If they do get symptoms they may notice a discharge from their penis and may have some discomfort in passing urine. The discharge can be clear, creamy or yellow. Sometimes they may just notice a slight itch in the urethra (water pipe). Sometimes the discharge may only be noticeable first thing in the morning. Occasionally if the infection spreads it can cause pain in or around the testicles, or pain on ejaculation (coming).

If the infection is in the back passage (rectum) it may cause some soreness and sometimes discharge.

Throat infection may cause either a sore throat or no symptoms at all.

Where does the infection go in men?

If the infection is not treated in men the chlamydia organism can spread to the epididymis, which is found in the scrotal sac around the testicle. Usually it only affects one side. It causes inflammation called epididymitis. This causes swelling and pain of the epididymis.

Chlamydia is a common cause of epididymitis in men under the age of 35. In older men other causes are more common. In some other countries gonorrhea is the most common cause of epididymitis in men under the age of 35. Occasionally men with a certain genetic susceptibility who get infected with chlamydia may suffer arthritis, eye problems and recurrent inflammation of the urethra. This is a rare condition called Reiter's syndrome.

What symptoms do women get?

In two thirds of the women infected there are no signs or symptoms at all. That's right, in many women there is no way of knowing you have the infection without being tested. Other women may notice a vaginal discharge, or some itching or soreness in that area. If the infection spreads beyond the cervix they may notice some discomfort or even severe pain in the lower abdomen. The pain can be worse during sexual intercourse. If the infection goes further they may be thought to have appendicitis or even an inflamed gallbladder. When the infection gets to the uterus the inflammation may cause irregular bleeding, especially if the woman has an intrauterine contraceptive device. Some women may experience pain when they pass urine or a feeling of having to pass urine more often.

Where does the infection go in women?

The infection occurs in the tall columnar cells of the cervix and from there can spread up to the cells lining the uterus and then spread into the cells lining the fallopian tubes. In at least 40% of the women who have the infection it has spread up to the uterus. The infection can spread even further to the lining of the abdomen and around the liver, where it can mimic gallstones. Occasionally the infection is found only in the urethra.

Chlamydia can spread from the cervix without the infected person even knowing about it, but it is important it be treated before it spreads further than the cervix.

If you have just given birth to a baby and have the infection, apart from the baby having a 70% chance of getting infected, it is quite likely the infection will spread into your uterus causing excessive bleeding and then spread up into your tubes after the delivery. This usually occurs at least one week after delivery.

How do I find out if I might have chlamydia?

The only way to find out if you have chlamydia is to be tested. It can infect the urethra, cervix, rectum, and tonsils or the remains of the tonsils if you've had them removed. Where it infects depends on what parts of the body you have used for sex. To test for chlamydia the doctor has to collect some of the cells it is in on a swab and then send them to a laboratory where tests can be done to see if the infection is present. Sometimes the test is to actually grow the organism, and sometimes it is an antigen test which looks for parts of the organism. Unfortunately this last test sometimes gives false positive readings: it says you have the infection when you don't really have it. Usually though it's safer to be treated than mess around with other tests.

There are no false positive results if the organism is grown – if it is grown from you then it's definite that you have got it. Sometimes however you may have the infection but not in the cell samples collected by the doctor. The test then would give a false negative reading. If it all sounds complicated, it is. This is why there are doctors who specialise just in treating conditions like this.

Women who are having an intrauterine device inserted should consider being tested for chlamydia first. Insertion of intrauterine devices makes spread of an infection into the uterus and up into the tubes more likely. Similarly women who are going to have a pregnancy terminated should be tested for chlamydia prior to the procedure.

What happens if chlamydia doesn't get treated?

For women, the most serious danger from chlamydia is that it might spread into the fallopian tubes, where it causes inflammation and scarring and eventually blockage of the tubes so the egg may not be able to get down to the uterus. The inflammation that chlamydia causes can be so mild that it is unnoticed even though it is causing damage.

In Australia in 1987, of the women who applied for the specialized in vitro fertilization treatments, 55% did so because of blocked tubes, half of which were due to previous infection with chlamydia.

Chlamydia is the major cause of pelvic inflammatory disease (PID). Fifty per cent of cases of PID are due to *Chlamydia trachomatis* infection. Women with PID are more likely to develop an ectopic pregnancy, which means the fetus grows in the wrong place, commonly in the fallopian tube rather than in the uterus. Women who develop PID may develop chronic lower abdominal pain and pain whenever they have sexual intercourse. See Chapter 14 *PID (Pelvic Inflammatory Disease)* for more information.

For men the most serious danger is that they might pass the infection on to a female partner, who may develop PID and become sterile. Rarely men may also develop epididymitis. If this involves both sides the man can be left infertile, but this is very rare.

What treatment is available?

Tetracycline antibiotics kill the chlamydia infection, but they cannot be taken if you are pregnant or breast feeding. In these cases erythromycin is the drug of choice. The treatment should be taken for at least 10 days. If the infection has spread you will need to be treated for longer. Following is a list of the recommended doses of the commonly prescribed antibiotics which will cure chlamydia infection. Most commonly you will be advised to take the drugs listed below for only seven days. I strongly recommend the longer periods shown, to cover secondary complications which may not be recognised at the time. Ask your doctor.

Drug	Dose	How often
Doxycycline	100mg	twice daily for 10 days
Tetracyclene	500mg	four times daily for 10 days
Erythromycin	500mg	four times daily for 14 days

If your doctor gives you doxycycline you should remember to stay out of the sun, because some people can develop an extremely bad sunburn through the drug making the skin more sensitive to sunlight than usual. If you have to be out in the sun wear complete block out sun cream, a hat and wherever possible long pants and a long sleeve shirt.

It is important not to have sex while you are on treatment even if your partner is receiving the same treatment. This is for two reasons. You may get better faster than your partner and then catch the infection back again. Having sex may also carry the infection higher up into the uterus. The higher the infection goes, the longer the course of antibiotics needed to get rid of it. Treatment for complicated infection is discussed in Chapter 14 *PID (Pelvic Inflammatory Disease)*.

To be sure that the treatment has been totally successful you must visit your doctor three weeks after treatment to be retested.

Should my partner be treated too?

Your partner must be treated or they may re-infect you. They should also have tests to make sure they don't have any other STDs and that they don't have any of the complications of chlamydia which require additional medication and a longer course of treatment.

What happens if I'm pregnant and have chlamydia?

If you have recently caught this infection you may go into labour early. See Chapter 20 *STDs and Pregnancy*.

Can it affect my baby?

Yes. Sometimes the baby may be smaller than it should be. There may be problems with the baby's eyes, lungs and ears. Lung infections may cause problems later in childhood. See Chapter 21 *STDs and Your Baby*.

11

EPIDIDYMITIS

KEY CONCEPTS

Epididymitis Inflammation of the epididymis.

Infertility Inability to fertilise an egg (ovum) so that pregnancy occurs.

Predisposing factors Things which make something likely to happen. In this chapter examples are infection or underlying disease of the prostate.

What is epididymitis?

The epididymis is a coiled tube about six yards long which carries the sperm from each testis to the part of the body where the ejaculate comes from. See Chapter 3 *Normal Anatomy and STD Examinations* for more detail. The epididymis looks like a small sausage and is usually found on the back part of each testis. Epididymitis is due to inflammation of the epididymis.

What causes epididymitis?

In sexually active men under the age of 35 the most common cause of epididymitis is infection with a sexually transmittable disease, especially chlamydia and gonorrhea. It is usually preceded by the symptoms of non-specific urethritis (NSU, see Chapter 13) including a discharge from the penis, but this is not always noticed.

In men over the age of 35 the most common cause is infection with bacteria from the bladder. Occasionally it can be due to chlamydia or gonorrhea. In this group of men there is often an underlying abnormality such as chronic prostatitis, prostatic stones, or an enlarged prostate causing a blockage to the outflow of urine.

What are the symptoms of epididymitis?

The onset of epididymitis can be sudden or slow. It is accompanied by severe pain in the scrotum and sometimes in the inguinal (groin) region. Prior to this there may have been a discharge from the penis or discomfort, burning or passing urine more often than usual.

The scrotum may become red and swollen. The longer you go without treatment the more the swelling increases. The swelling starts first at the tail of the epididymis at the bottom of the testicle and then spreads up to involve the head or top part of the epididymis. Sometimes the swelling and infection can spread to the testicle, and a collection of fluid called a hydrocele can form.

It is important to visit your doctor as soon as you notice pain in your scrotum so the doctor can treat you quickly and make sure things do not get worse.

What other illnesses look like epididymitis?

When the swelling is quite severe it is difficult to know exactly what is going on. Sometimes in men the testicle can twist in the scrotum and cut off the blood supply. This is extremely painful, and rapid swelling occurs. Sometimes it is not possible for the doctor to know whether this has happened without an operation to look inside. If the testicle has twisted and cut off its blood supply it is a medical emergency because the testicle will die in four hours. If you have pain in the scrotal sac see your doctor or local emergency department pronto.

Sometimes cancer of the testicle can mimic epididymitis, but the pain from cancer of the testicle does not usually happen as quickly as the pain from epididymitis.

How is epididymitis diagnosed?

The diagnosis of epididymitis can be difficult if there is a lot of swelling. If there is a discharge from the penis this tells the doctor there is inflammation of the urethra, and helps make the diagnosis easier. Tests can be taken from the eye of the penis to diagnose chlamydia or gonorrhea. Urine tests will let the doctor know the cause of the infection in many other cases.

What is the treatment for epididymitis?

Epididymitis is treated with antibiotics to kill the infection, pain killing tablets, and with bed rest and elevation of the scrotum by placing a towel under it, to reduce the swelling and pain. You should remain in bed until all the pain has gone. The earlier you see your doctor and receive treatment the sooner you will be better again. Remember that rest in bed means exactly this. You should not have sexual intercourse or masturbate until all the pain and swelling has gone. Make sure you have checked with your doctor whether your partner needs to have treatment too.

Will I become infertile?

Epididymitis can cause infertility, especially if the inflammation involves both sides. Infertility can also occur after infection with gonorrhea or chlamydia even if the person does not know they have these infections. The good news is that the damage is sometimes able to repair itself over time. Remember, for a woman to get pregnant only one sperm needs to reach one egg. Usually tests for infertility are only done if your partner has difficulty becoming pregnant.

Should my partner be tested?

If your epididymitis is due to either chlamydia or gonorrhea your partner should be tested and then treated. This will make sure they do not have any of the complications of infection such as pelvic inflammatory disease, which needs more and different antibiotic treatment. Testing of the partners of men under the age of 35 with epididymitis is important because it may reveal the cause of the infection.

12

GONORRHEA

KEY CONCEPTS

Antibiotic resistance   Normal antibiotics no longer work and new antibiotics have to be used.   Often antibiotic resistance involves resistance to more than one type of antibiotic.

Asymptomatic infection Infection which occurs without the infected person being aware they have the illness.   The disease is still there, it can still cause damage to them and they can still pass it on.

Disseminated infection   Infection which is widespread throughout the body.

Gram negative diplococci The appearance of certain bacteria including the gonorrhea organism under the microscope when a special stain called a gram stain has been used.

Neisseria gonorrhea e   The organism which causes gonorrhea.

Pelvic inflammatory disease Inflammation of the fallopian tubes.   This may result in sterility.

Sterility   Inability to fertilize an egg so that pregnancy occurs.

What is gonorrhea?

Gonorrhea is a sexually transmittable disease caused by a bacterium called *Neisseria gonorrheae*.   It is named after Dr Albert Neisser who discovered it in pus from patients in 1889.   The disease mainly affects young people in the age range 15 to 24 years. It is a clever germ with little arms called pili which latch onto body surfaces, particularly tall cells called columnar cells which line the cervix, urethra and rectum.

Slang names for gonorrhea are 'the clap' and 'the jack'.

Gonorrhea is an age old disease. It was written about in the book Leviticus in the Bible. Hipprocates (the 'father of medicine') wrote about gonorrhea in the fourth century BC. He called it strangury and was aware that it resulted from 'the pleasures of Venus'. The term gonorrhea was coined by Galen in the second century. The term clap probably originated in the middle ages and may have been derived from the Les Clapier district of Paris where many prostitutes lived.

How is gonorrhea caught?

Gonorrhea is caught by having sex with someone who has it. The trouble with gonorrhea is that lots of people who have it don't know they are infected. Up to 80% of women who have gonorrhea may have no symptoms whatsoever. Some men may have no symptoms either. This means you could catch the infection from someone who hasn't noticed that they have it.

Gonorrhea can be caught and carried in the urethra and cervix in women, in the penis in men and in the rectum and throat in both men and women.

A man has a 20% chance of catching gonorrhea from a woman who has it if he has vaginal intercourse with her. If he has sex three more times the chance of him catching the infection is increased to 60% to 80%. If a woman has sex with a man who has gonorrhea the chance that she will get the infection is higher (approximately 40%) than the other way around.

How long does it take to know if you have caught gonorrhea?

It takes two to 14 days for gonorrhea to grow in large enough amounts inside you that you notice something. Most commonly symptoms are noted within two to five days of catching the infection. However often people who have gonorrhea have no symptoms whatsoever.

How do you know if you have gonorrhea?

The only way to know for sure whether you have the infection or not is to be tested by a doctor. The only way the doctor will know will be by doing special tests. It is not possible for anyone to say you have gonorrhea just by looking.

In men, the infection may not show any signs at all wherever it is. If there are signs there may be a pus-like discharge from the penis and pain passing urine. If the infection is in the rectum there may be an anal itch and severe pain in the back passage, as well as anal bleeding and discharge. You can only get gonorrhea in the rectum if someone has inserted their penis in your anus. If you have gonorrhea of the throat you may develop a sore throat.

Up to 35% (sometimes higher) of men with gonorrhea have infection with chlamydia as well.

In women there may be no symptoms. If there are, there may be a discharge from the vagina which may be yellow or clear in color, and there may be a smell associated with the discharge. There may be pain passing urine or you may feel as if you want to pass urine more often than usual. If the infection spreads inside the woman there may be pain in the lower abdomen or lower back. Sometimes there may be bleeding in between periods, or the menstrual period may be heavier than usual. The glands called Bartholin's glands which create lubricating fluid during sex and are located at the opening of the vagina may occasionally become infected and swell up. Sometimes other glands around the urethral opening swell up if they become infected.

The infection can spread further into the blood stream causing high temperatures and infecting joints in the body. The most common joints to be involved are some of the finger joints, the wrists, knees, ankles, and elbows. Often there is a rash as well. Rarely in women the infection can spread up to the surface of the liver and cause a condition called the Fitz-Hugh-Curtis syndrome. (This was named after two Americans, Curtis and Fitz-Hugh.) When this happens the person notices abdominal pain, which may be worse when breathing deeply or coughing, and sometimes is also felt in the right shoulder. The Fitz-Hugh-Curtis syndrome can also be caused by chlamydia.

What are the complications of gonorrhea in women?

Women may develop infection which spreads up through the cervix into the uterus and then up into the fallopian tubes, which can swell up with pus. When this happens the tubes end up getting blocked and rope-like cords may develop, tying the tubes and womb to other parts of the body, for example the bowel.

Severe infection of the tubes like this may result in sterility. (See Chapter 14 *Pelvic Inflammatory Disease*).

What are the complications of gonorrhea in men?

Men may develop narrowing of the urethra, or difficulty getting an erection. If the infection spreads to the epididymis or testicles sterility may occur due to blockage of the tubes that carry the sperm. Untreated gonorrhea may result in acute epididymitis (see Chapter 11 *Epididymitis*). Rarer complications include chronic prostatitis and infections of certain glands on the penis called Tyson's glands and Cowper's glands. These are small glands that open into the penile urethra (see Chapter 3 *Normal Anatomy and STD Examinations*).

Further complications of gonorrhea affecting both men and women

Infection can cause sterility. Occasionally eye, heart, nervous system and joint problems may occur. If infection occurs in the eye this is extremely serious and must be treated quickly or blindness may result.

How is gonorrhea diagnosed?

Your doctor will ask what symptoms you have noticed. They will examine your body and genitals to see how far the infection has spread, and where it has spread to. They should check and make sure there are no other sex diseases present, as it is very common to catch more than one sex disease at the same time.

In men the doctor will take a sample of the pus from the end of the penis and place this on a slide to send to a laboratory. Another sample of pus will be taken from inside the penis, using a cotton wool swab. This sample will be used to grow the infection so it can then be tested against different treatments, to make sure the treatment you have been given will work.

If the rectum or mouth has been used for sex, then the doctor will take cotton swabs to grow the organism from those places.

You must tell the doctor about the parts of the body you have used during sex because the routine treatments do not always get rid of the infection if it is in the rectum or throat.

The only certain way to say that you have gonorrhea is for the organism to be grown and then tested in a laboratory to make sure it is gonorrhea and not other germs that may look the same under a microscope.

In women, the doctor will take swabs from the urethra, cervix and rectum to look for the organism under the microscope, and will then try to grow the organism. For women, the rectum is checked even if they have not had anal sex because the infection sometimes spreads there via moisture occurring during vaginal intercourse.

The doctor will try and grow the infection from the throat if you have used your mouth for sex and taken the penis into your mouth or swallowed vaginal secretions. To take proper swabs from your throat the doctor has to take a swab that touches both the left and right tonsils (or where they would be if you have had them removed) and the back of the mouth. This may make you feel like you want to cough but does not hurt. In fact none of the tests hurt except for the ones that are taken from the urethra in both men and women.

If the infection has spread into your blood (disseminated infection) the doctor will admit you to the hospital and take blood from you to try and grow the organism from the blood.

Remember that when the doctor sees you, they will not know exactly what is wrong with you until they get the results back from the laboratory, and the first tests only indicate that you probably have the infection.

The first tests look for the infection in the cells on the slide. If gonorrhea is present, pairs of kidney shaped germs are seen inside the white blood cells. These are called gram negative diplococci. There are other infections that can look like this so it is not until the infection has been grown, which takes about two days, that the doctor can definitely say that the infection is gonorrhea. The organism is very fussy about the way it grows in the laboratory, so you need a special set up to grow it. Because the infection is such a serious one the doctor will give you treatment as soon as it looks as though you might have it.

In women who have had sex with someone who has gonorrhea, it is usual for the doctors to do two lots of tests two days apart for them to be sure the infection is not present. In men, one lot of tests is enough, provided they are properly taken.

Figure 12.1 Gram negative diplococci

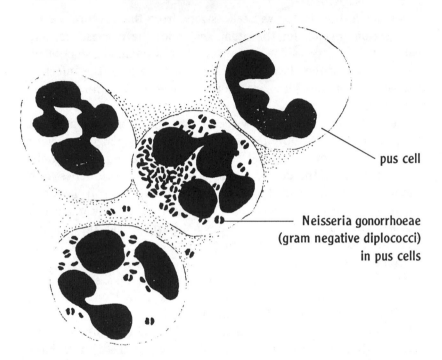

pus cell

Neisseria gonorrhoeae
(gram negative diplococci)
in pus cells

Other tests such as for chlamydia and syphilis and possibly HIV infection will be done at the same time. If the doctor does an HIV test this will be discussed with you first and it will only be done if you agree to having the test. In many STD clinics it is now routine to be offered an HIV test at the same time you have other tests for STDs.

Syphilis takes from nine to 90 days (three months) to show up in the blood), and HIV infection takes up to three months and occasionally even longer to show up in the blood if it has been caught sexually.

I've been told I've had sex with someone who has gonorrhea, what should I do?

If you get a call from a sex partner who says they have gonorrhea, or a call from a health worker to say you have had sex with someone with gonorrhea, you should go straight away to either your local doctor or an STD (Sexually transmittable Disease) clinic to be tested. Do not put this off: the longer you have the infection the more likely you are to develop more serious consequences or pass it on to someone else.

What treatment is available?

Many types of gonorrhea are sensitive to penicillin and can be treated with a single dose of amoxycillin, which is a penicillin antibiotic, and probenicid, which is a drug which keeps the amoxycillin levels in your blood high. If the infection is in the throat or rectum the treatment needs to be given for longer.

Some strains of gonorrhea have developed an enzyme called penicillinase which stops penicillin from working. In these cases treatment is with an injection of an antibiotic which is called ceftriaxone.

If the gonorrhea was caught by having sex with someone from overseas, South East Asia for example, there is a high likelihood the organism will not be killed by a penicillin antibiotic. The doctor is likely to treat you with an injection of ceftriaxone. The treatment you will be given depends on the type of gonorrhea most commonly found in the community you acquired the infection from.

Some doctors will treat you for the infection based on you having had sex with someone who has it, others will do tests and only treat you if the organism is grown. Because chlamydia and gonorrhea often occur together, your doctor will give you treatment for chlamydia at the same time.

If you have one of the complications of gonorrhea you may need to be admitted to the hospital for intravenous treatment or you may need treatment with several different antibiotics at the same time. You should avoid having sexual intercourse while you are being treated, even if your partner is being treated. This is because one of you might get better faster than the other and pass the infection back.

Gonorrhea, pregnancy and babies

See Chapter 20 *STDs and Pregnancy,* and Chapter 21 *STDs and Your Baby.* Gonorrhea can cause serious harm to babies.

How can I avoid getting gonorrhea?

The only real way is to make sure your partner has tests. Ask them to have checks for chlamydia, syphilis and HIV infection at the same time. All of these infections commonly occur in people who don't have a clue that they are infected.

If a condom is worn, this is extremely good protection against gonorrhea, provided it is put on at the start of sex and does not break. Condoms will not, however, give you complete protection against genital warts, herpes or some other STDs. Being on the oral contraceptive pill or using an intrauterine contraceptive device offers no protection against catching gonorrhea.

The fewer people you have sex with the lower your chance of catching an STD like gonorrhea.

13

NSU
(NON SPECIFIC URETHRITIS)

KEY CONCEPTS

Asymptomatic infection Infection which causes no symptoms so that the person is unaware they have the infection. The disease can still cause damage to them and they can pass it on.

Cervicitis Inflammation of the cervix.

Chlamydia trachomatis The organism which causes genital chlamydia infection and 50% of NSU infections.

Epidemiological treatment Treatment of the sexual partner at the same time the person with the disease is treated.

Urethra The tube through which urine passes on its way from the bladder.

Urethritis Inflammation of the urethra.

What is NSU?

NSU stands for Non Specific Urethritis. A diagnosis of NSU means that a man has inflammation of the urethra due to an infection, but the exact nature of the infection is not known. The cause may be discovered later. Up to 50% of the time it will be *Chlamydia trachomatis*. Other causes are viral infections, *Ureaplasma urealyticum*, and *Mycoplasma hominis* (these are discussed later). Once the cause is found, it is called by the name of that infection and is no longer called NSU.

How is NSU diagnosed?

If you have NSU, you may notice a discharge from the eye of the penis. It can be watery, but also it can be white or yellow in color. Your doctor will make the diagnosis by looking at some of this discharge on a glass slide. If there are more than four or five cells per high power field and no gonorrhea bugs the doctor will tell you that you have NSU. Sometimes a urine sample is examined to see if there are threads in the urine. These are collections of cells caused by inflammation, that string together in the tiny glands (Littre's glands) lining the urethra.

If you have symptoms you think may be due to NSU it is wise to be checked by a doctor.

How is NSU caught?

Usually NSU is caught by sexual intercourse, resulting in transfer of an infection, most often chlamydia.

Sometimes NSU occurs after you have been treated for gonorrhea. This is called post gonococcal urethritis (PGU), and is usually due to double infection with one of the organisms that causes NSU, most commonly chlamydia.

In rare cases, NSU can result from changes in a female partner's bacteria in the vagina due to stress or taking a course of antibiotics.

Also rarely, NSU can be caused by recurring genital herpes, stress or unusual inflammatory conditions.

More about Ureaplasma urealyticum and Mycoplasma hominis

These germs are found in the genital region of men and women. For many people, having these organisms is quite normal. They are fairly common in new born babies, but tend to get less common with age. When sexual activity starts they become more common again. The more sexual partners a person has, the more likely they are to carry either of these germs.

Whether either of these organisms is a cause of NSU is a quite confusing issue, with some studies saying yes and some saying no. Overall, at the moment, it is thought that *Ureaplasma urealyticum* can be a cause of urethritis in some cases, however if the germ is found in someone who has NSU you cannot be dogmatic and say it is the cause of the NSU!

In women it is thought that *Mycoplasma hominis* may cause pelvic inflammatory disease and sometimes be the cause of fever after a spontaneous abortion, and after delivery of a normal baby. *Ureaplasma urealyticum* is thought possibly to have a role in the fever following Caesarean section and fever after birth. Some studies suggest it may be a cause of recurrent spontaneous abortion, stillbirth and also of low birth weight.

There is still not enough evidence to say that if you have these germs you should be treated for them. This is because many people seem to have them without any problems. However, if you have symptoms that could be due to these infections and chlamydia has been ruled out then it is reasonable for these germs to be treated.

How do I find out if I have got NSU?

If you have symptoms such as pain passing urine or a discharge from the penis, you should see your doctor. It is best to not pass urine for four hours before. If you have a discharge only first thing in the morning, book an early appointment and don't pass urine until you've seen the doctor. Passing urine can wash away the signs of infection, making the tests useless.

Your doctor will smear some of the discharge on a slide. A diagnosis can be made quickly. You should also be tested for gonorrhea, chlamydia and genital herpes. For these tests, samples taken from the urethra are sent to a laboratory and it takes a while to get results. Meanwhile you will probably be started on some treatment and asked to get your partner in for tests and treatment too.

What treatment is available?

Treatments vary depending on the cause of NSU. The most common treatment is a tetracycline antibiotic. Some infections are not sensitive to tetracycline and in these cases the treatment will have to be changed. See Chapter 10 for chlamydia treatment.

It is wise not to have sex while you are on treatment, in case you catch the infection back again. In women the infection which caused the NSU can be spread higher up during sexual intercourse, and so become more serious.

Should my partner be treated too?

Your partner should definitely be tested and treated (this is called epidemiological treatment). The sooner you get your partner in for tests and treatment the sooner the infection is cured and the sooner you will be able to start having sex again.

Many doctors just give the partner treatment without doing any tests. I find that tests from one person may not always reveal the reason for the problems. If the other partner can be tested there is an increased chance of finding the cause and getting the correct treatment.

A good example of this is with trichomonas infection. This is more commonly detected in women than men. If the male goes for tests the doctor will find inflammation and – in the absence of other information – will probably prescribe treatment with a tetracycline antibiotic. This will not cure trichomonas infection: either metronidazole or tinidazole is required. If the female does not have tests she will end up being given the wrong treatment too, for the symptoms she may eventually develop. If, however, the female partner has tests done the doctor will find the trichomonas and both partners can be given the correct treatment.

Knowing the exact cause is not only useful in ensuring the correct treatment is given, it also means you can be accurately tested later to make sure the infection has gone.

My NSU keeps coming back

There may be several reasons for this. The first thing to check is that you haven't caught the infection again from your partner. Has your partner been to the doctor and been examined, had tests and been given treatment? Did you continue to have sexual intercourse while you were on antibiotics? Even if you are both taking tablets one of you can get better more quickly than the other and thus pass the infection back again.

Sometimes a different antibiotic needs to be tried for the particular organism that is causing your problem.

Alcohol can cause delayed healing or an apparent recurrence. The reasons for this are not really understood.

Up to 20% to 30% of men can have persistent symptoms of NSU after a course of antibiotic treatment. However, provided they have taken the full course of antibiotics prescribed and they have not become re-infected, most men with even persistent symptoms will soon get better.

Can women get NSU?

The female counterpart of male NSU is cervicitis or inflammation of the cervix, the cause of which is not apparent until tests are done.

Whatever underlying infection is causing a man's NSU may also cause cervicitis in his partner. The female cannot get NSU, but she can get cervicitis by catching the man's underlying infection. Similarly, a man cannot get cervicitis, but he can get NSU by catching a woman's underlying infection.

With cervicitis the cervix may look swollen and inflamed, and have a discharge. It may bleed if it is touched. The medical name of this condition is NSGI, which stands for Non Specific Genital Inflammation. The diagnosis is made by looking at cells taken from the endocervix and smeared on a glass slide. If there are more than 10 white blood cells per high power microscope field and no gonorrhea organisms are seen, the diagnosis is cervicitis.

Women who have been diagnosed with cervicitis are often treated for presumed chlamydia infection, because it is such a serious infection if left untreated.

Tests which count the number of cells on the cervix are not accurate if taken around the time of the menstrual period.

14

PID
(PELVIC
INFLAMMATORY DISEASE)

KEY CONCEPTS

Dyspareunia   Pain during sexual intercourse. This can be superficial due to problems at the opening of the vagina, or deep where it can be due to PID, the position of sexual intercourse or other causes.

Ectopic pregnancy   A pregnancy which occurs outside of the normal place in the uterus.

Sterility   Inability to become pregnant.

Superinfection   When an area already infected with one organism becomes infected with other organisms.

Tubal infertility   Inability to become pregnant because of a malfunction of the fallopian tubes.

What is PID?

PID stands for pelvic inflammatory disease. The name may not sound very threatening, but PID is a serious complication of some sexually transmittable diseases that affect young women. All women need to know about this one.

PID is the result of infections that cause inflammation of the female genital tract. The term includes inflammation of the uterus, fallopian tubes and ovaries. PID is nearly always due to infection that travels up through the vagina into the cervix and then into the uterus, up into the tubes and so on.

In rare cases, infection of the fallopian tubes can occur from a spread of infection from the appendix or from a serious infection in the blood, rather than being sexually transmitted.

When the infection gets into the fallopian tubes the inflammation may cause scarring and subsequent blockage of the tube so that eggs from the ovary cannot travel down to the uterus. Often what happens then is the sperm and egg meet in the fallopian tube and the fertilised egg grows in the tube instead of the uterus. When this happens it is called an ectopic pregnancy. The tube is only small and not built to expand so as the pregnancy develops, it causes pain and may burst, resulting in severe bleeding and a breakage of the tube. This is a medical emergency and sometimes women die from losing blood because they do not get to hospital in time. Once at the hospital they need an emergency operation to stop the bleeding and remove the pregnancy. Sometimes the tube can be sewn back together, but other times it has to be removed because there has been so much damage. If the ectopic pregnancy is found before it bursts it may be possible to remove the pregnancy from the tube without having to remove the tube.

It is easy to test for the organisms that cause PID (most commonly *Neisseria gonorrheae*, *Chlamydia trachomatis*, and *Mycoplasma hominis*). Early treatment will reduce the chance of complications occurring.

What makes PID more likely to occur?

The cervix usually acts as a barrier to infection by producing mucus which flows down into the vagina. This mucus contains enzymes that break up organisms. Certain conditions such as abortion, miscarriage, childbirth, use of an intrauterine contraceptive device (IUD) and operations on the cervix make it easier for infection to get through the barrier.

After a termination of pregnancy the risk of PID is 2% but this increases up to 10% in women who have an undetected sexually transmittable disease. The risk of PID due to an intrauterine contraceptive device usually occurs at the time the device is inserted.

How does the infection get there?

Infections are thought mainly to piggy back themselves on sperm during sex, to get through the cervix into the uterus and higher into the fallopian tubes. *Trichomonas vaginalis*, which is a very common STD (See Chapter 17 *The Other STDs*), is also thought to carry infection upwards. The contractions of orgasm may also encourage infections to be drawn up into the uterus.

Spread of infection through the cervix is more likely to occur at the time of menstruation because the endocervical canal is open at this time.

What are the causes of PID?

The most common causes are infection with the organisms which cause chlamydia, gonorrhea and another less well known organism called *Mycoplasma hominis*.

Chlamydia trachomatis is thought to be the cause in at least 50% of cases. *Chlamydia trachomatis* by itself causes a low grade inflammation and damages the lining cells of the tubes. Some studies have shown that 10% of all cases of chlamydia infections in women go on to develop PID.

Of women who are infected with gonorrhea, 10% to 15% will develop PID if they are not treated. The organism which causes gonorrhea causes severe inflammation, high temperatures and severe pelvic pain. Superinfection with other bacteria that live inside the body, particularly those which don't need oxygen to grow, is common.

Mycoplasma hominis is an organism that can occur in men or women without causing disease.

How common is PID?

PID is increasingly common in Western societies. Infection with chlamydia is the most frequent cause. In industrialised countries, ten to 13 of every thousand women of reproductive age are infected. Twenty women in every thousand in the age group 15 to 24 are affected. Many countries are unaware how bad the problem is because PID and chlamydia are not notifiable diseases. In most countries the importance of chlamydia and its complications has not been recognised.

How do I know if I have PID?

If you have PID you may notice a vaginal discharge which can vary in color from white to yellow to brown or greenish. You may notice some unusual bleeding or an odor. Your period could be longer or heavier than usual, or there may be spotting in between the periods. Sometimes you may notice that it hurts deep inside when you have sex. Occasionally you may notice pain when you pass urine.

Some women who have severe infection which spreads up the back of the abdomen can get pain around the liver that mimics inflammation of the gallbladder (cholecystitis). The medical name for this particular inflammation of the liver is the Fitz-Hugh-Curtis syndrome. Inside the abdomen of women with this condition there are string-like attachments, called violin string adhesions, which go from the outside of the liver to different parts of the internal body organs. They are caused by inflammation.

Some women have such severe pain in the lower part of the abdomen that they are mistakenly thought to have appendicitis. Others have a high temperature because of the infection.

Finally, sometimes there is unfortunately no warning at all. This is particularly likely to occur with chlamydia infection.

If you have any of the symptoms above or suspect that you may have been exposed to infection you should go to a doctor or STD clinic and be tested.

How is PID diagnosed?

PID is a difficult disease for doctors to diagnose with certainty. The surest way is for the doctor to look inside your abdomen with an instrument called a laparoscope. This clever instrument is a long tube with a light at one end and an eyepiece at the other. It can be inserted into the abdomen through a very small hole made under a general anaesthetic. By doing this the doctor can actually see if the fallopian tubes are inflamed or swollen with pus, or if there is pus in the pelvis.

Not all patients want to have a laparoscopy, nor are there always facilities for this to be done, so often you will be advised to have treatment with antibiotics which will stop the infection if you have it, without its presence having been absolutely proven.

If a laparoscopy is not done, the diagnosis can be wrong up to 35% of the time. Conditions which can be mistaken for PID are appendicitis, endometriosis, bleeding from an ovarian cyst and ectopic pregnancy.

The doctor may take your temperature if it is thought you are quite unwell, and will do blood tests to see if the white cell count in your blood is higher than normal.

You should also have tests taken from the genital region to try and find out the cause of the inflammation. In addition to the common causes there is usually super-infection with a lot of other bacteria. The tests taken from the cervix show an increased number of inflammatory cells on smears that are made on glass slides. Normally there are less than ten white blood cells on a smear from the inside lining of the cervix (endocervix) but in PID there are more than ten.

When the tests are done to see what infection it is that you have, your doctor will also feel inside your vagina to see if there is pain in the pelvis or if there is a lump which may indicate either a tube full of pus or an ectopic pregnancy, or an ovarian cyst.

Figure 14.1 Acute salpingitis or tubal inflammation

fallopian tube red and swollen   fallopian tube normal

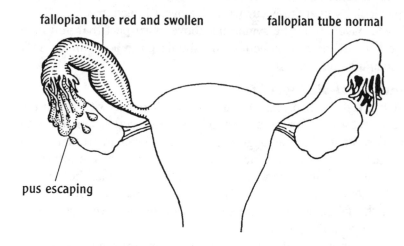

pus escaping

Sometimes your doctor will arrange for an investigation called an ultrasound. Sound waves that you can't hear are used to draw a picture of the inside of some part of your body. This test doesn't hurt although it can be uncomfortable. It is used to see if there are lumps or swellings that may need special treatment.

If you have an intrauterine contraceptive device (IUD) the doctor will probably decide that this should be removed sometime after the antibiotics have been started. Most specialists who treat this condition insist that any IUD be removed. This makes the treatment work better with less chance of later problems.

The earlier the infection is treated the better for you because there is less chance of scarring and complications occurring. If the pain is very bad, or the infection thought to be very severe, you may be admitted to the hospital for rest and powerful intravenous antibiotics that can kill the multiple possible causes of the infection.

What are the complications of PID?

The complications of PID are extremely serious. All of them can be reduced by early diagnosis and treatment, so if you suspect you may have PID, act quickly to get treatment. If you wait to see how it goes you could be doing your body irreparable harm.

If you develop PID just once you are then six to ten times more likely than other women to get it again. Each time you have another episode the chance of becoming infertile because of blockages in the tubes increases. The first episode of PID is associated with a one in six chance of becoming infertile. After that the risk doubles each time increasing to 35% after two episodes and 75% after three episodes. The chance of having an ectopic pregnancy after an episode of PID is increased by seven times and increases more after each subsequent episode.

A single episode of PID will leave you with a one in five chance of chronic pain in the pelvis, and a two in five chance of pain deep inside when you have sex (the medical term for this is deep dyspareunia). This occurs because the inflammation causes adhesions that are like tight ropes that stick the insides of you together and won't let them move around properly. Can you imagine hurting each time you have sex?

The chance of having some problem with your period is four out of five during an episode of PID. This problem usually goes away when the infection is treated, but some women do develop painful periods after they have had PID.

If you add up all these chances you will see that while PID itself is bad enough, the chances of your having unpleasant complications are very high and they skyrocket with second and third infections.

All this means that if you get PID you must try extremely hard to make sure you never get it again. If you are not in a regular relationship this means going to the extent of asking your partners to have an STD check up that includes testing for chlamydia and gonorrhea before you have sex with them. Even then still use a condom until you can trust them to know they are not going with anyone else as well.

It probably helps to be a little paranoid about your partners because that is going to protect your chances of having a normal sex life and a family. If your partner is not interested in helping you out by being tested and wearing condom s, then I advise you for the sake of your health for the rest of your life, to consider abandoning the relationship. It is better to do this at the start than further down the track when you get PID again.

This may sound a little tough, but it seems that every body has its own weakness. Some people get hay fever, others get sinusitis and others keep getting chest infections or stomach pains. Your weakness once you have had PID is right where the infection was. Unfortunately for you, the consequences are much more serious than just a bout of hayfever.

What are my chances of getting pregnant after PID?

A lot of women worry unnecessarily about the consequences of PID. Remember, all you need to get pregnant is for one egg and one sperm to meet in the right place. When and if you have trouble becoming pregnant is the time to start worrying.

In the meantime, if you have had an episode of PID your number one priority should be to make sure that you never have another episode. Make sure your partner is tested and treated and make sure new partners are not infected before you start a sexual relationship with them.

If the worst comes to the worst and you have trouble getting pregnant there are alternative treatments such as microtubal surgery or failing these you can join an in-vitro fertilization program.

Should my partner be tested if I have PID?

Yes. Your partner most certainly should be tested as there is a chance of finding the infection in him. This will tell the doctors what your infection is if they have not been able to find the cause. If your partner has an infection which is not treated you will catch it back from him as soon as you leave hospital or stop the antibiotic treatment. You will get sick again and start immediately on your second and much more dangerous episode.

The most common infections in male partners of women with PID (for which the cause cannot be found) is infection with chlamydia or gonorrhea .

Quite commonly chlamydia and gonorrhea can occur in the male with no symptoms whatsoever. Often it is hard to get your partner tested and treated when they don't feel anything wrong with them. If he does notice something wrong it will probably be a discharge from the end of his penis when he wakes up in the morning or at other times of the day and he may have discomfort when he passes urine. Unfortunately tests need to be done regardless of whether your partner has noticed anything or not.

If the relationship has broken up, it is still important to make sure he gets tested, otherwise his next girlfriend might get the same problem.

Usually your partner will be tested once they understand how serious the problem is. STD clinics have health workers who can help tell a person they may have an STD and that they need to be tested. You can ask their advice and help in going about it. Maybe they'll tell your partner for you if you don't want to.

What is the treatment for PID?

PID should be treated with several antibiotics. These antibiotics should kill gonorrhea, chlamydia, a wide variety of other bacteria that can be involved, and also the bacteria that grow without oxygen (anaerobes). The treatment usually needs to last for at least two weeks and sometimes it needs to be given for as long as a month.

Often treatment can be given as an outpatient as long as you are reviewed every few days (certainly at least every week). This is to make sure you are getting better and are not developing complications that might need special treatment, for example a tube full of pus which needs to be drained by operation.

Are there any sorts of contraception that alter my risk of PID?

Women who are under the age of twenty five or women who have not yet had children should think twice about having an intrauterine device for contraception because of the possibility of PID occurring at the time of insertion or later if they catch a sexually transmittable disease.

The oral contraceptive pill may make it more difficult for an infection to pass through the cervix if you catch an infection. It probably does this by making the cervical mucus thicker and therefore harder for the infection to work its way through, and also by reducing the amount of bleeding during menstruation.

Barrier methods of contraception such as condoms and a

diaphragm with a spermicide reduce the risk of catching or passing on an infection that causes PID.

I recommend that both partners always have an STD check and HIV test before they start a sexual relationship. This is the surest way to protect your ability to become pregnant and have a family when the time is right for you.

Some people however are too embarrassed to ask their partner to have a test. In these cases you should use one of the barrier methods of contraception that are mentioned above. Even if you are on the oral contraceptive pill, if you have a new partner it is a good idea to insist on using condoms until you are sure they have not got an infection they can pass on to you.

Not many people realize that very serious infections can occur in someone without them knowing it. They might not be showing any symptoms but they can still pass the infection on to you — and it could do you far more harm than it currently appears to be doing them. If they care for you, they won't want to subject you to that risk.

15

PROSTATITIS

KEY CONCEPTS

Acute prostatitis   Prostatitis which occurs quickly.

Chronic prostatitis   Prostatitis which persists for a long time.

Infectious prostatitis   Prostatitis due to an infectious organism.

Noninfectious prostatitis   Prostatitis due to non infective causes.

What is prostatitis?

Prostatitis is inflammation of the prostate gland. This gland is found only in males, at the bottom of the bladder and wrapped around the urethra (the tube which carries urine out of the bladder). See Chapter 3 *Normal Anatomy and STD Examinations* for an explanation of the prostate and what it does. There are two types of prostatitis: infectious and non infectious.

As men grow older, the chance they will develop prostatitis gets higher and higher but luckily in most cases it causes no problems. Lots of men do not even know they have the inflammation.

When there is inflammation it collects in the tubes within the prostate and makes them swell up with secretion and pus cells. These tubes empty into the urethra. In most men however prostatitis is not a serious problem and often settles with appropriate treatment.

What causes prostatitis?

Infectious prostatitis is caused by germs. Some of these germs are the common cause of urinary tract infections in men and women. The names of some are: *Escherichia coli, Proteus mirabilis, Klebsiella* and *Pseudomonas* species.

Very rarely prostatitis is due to sexually transmitted infections such as *Trichomonas vaginalis* and *Chlamydia trachomatis*. *Ureaplasma urealyticum* has been found to be a cause of prostatitis in some cases. See Chapter 12 *Gonorrhea*, Chapter 17 *The Other STDs* and Chapter 10 *Chlamydia* to find out more about these infections.

In the old days before antibiotics, prostatitis was a common complication of gonorrhea. It resulted in infection spreading into the blood. In addition, pus would gather into formations called abscesses and then breakdown, creating connections between the urethra, rectum and surface skin. After the inflammation settled down, the person could be left with a feeling that when they wanted to pass urine they had to do so in a great hurry, they may have had pain when they passed urine, as well as frequent pain just above the pubic bone. For some, when they passed urine it was like a trickle from a watering can. The days before antibiotics were certainly the bad old days!

The cause of noninfectious prostatitis is not known. Sometimes it is thought to be due to stress. Other possible causes are some urine flowing backwards into the prostate instead of forward down the urethra and inflammation in an enlarged prostate gland (enlargement occurs in all men as they grow older). Rarer causes include inflammation of blood vessels and swellings in the prostate called granulomas.

What are the symptoms of prostatitis?

Acute prostatitis is very painful. It develops quickly and makes you feel quite unwell with high temperatures, hot and cold flushes, a feeling of wanting to pass urine more often than usual, and occasionally blockage of the urethra due to swelling, so the bladder fills up with urine which cannot get out easily.

Chronic prostatitis occurs more slowly. Some men with this condition have no symptoms all. Others may notice they pass urine more often than usual, or that when they want to pass urine they must do so in a hurry. Others may have bladder problems and notice they continue to dribble urine after they have urinated, or that it hurts to pass urine. Some notice a watery discharge. Others may get pain after ejaculation. The pain is usually felt just above the pubic bones, but sometimes is felt in the testes, penis, groin, upper thighs or the area between the genitals and anus (the perineum).

When the prostate is inflamed, the secretion it makes is more alkaline than usual and contains less zinc, which causes the sperm to be less mobile. There is also less of the enzyme (called lysozyme) which breaks down germs. This may be why germs can get into the prostate.

How do I know if I have prostatitis?

Prostatitis is sometimes difficult to diagnose. Your doctor will ask you what symptoms you have noticed and will examine your genitals to see if there is any tenderness or lumps or bumps. Your doctor may feel your prostate gland to see if it is larger than normal, if it is sore, or if there are lumps in it. This is done by the doctor inserting a finger with a glove on it into your rectum while you are lying on your side with your knees pulled up to your chest. This test does not hurt unless the prostate is acutely inflamed. You should tell the doctor if it is hurting.

There are a series of tests available. Usually you will be tested to make sure your symptoms are not due to a sexually transmittable disease. Then you will be asked to do a urine test. Rarely a three part urine test is requested: firstly you are asked to pass about 10ml of urine into a jar, then some into the toilet, then 10ml into a second jar. Then the doctor will massage your prostate and collect the prostatic fluid from the end of the penis on a glass slide. Finally you will be asked to pass 10ml more urine into a third jar. If you still have some urine left you can then finish into the toilet. Try not to put more than 10ml of urine into the jars or it can interfere with the results.

At the laboratory the fluid in the jars is examined for pus cells and germs grown in it. Which of the three samples grows the most germs gives a good indication of whether the infection is in the urethra, bladder or prostate.

What treatment is there?

Treatment for prostatitis is with antibiotics. Even if the infection is not found to be caused by a germ, many people will get better, with their symptoms disappearing. If the prostatitis is thought to have occurred after an NSU infection, then a course of doxycycline or minocycline for two to three weeks is warranted. If you have symptoms of NSU, chlamydia or gonorrhea (see Chapters 12, 9 and 11 respectively) see your doctor for treatment straight away to reduce your chance of developing complications.

Do I have to use condoms?

If you have developed prostatitis after an episode of NSU it would be wise to wear condoms for a while until you know that you are better. It is important to allow your body time to heal without the risk of becoming infected again.

How long does it take to get better?

With acute prostatitis you should start to feel better within a week, although you will be given antibiotics for longer than this. In chronic prostatitis you may need to take the antibiotics for a long time. One of the reasons for this is that the antibiotic has to build up in concentration within the inflamed part. Because of the blockages in the tubes caused by the inflammation it can take quite a while for things to settle down.

It's best to avoid alcohol during treatment. If you drink too much it dilutes the antibiotic so it will not work. Also, alcohol dehydrates the body and will tend to dry up the inflamed secretion, thus making it harder for the body to remove the areas of inflammation. Finally, if you drink too much alcohol you might forget about wearing condoms. Your body needs a break and a chance to get better.

Should my partner be tested?

If you are in a stable relationship and your prostatitis developed after an episode of NSU, then you should ask your partner to see a doctor for tests and treatment. This will reduce the chance of any organism that may have caused your problem re-infecting you, even though it is probably not causing any symptoms in your partner. Such is life.

16

SYPHILIS

KEY CONCEPTS

Chancre   The ulcer which occurs in the first stage of syphilis (pronounced 'chank-er').

Congenital syphilis   The infection transmitted to babies by mothers who have untreated syphilis during pregnancy.

Latent syphilis Syphilis infection which is active in the body but shows no symptoms or signs and can only be detected by a blood test.

Primary syphilis   The first stages of infection with syphilis when a chancre is present.

Secondary syphilis   Further active infection with syphilis which happens after the first stage and before the infection becomes hidden.

Tertiary syphilis   The last stages of syphilis where it may affect the skin and bones, heart and brain.

Treponema pallidum   The organism which causes syphilis.

The history of syphilis

There are two theories about the origin of syphilis. The Columbian theory is that the disease was caught from natives in the West Indies or from American Indians by the crew of Christopher Columbus' ship and that they imported it to Europe on their return from America in 1493. As it was a new infection in Europe the people had no immunity. It spread rapidly and was called the Great Pox in the late fifteenth century.

The other theory is that syphilis changed from being an infection found only in the tropics to one which was spread by sexual intercourse in countries where clothes were worn. Supporting this theory, the organisms which cause the tropical disease yaws and the organisms which cause syphilis look exactly the same under the microscope and cause the same reaction in the blood.

Syphilis was called the 'Italian disease' by the French and the 'French disease' by the Italians. Eventually it was named after a poem written by Fracastorius in 1521, in which he described a shepherd named Syphilis who had the disease.

In the eighteenth century it was thought that syphilis and gonorrhea were due to the same infection. It was known they were caught by sexual intercourse. Research was done by infecting people with secretions from patients with the disease. It was not until 1838 that it was confirmed that syphilis and gonorrhea were definitely different infections.

Treatment for syphilis in the early days was quite toxic, being with mercury, arsenic and bismuth. Luckily in 1943 penicillin was discovered and it is still the best treatment for syphilis.

Syphilis is on the increase in some countries. In the United States the number of young people with syphilis infection is increasing. Syphilis is a common infection in underdeveloped countries. Some studies have reported up to 22% of women tested showed evidence of being infected. In these countries a large number of babies die from the infection. The numbers of babies being born with syphilis is increasing again, just when health officials thought the problem was under control.

What causes syphilis?

Syphilis is due to an organism called *Treponema pallidum.* Treponema comes from a Greek word meaning 'a turning thread'. Pallidum comes from a Latin word meaning pale. Under a microscope the organism looks like a tiny snake. It moves in a characteristic way. It has lots of spirals, and moves by bending in the middle, rotating like a corkscrew, and compressing and expanding like a coil. Sometimes when it is compressed the centre part buckles out and forms a U shape like the slinky toys you may have played with. The organism multiplies by dividing itself in half every 30 to 36 hours. Because it is approximately a day and a half between multiplying, the treatment which is given to kill the infection has to be given over a long period of time so that the organisms that are multiplying at any time during the day are killed by the antibiotic. See the section on treatment.

The organism does not live very long outside the body, so if a doctor wants to test for syphilis by looking for the organism in secretions the fluid must be kept at body temperature and examined under a microscope within 20 minutes. It is not easy to grow the organism but specially equipped laboratories can grow it in rabbits.

The organism is killed by antiseptic and even ordinary soap and water. Unfortunately you cannot cure yourself this way as the organisms will have burrowed deep inside you. What this does mean is that if you have caught the infection but have scrubbed and cleaned the sore before you go to the doctor for tests, you may initially appear negative. The test looks for the organisms on the surface of the ulcer and it only detects them if they are alive. Often the doctor will ask you to not use soap on the sore and return the next day for more tests.

Figure 16.1 Treponema pallidum in body tissue as seen though an electron microscope

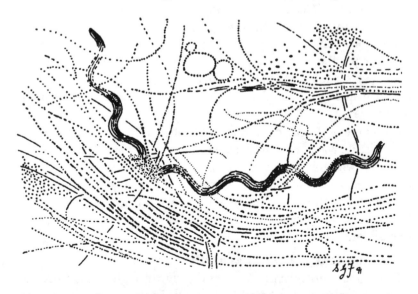

Syphilis is highly infectious. Contact with 50 to 60 organisms is enough to cause an infection. As soon as they get into the body they start multiplying and wriggling around and getting into every part of the body.

How is syphilis caught?

Syphilis is caught by having sexual intercourse with someone who has syphilis and is infectious. The sores of the person with syphilis are rubbed against the other person, and the organism is transferred.

Syphilis is also spread by blood, so occasionally it is caught by sharing needles with someone who is infected.

The organisms which cause syphilis live in the blood and any fluid which oozes from the sores of someone with syphilis in either stage one or two of the disease (see below).

In women these sores may all be inside where they can't ordinarily be seen. This means that a man can catch the infection from a woman without knowing that the woman has the infection. Wearing a condom may reduce the chances but it is still possible to catch syphilis from sores on parts of the body not covered by the condom, or rubbed onto parts of the body not protected by the condom. For example, if the infection in the first stage is on a man's scrotum, a condom will not stop the infection being passed on. Similarly if the infection is on a woman's vulva, a condom will not stop the scrotum or mouth coming in contact with the sores.

It is infections like syphilis, genital herpes and genital warts which make the doctors say condom s will reduce your chance of getting a sexually transmittable disease, but will not completely eliminate the risk. Condoms only work on the part of the body they cover.

It is common to catch syphilis without getting any symptoms so it is wise to have a syphilis blood test if you have had sex with someone who might be infected or if you are found to have some other sexually transmittable disease. It can take up to three months for the infection to show up in your blood so you should have a test early and then have a follow up blood test three months later.

What happens if I catch syphilis?

The syphilis organism enters your body through a tiny break in your skin. Usually the break is so small that you cannot even see it. From there it spreads in the lymph channels to the closest lymph nodes. Within 24 hours the infection enters the blood stream and starts spreading throughout the body, including the brain.

There are four stages of syphilis, called primary, secondary, latent and tertiary syphilis.

Syphilis and HIV

People who have HIV infection tend to have more severe syphilis, and it enters the tertiary stage sooner. HIV makes syphilis worse and, unfortunately, the reverse is also true: having syphilis speeds up the growth of HIV.

This is just another reason why if you are found to have syphilis it is a good idea to be tested for HIV infection as well. If you have both infections you are usually given stronger treatment and may have additional tests done to see if the infection has spread to the brain.

Another complication is that syphilis can be more difficult to diagnose if the person also has HIV infection: not all the tests are as reliable in this double-infection situation.

All this means that if you have HIV infection and suspect you may have caught syphilis, you must act immediately to be tested and start treatment. Sometimes if you have had treatment in the past for syphilis and later catch HIV, you will be advised to be retreated for syphilis with antibiotics that work against infection in the brain.

Primary syphilis

Within nine to 90 days of having caught the infection the person usually develops a sore called a 'chancre' at the place on their body where they first caught the infection. The chancre starts off as a tiny red pimple or flat spot which then becomes an ulcer. It can be quite small but can be as big as five centimetres (two inches) wide. Usually there is only one sore, but some people may have more than one.

Usually the infection is on the genitals, but it can be on any part of the body including the mouth. In men the most common place for the chancre to occur is on the penis near the tip. In women the chancre usually occurs on the cervix or high in the vagina, hidden from view. Sometimes the chancre can occur around the anus, or on the lips or inside the mouth. This can happen if these parts of the body have been used for sexual intercourse. The lymph glands in the region are usually swollen, but like the sore, they do not hurt.

In women, because the chancre may occur inside the genital organs, they may not know they have the infection until they go onto the next stage.

Most people do not feel sick and often the sore does not hurt.

The person becomes infectious as soon as they have enough organisms in their body in one area to infect another person.

The chancre is highly infectious for all the time it is present. The secretions which ooze out of it are loaded with the tiny snake-like organisms that cause syphilis.

Figure 16.2 A chancre

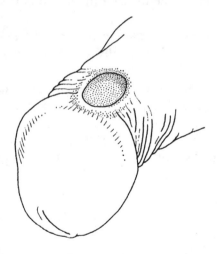

If the chancre is not treated, it goes away within two to eight weeks (sometimes longer if it is big). This does not mean you are better. Unfortunately what is happening is that the infection has gone inside your body where it is growing and spreading, getting ready for the next stage of infection. You are still infectious.

Secondary Syphilis

The second stage of syphilis occurs from one to six months (commonly six to 12 weeks) after the first signs of infection. By this time the infection has spread throughout the whole body.

You may feel ill with high temperatures, generalised aches and pains, a headache and a general feeling of being unwell. When this happens you usually do not feel like eating. The original sore may return and there may be other sores in the mouth and genitals.

You may notice your hair starting to fall out and bald patches appearing, your eyebrows thinning, swelling of many of the body's lymph glands and warty type lesions in the genital regions. Sometimes these can occur under the breasts of large women, or in the armpits or around the anus. Rarely they occur at the corner of the mouth. These warts look like the warts due to the human papillomavirus so sometimes a mistake can be made in diagnosing the infection. This is another reason if someone has genital warts doctors like to do a blood test for syphilis.

Often there will be a rash. This can be anywhere but most commonly it appears on the palms of the hands and soles of the feet. The rash can be flat, pimply or a mixture of blotchy and raised areas. It may break down into sores which ooze fluid filled with the tiny snake like organism.

Typically this secondary stage can last intermittently for two years. It is the most infectious stage of the disease.

If they are not treated the infected person remains highly contagious for some time into the next stage called the latent stage. Pregnant women can pass on the infection to their baby in this stage even if they do not have symptoms.

Latent syphilis

If it is not treated during the first and second phases the syphilis infection can hide away in the body for many years. This is called latent syphilis, which means it is quiet or hidden. In this situation you feel well, but you will be infectious for the first few years. The only way of finding out you have the infection at this stage is to have a blood test.

Early latent syphilis is up to two years of no symptoms. Late latent syphilis is from at least two years of latent infection, up to the development of the third stage.

If the infection is not discovered, then you may be lucky and have no further problems. Women with latent syphilis can however pass it on to their babies for up to nine years after they caught the infection, if they were not treated. Treatment will stop the infection being passed on to the baby. See Chapter 20 *STDs and Pregnancy* and Chapter 21 *STDs and Your Baby.*

Tertiary syphilis

If it is not treated the syphilis may advance to its fourth and final stage, which is not pleasant. People who have never been treated for syphilis can pass into this stage any time from three to 20 years after the first infection. Not all people with syphilis which has been untreated will go on to this stage, but it is not a good lottery to enter.

Tertiary syphilis can take three forms known as cardiovascular syphilis, neurosyphilis and benign late syphilis.

In benign late syphilis, lumps start to grow. They can be:

- On the skin, where they can stick out and ulcerate.
- In the mouth, nose and throat, where they can break down to cause deformity of the nose, hoarseness and painful ulcers which interfere with eating.
- In the bones where they can cause pain and sometimes ulcers.
- In the eyes, causing pain, difficulty seeing things properly, loss of eyesight, excessive watering and irritation by bright lights.
- In other parts of the body such as the testicles and liver, though this is less common.

Cardiovascular syphilis affects men more often than women. They may have no symptoms until the heart is severely affected. Most commonly syphilis will affect the aorta which is the blood vessel that leaves the heart carrying blood which has been oxygenated in the lungs. If the aorta is affected close to the coronary arteries (the blood vessels which supply blood to the heart), they can become narrowed resulting in chest pain. This is commonly known as angina. Most angina is due to blood vessels being narrowed by cholesterol deposits but occasionally syphilis can be the cause.

Where the aorta is affected close to the aortic valves of the heart, the valves can become leaky, allowing blood to run back into the heart when it is being pumped out into the body. This condition is called aortic regurgitation. When this is mild it is only detected by changes in the blood pressure readings and listening to the heart. As it becomes more severe the person may develop shortness of breath on exercise and may also develop breathlessness when they lie flat in bed at night. Severe involvement of the aorta can cause expansion of the wall of the aorta so it looks like it has a balloon on it. This condition is called an aneurysm. If the aneurysm gets large enough it will burst just like a balloon and the person will die. Sometimes other blood vessels develop aneurysms.

Neurosyphilis can affect the brain and nervous system. If you develop syphilis of the brain there are several ways it can affect you. One way, called meningovascular syphilis, affects the lining of the brain especially around the blood vessels. The person may develop a headache which may be present for weeks or months. There may be variable signs such as a stroke which can affect one part of the body or a side of the body. They may develop ringing in the ears, a sensation of the room spinning around them, and deafness. If the arteries affecting the spinal column are affected the persons legs may become stiff and eventually paralysed. If the involvement is high up in the spinal column the muscles in the hands may be weakened and wasted. Other parts of the spinal cord may be affected and the person may lose control of their bladder and bowel.

In another form of syphilis-related brain disease, called general paralysis, the symptoms do not usually develop until at least ten years after infection. The person may become more tired than usual, and irritable. They may have difficulty concentrating and trouble sleeping. Often it is not the infected person who notices the problem, but friends and family who recognise unusual behavior and changes in the personality. The memory gradually deteriorates and the person's moods change quickly. They have no insight into their illness and are totally unaware there is a problem. This can cause great hardship for the family and friends. Finally they can become disorientated, not knowing where they are, may have fits and may have thoughts about themselves that are totally inappropriate.

Often people at this stage have a feeling of well being. They may have thoughts that are called delusions of grandeur. They might tell you that they were a very important person such as the president. They may tell you they own a Rolls Royce or that they were the best salesman of the year. Occasionally they may become paranoid and frightened that everyone is against them.

Eventually the brain deteriorates so much that the person is unable to look after themselves and becomes bedridden, incontinent of feces and urine and unable to do anything for themselves. When these people die, if they have an autopsy performed, the brain is found to be shrunken down to a much smaller size than it should be.

Another form of brain involvement is called tabes dorsalis. In this condition particular parts of the brain and spinal column are affected. The ability to know where parts of the body are in the dark is lost. Infection is often first diagnosed because the person starts bumping into things when they get up at night to go to the toilet. The person may develop what are called lightening pains, where there is a stab of pain on one part of the body which shifts without warning to somewhere else. This pain is very distressing and very difficult to treat. Sometimes the pain can be severe and may be mistaken for a medical emergency, leading the doctors to think the person needs an operation for, say, a burst ulcer or appendix.

The person may start to feel as if they are walking on cotton wool, or that ants are crawling all over their skin. Sometimes they become incontinent of urine when their bladder is full and, in the old days, died of kidney and bladder infections. When the person walks they may be unsteady on their feet and may slap their feet on the ground because they cannot feel properly where their feet are. Because of the lack of feeling severe ulceration may develop. Sometimes they may also lose their eyesight. When they lose awareness of their body, they do things with their arms and legs that over stretch the joints and cause swelling and degeneration of the joints. The joints can become grossly deformed but luckily for the patient are quite painless.

Unfortunately in the advanced stages of syphilis where the damage is due to scarring from long standing infection, treatment only stops further damage to the body, but cannot repair the damage already caused. That's why it is so important, if you think you might have caught syphilis or you think one of your friends may have had sex with someone who is likely to have the infection, to go and get a blood test, or encourage your friend to get the blood test. It's so much better to have the blood test and be cured than to slowly rot away on the inside, just because you are too scared to have a needle or are too embarrassed to see a doctor.

Usually doctors are really pleased to see people being brave and sensible about having a check. Occasionally you might see one who will tell you off for being in the situation you got yourself into, but deep down they are just trying to help you and are hoping, like you, that you have not caught a sexually transmittable disease such as syphilis.

How do I find out if I have syphilis?

In the early stages of the disease, tests are made on fluid taken from the chancres or sores and examined under a microscope for the characteristic snake-like organisms. This can only be done in places where there is a laboratory set up for this purpose. It takes training to be able to recognise the organism and a special light setting on the microscope called 'dark ground illumination'. The laboratory person sits in a dark room with just the microscope light on. It can take a long time even for an experienced person to find the syphilis organism and they can spend up to 20 minutes looking at one slide.

In addition, a blood test is taken. This is usually positive early in the infection but sometimes it can take up to three months for syphilis to show up in the blood, so the test will have to be repeated a few months later. Occasionally if someone is infected with HIV the test may not become positive until much later.

In the later stages of syphilis a spinal fluid examination is usually necessary to see if there is involvement of the brain. In addition examination of the heart and a chest X ray and sometimes bone X rays are required.

Despite all this it is sometimes difficult for a doctor to decide if you have syphilis, what stage you are in, or how effective any past treatment has been. In these situations you will most likely be referred to an STD specialist.

It is common to catch syphilis without knowing you have caught it, so it is wise to have a syphilis blood test even if you don't have any symptoms, if you have had sex with someone who might be infected or if you are found to have some other sexually transmitted disease. You should have a test straight away and then make sure you have a follow up blood test three months later.

There is a combined test for syphilis and HIV infection. You will be asked for your permission before this is done. It is a very sensible idea to have both tests at the same time. It means just one needle for the blood test, but a little extra blood is taken.

People who catch syphilis need to make sure they have not caught HIV infection or another sexually transmitted disease at the same time. People who have infection with both HIV and syphilis can pass either on very easily, probably more easily than someone who has just one infection by itself. One of the reasons for this is that the sores of syphilis will also contain HIV if it is present.

What treatment is available?

Syphilis is curable with treatment. The best treatment is penicillin given either intravenously or by daily injection for ten to 21 days depending on the stage of infection. With treatment given this way the penicillin gets into the brain in large enough amounts to kill the organisms if they are there. Treatment with only two or three penicillin injections does not kill the organisms which have reached the brain. (There are however some people who need this sort of treatment, which is given as a compromise, because they are unable to have injections over a long time.)

If you have both HIV infection and syphilis then you may be treated in hospital with intravenous penicillin or be retreated with higher doses and a longer course of treatment. This treatment makes sure the penicillin reaches any organisms which may have hidden away in the brain.

There is alternative treatment if you are allergic to penicillin.

When you start on treatment it is quite common to feel unwell with temperatures, aches and pains and a headache. This reaction is called the Jarisch Herxheimer reaction. It can occur for one or two days of treatment. It results from the reaction the body makes against the syphilis organisms when they are killed. In the third stage of syphilis, this reaction can cause problems if it is too severe and usually the doctor will start you on a course of prednisolone (a drug which reduces the amount of swelling and inflammation) 48 hours before starting the penicillin treatment. The prednisolone dose is reduced over the next week then stopped.

After being treated for syphilis, you will be asked to have regular checks to make sure the treatment has worked. These checks are carried out for many years, especially if you have been found to have HIV infection. For the rest of your life, your blood will show evidence that you have been infected with syphilis. Of the tests used to diagnose syphilis, some will become negative with treatment but some stay positive. Interpreting the blood test results for syphilis is difficult and is best done by people who are used to dealing with the infection.

If I don't receive treatment, for how long will I be infectious?

If you don't get treatment you will be infectious for about four years.

An exception is if you are a woman and become pregnant in which case the syphilis organism can pass into the placenta many years after the initial infection.

If you are also infected with HIV and have never been treated for syphilis then it is quite possible that you will remain permanently infectious and pass on syphilis to anyone you have sex with, unless you are treated. It is not known if it is possible for people who have syphilis and HIV to become infectious again after they have been treated. Researchers think this unlikely but it is a possibility. This is why people with HIV infection who have had syphilis are kept under regular syphilis review, as well as being monitored for other infections.

Who should be tested for syphilis?

Any person who has sex with someone who is known to have syphilis should have a test. A person who has sex with someone who is known to have any sexually transmitted disease should have a test, because syphilis often occurs in conjunction with other infections. A person who catches any sort of sexually transmitted disease should have a blood test for syphilis, for the same reason.

Women who are pregnant should have a test early in their pregnancy to ensure they do not have the infection and either infect their unborn baby or miscarry. See Chapter 20 *STDs and Pregnancy*. People who have HIV infection should also be tested for syphilis, because of the particularly severe effects it can have on them if not treated.

How does syphilis affect babies?

The syphilis organism can pass through from the mother's blood to the baby's blood at any stage in the pregnancy and cause growth deformities in the baby. The baby may be born dead.

If syphilis in the mother is not treated it is very likely that the baby will be born infected. Many places test mothers for syphilis early in the pregnancy so that treatment can be given. In some high risk communities the mother may also need to be tested part of the way through pregnancy. Treatment early in pregnancy will stop the baby having illness due to syphilis and the baby will be born normal. See Chapter 21 *STDs and Your Baby.*

Section Four

The Other STDs

17

THE OTHER STDs

Balanitis and Balano-posthitis

What is balanitis?

Balanitis is an inflammation of the skin on the head of the penis. Balano-posthitis is inflammation of the head and neck of the penis.

What does balanitis look like?

Most commonly there is redness of the glans (head of the penis) and the area below it. This may ulcerate or become severely inflamed causing a smelly discharge from the skin. Candidia or thrush is a common cause (see Chapter 9)

How is balanitis caught?

The most common cause of balanitis is not cleaning under the foreskin on a regular basis. Men who have not been circumcised should keep the area under the foreskin clean by retracting the foreskin (pulling it right back) and washing the skin clean each day. There is no need to use soap, which can cause skin irritation in some men. The important thing is to wash away the smegma — the white cheesy stuff that is made by the glands around the head and neck of the penis.

A similar condition to balanitis occurs in women, causing vulval irritation. It may be due to not washing the vulva regularly.

Another common cause of balanitis is the organism which causes thrush, *Candida albicans.* Bacteria can also cause balanitis. You can get candidia from your partner, even though it may not be troubling them. Doing a lot of sport and getting quite sweaty in the genital region can also encourage candidia. Because candida likes sugar, infections caused by candida are more common in patients with diabetes as they have sugar in their urine.

There are many other less common causes of balanitis, including chemical irritation and drug reactions.

What treatment is available?

The main aim of treatment is to keep the glans and foreskin clean and dry. If you can retract the foreskin easily you should clean the glans and area under the foreskin two or three times a day, and than gently dab it dry. Make sure the skin is completely dry before you roll the foreskin back. You can use a fan, hair dryer or the heat from a reading light to dry the skin more rapidly.

If you cannot retract the foreskin easily do not force it or you might not be able to get it back to normal. If you do force it and then can't get the foreskin back over the glans, go down to your local hospital and see a doctor. Sometimes an operation is needed.

If you get balanitis easily you should retract the foreskin and clean the area every time you wash or have a shower. Always retract the foreskin when you urinate.

When can I start having sex again?

You should avoid having sex until the infection has cleared up. Having sex while the penis is inflamed makes things worse because it tears the skin and the moisture slows down healing.

Should I get tested for other sex diseases?

Your doctor can advise you on this. If your infection is obviously just due to candida then further tests may not be called for. If you have multiple partners or have just changed partners it is a good idea to have a full STD check.

Chancroid

What is chancroid?

Chancroid is a sexually transmitted infection that causes genital ulcers. It is very common in tropical countries such as some parts of Africa and South East Asia. Usually it is only found in Western countries in people who have caught it overseas.

What symptoms does chancroid cause?

The first thing noticed is usually a small pimple on the genitals, which is quite sore. Soon this develops into one or more ulcers which grow quickly and can be extremely painful. Often the glands in the groin swell up and become sore.

In women there may be no symptoms because the ulcer is inside and not noticed, otherwise it may cause pain passing urine, a vaginal discharge or pain on sexual intercourse. If anal sexual intercourse has been performed there may be pain passing bowel motions or bleeding from the back passage. There is often more than one ulcer and these can grow quickly to join together to form giant ulcers. It is not uncommon for the inguinal glands on one side to swell up full of pus.

Luckily this infection does not spread further than the genital region and close by lymph nodes.

Figure 17.1 Chancroid

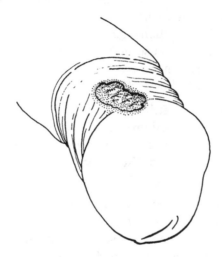

How long will it take to find out if I have caught it?

Within four to seven days of having caught the infection (no quicker than three days and rarely longer than 10 days) symptoms will develop. The ulcers caused by chancroid can be confused with the ulcers of syphilis, genital herpes and granuloma inguinale.

How is the diagnosis made?

Some of the fluid and cells from the sore are placed on a glass slide and sent to a laboratory. It takes special skill and training to be able to recognise chancroid. Under the microscope it looks like a pair of dumbbells which have been bent in the middle. The laboratory may try to grow the organism but this is difficult and often not successful.

What treatment is available?
Chancroid infection can be cured by antibiotics. The current recommended treatment is with an injection of ceftriaxone. The good news is that once you start antibiotic treatment the ulcers start healing almost straight away. Sometimes a swollen lymph gland needs to have the pus drained out.

Be sure that you are tested for other STDs such as gonorrhea, chlamydia, HIV and syphilis which commonly accompany chancroid.

Should my partner be treated too?
Your partner should at least be tested for chancroid and in many situations they should be treated too, otherwise you are going to end up catching the infection again soon! Remember that in women the infection may cause no immediate symptoms because it can occur inside. You may need to twist your partner's arm to go for tests when they feel perfectly well.

When can I have sex again?
Once the ulcers have healed up and you have finished the course of antibiotics you can have sex again, provided none of the tests for other sexually transmitted disease has become positive in the meantime.

What treatment can I have if I am pregnant?
Treatment in pregnancy poses no problem except that tetracycline antibiotics have to be avoided. Please have tests to make sure you do not also have infection with syphilis, gonorrhea or chlamydia which may harm the baby.

Donovanosis (granuloma inguinale)
What is donovanosis?
The organism which causes donovanosis is a bacterium called *Calymmatobacterium granulomatis*. In Australia it is found mainly in the hot sandy desert and very northern areas. Aborigines used to treat the infection with a powdered extract of the bloodwood tree (Eucalyptus corymbosa). It is also common in India, some parts of Africa, the Caribbean and other tropical and subtropical countries. The infection was first recorded by a man named

McLeod in 1882. He described it as an 'ulcerating granuloma of the pudenda'. In 1905 Donovan described the changes in the cells which are now called Donovan bodies.

How is donovanosis caught?
Donovanosis is caught by having sex with an infected person. Fortunately it is not too infectious so if you have sexual intercourse with someone who has this infection you might be lucky and not catch it.

Figure 17.2 Donovan bodies in a white blood cell

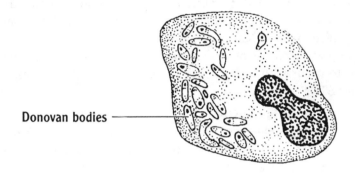

Donovan bodies

What symptoms does donovanosis cause?
Donovanosis starts out as one or more small lumps. Usually they are in the genital region. They can be outside the body or inside and can spread to the inguinal (groin) region. Rarely the infection can spread to other parts of the body such as the mouth and lips, the liver, lungs and bones.

The small initial lumps ulcerate to form beefy looking but painless growths. These growths continue to get bigger and bleed easily if they are knocked. Women may notice irregular bleeding or blood in their urine. Sometimes other bacteria invade the sore causing the lesion to smell and have an ooze of liquid from its surface. Sometimes the growths look like genital warts or the warts caused by syphilis and sometimes they may even look like cancer. The ulcers often become infected with other organisms causing pus and a foul smell.

In women if the growth is on the cervix it may not be noticed. It can grow to quite a large size during pregnancy and cause obstruction to delivery of the baby via the vagina. However the main danger is that it weakens the cervix so it tears and bleeds excessively during childbirth. This bleeding may be very difficult to stop.

How long will it take to find out if I have caught donovanosis?

This is difficult to say exactly but it could take as long as 80 days to show.

How is donovanosis diagnosed?

A small piece of the growth is crushed on a slide and sent to a laboratory for an expert to examine. Under a microscope the germs which cause the infection appear in groups called 'Donovan bodies' which look like safety pins inside cells.

It is very common for other infections including gonorrhea and syphilis to occur with donovanosis, so you should also be tested for other STDs

What treatment is available?

The most commonly used treatment is a course of antibiotic tablets. A tetracycline or sulphonamide are most commonly given, until the lesions have healed. This can take quite some time. Often the tablets need to be taken for three to five weeks. It seems that a new antibiotic called ceftriaxone is also useful in treating this infection. This antibiotic is given by injection.

When treatment is started you will notice the sores starting to heal within three to seven days, but you must continue the treatment until the sores have completely healed otherwise they will come back. Often there is some scarring due to the infection. This can be just white patches of skin, but in more severe cases where the person did not go for early treatment there can be shortening of part of the penis, blockage of the penis or a deep hole where the infection was. Early treatment will reduce or prevent scarring.

Should my partner be treated too?

Donovanosis is not too infectious, but it is dangerous and it is commonly associated with other more infectious STDs, so your partner should certainly be tested for donovanosis and other STDs. If the infection is not found it is unlikely that your partner will receive treatment. It is not uncommon for the partner to be uninfected.

When can I have sex again?

As soon as the ulcer has healed you can start having sex again, provided you make sure your partner has been checked and that they have finished any treatment they were given. It is important to take the treatment until the sore has completely healed otherwise it is highly likely it will come back.

What treatment can I have if I am pregnant?

The usual tetracycline or sulphonamide treatments cannot be used because they may harm your baby. Alternative treatments are available, but they may have to be given in hospital.

Lymphogranuloma Venereum (LGV)

What is lymphogranuloma venereum?

Lymphogranuloma Venereum (LGV) is a sexually transmitted infection that is mainly a disease of lymphatic tissue. The organism which causes it is a type of chlamydia. Lymphogranuloma venereum is commonly found in some parts of Africa, Asia, Australia, South America, India and the Caribbean. Most of the cases of LGV diagnosed in Western countries are in people who have caught it from sexual intercourse with a person from overseas.

What symptoms does lymphogranuloma venereum cause?

The infection enters through breaks in the skin which are sometimes so small they are not even noticed. Where it enters the skin it may cause a swelling or ulcer which is commonly not noticed. During the early stages of the infection there can be discomfort on passing urine, which may be diagnosed as non-specific urethritis. Inflammation of the cervix (cervicitis) is also common during the initial stages. This heals quickly leaving no scar.

The germ then spreads in the lymphatics to the closest lymph nodes. It grows in these lymph nodes, producing a swelling filled with pus which bursts and spreads to more lymph nodes.

Swelling of the inguinal lymph nodes in the groin is the most common reason for people with the infection to go to their doctor. When the node bursts a lot of damage can be caused, including holes appearing inside the body where they shouldn't be. These holes between body organs are called fistulas. An example of a fistula that can be caused by LGV is a hole that joins the bowel to the vagina, with obviously unpleasant results. Holes from the abscesses to the outside of the skin, called sinuses, also occur.

While the body is fighting LGV infection the person will feel unwell and have high temperatures. The body fights hard against the infection but scarring occurs in the lymph glands and the lymph fluid is kept below the blockage. Because of this parts, of the body such as the legs, testicles or vulva can swell up. If the infection involves the back passage the person may notice itching, a discharge or bleeding and pain. Later on partial or complete blockage of the bowel can occur due to scarring. Sometimes a biopsy needs to be taken to make sure cancer is not present.

How long will it take to find out if I have caught it?

The first stage of lymphogranuloma venereum infection usually occurs within 12 days, but this stage is often not noticed and it is not until 10 to 30 days later, sometimes up to six months later, that the person notices swelling of the lymph nodes.

How is lymphogranuloma venereum diagnosed?

Diagnosis of LGV is made on a combination of factors: the observed symptoms, a blood test and growing the chlamydia organism. Other STDs should be looked for at the same time.

What treatment is available?

Treatment for lymphogranuloma venereum is usually with tetracycline antibiotics, particularly for the early and middle stages of the disease. In late disease, when scarring has occurred, surgery is sometimes required.

Should my partner be treated too?

Your partner should be fully examined for signs of the infection. If none are found a repeat check up and blood test should be done a few weeks later. Your partner should also be checked for other sexually transmittable diseases including HIV. Most doctors will only treat for lymphogranuloma venereum if they are sure the person has it, however in countries where there is a lot of this infection doctors commonly give treatment just in case. This sort of 'just in case' treatment is called prophylactic treatment.

When can I have sex again?

Depending how severe the infection is, you should be able to start having sexual intercourse again within two to four weeks, depending on how long it takes to treat you. The earlier the stage of the infection the quicker you will get better, once you start treatment.

What treatment can I have if I am pregnant?

Tetracycline antibiotics cannot be given in pregnancy, however there are other antibiotics such as erythromycin which can be used.

Molluscum contagiosum

What does molluscum contagiosum look like?

This infection looks like waxy pimples. Sometimes they are skin coloured or pink to red in color. Sometimes there is an area of redness around the spots. Many of them have a little hollow in the middle of them. They are filled with white material which comes out in a single lump if it is scraped out with a needle.

In children the infection is usually on the face, body, arms and legs. In adults the lumps are mainly on the genitals, thighs and lower abdomen. There can be just a few sores, but as many as twenty or more can grow.

People with HIV infection commonly get this infection. The pimple like lesions can then grow much bigger and have several white lumps in them. Sometimes with HIV infection the lesions are much more numerous. They can also occur on the face, and people grow beards to cover them up.

How is molluscum contagiosum caught?

Molluscum contagiosum is quite contagious. It is passed on by skin contact. Children commonly pick this infection up at school through normal, non-sexual contact, but in adults it is almost always spread by sex. Sometimes people in nursing homes get the infection. In this situation it is thought usually to be spread by non-sexual contact.

How long will it take to find out if I have caught it?

It takes on average four to eight weeks for the growths to occur, but it can be as short as one week and as long as 25 weeks. Remember the lumps are highly infectious and if you scratch them you will spread the infection more on yourself.

What causes molluscum contagiosum?

The organism which causes molluscum is a member of the appropriately named family of pox viruses. The virus is found in the secretions of the infection. No-one has succeeded in growing it in a laboratory, which means it is difficult to study.

Figure 17.3 Molluscum contagiosum

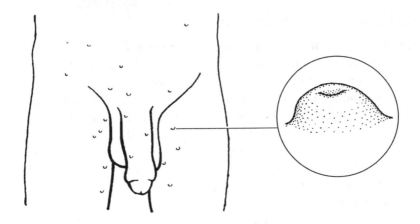

How is molluscum contagiosum treated?

The lesions may be left untreated. If they are not treated they will eventually go away but this may take up to several months. Usually they heal without scarring. There are no known long term problems.

They can be treated with liquid nitrogen, with trichloroacetic acid, or with a 0.7% solution of cantharidin. An older treatment was to scrape out the centre out of the lesions, but this is not used much these days. Retreatment is often needed, both to treat lesions which have not responded and to treat new ones that have developed in the meantime. Most people like them treated and your doctor can do this for you. After several treatments over two or three weeks the infection usually disappears. In some people the lesions may disappear sooner, in others they may take longer to go. The lesions in HIV infection can grow very big unless they are treated.

Pediculosis pubis (pubic lice or crabs)

What is pediculosis pubis?

Pediculosis pubis (pubic lice or crabs) are tiny crab-like creatures that live in pubic hair, and sometimes in other hair below the neck. It is extremely uncommon to find them in your eye lashes or eyebrows. They cannot live in the hair on your head.

Pubic lice feed on blood. To do this a crab fixes its mouth against the skin and stabs an opening. Its saliva stops the blood from clotting so blood is pumped by the victim's heart to the crab's stomach. Usually the crab defecates while it is feeding, leaving a dark red mess near by.

Figure 17.4 A pubic louse and egg

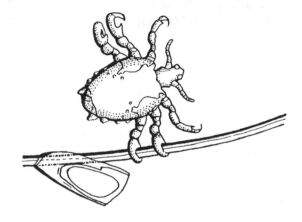

How are pubic lice caught?

Contrary to popular stories pubic lice are not caught from toilet seats. They are caught by the crab crawling on to you from an infected person. Mostly this happens during sex. Occasionally a crab may get lost in the bed clothes then crawl on to you.

Pubic crabs walk very slowly (a maximum of 100mm or four inches in a day), they do not jump and they live a maximum of 24 hours once they are off a body, so it is extremely rare to catch crabs any way other than by having sex with an infected person.

What are the symptoms of pubic lice?

Mainly pubic lice cause itching due to an allergic reaction to the bites. There are often little blue marks on the skin where lice have been feeding. Black dots appearing on the underpants is a common symptom. The dots are actually digested blood in lice excreta.

People who catch pubic lice often can't believe it when they see the infection, which looks like a small freckle. They find the freckles move and itch, and that when they take a closer look at them they have six legs. They may also see the tiny, shiny eggs, called nits, which stick on to the pubic hair. These eggs or nits stick so well that even after they are killed by treatment they stay attached until the hair grows out or you shave it off.

When the baby crab is ready to hatch out of its egg, it starts sucking in air and expelling it through its anus (the slang term is farting). This compressed air builds up in the egg behind the baby crab until there is enough pressure to propel it forward and out of the egg. This is the only creature I know of to be born by expelled air (farting).

How long will it take to find out if I have caught pubic lice?

You have to become sensitised to the bites before you know you have caught lice. This takes at least five days. Whether you notice them or not often depends on how many you have. Many people do not realize they have the infection until they start itching from a large number of bites.

What treatment is available?

Commonly people will shave to get rid of pubic lice, but this does not work and you end up being itchy from the hair growing back. Spraying them with insect sprays does not work either because this doesn't kill the eggs.

One treatment is with a solution called malathion 0.5% (Maldison). This is applied to all the hairy areas below the neck including the armpits, and washed off after 12 hours.

You can also use lindane, left on for eight to 12 hours and repeated a week later. Some doctors have reservations about using lindane because it accumulates in body fat. It is no longer the preferred treatment. If you are pregnant or are breast-feeding you should not use lindane.

Your clothes and bedclothes need to be washed in the hot cycle of the washing machine. Washing kills the eggs as well as the crabs. You need to make sure that your partner's clothes and bed linen are also washed, and that your partner is treated as well.

If you find the crabs on your eyelashes (an extremely rare event) cover them with vaseline. This chokes the little blighters.

Should I be tested for other sex diseases?

It is quite common to catch more than just crabs. Instead of just visiting the pharmacist and treating what you can see, you should visit your doctor or local STD clinic and make sure you have not also caught other infections that could cause you serious harm. Remember many harmful STDs may initially give you no symptoms at all, but can be completely cured if treated early.

Should my partner be treated too?

Yes. If you have public lice, the chances are high that your partner does too. Your partner should be treated when you are, and be tested for other STDs.

If your partner is not treated, you may get re-infected from them.

What treatment can I have if I am pregnant or breast-feeding?

Check with your doctor to find out what treatments are safe. Avoid lindane.

Trichomoniasis

What is trichomoniasis?

Trichomoniasis is due to an organism called *Trichomonas vaginalis* which belongs to a group of organisms called protozoa. Under the microscope it looks a little like a sting ray: it moves the same way and has a tail. Unlike a stingray it does not have a sting in its tail — though if you get this infection you might think it does!

The organism gets its food by engulfing or wrapping itself around whatever it wants to eat. It seems it can open a 'mouth' anywhere it likes.

Surprisingly, it can eat other STDs such as gonorrhea and chlamydia. Unfortunately this stomach turning appetite is not necessarily good for you. If you have combined infection with say trichomonas and gonorrhea and are treated for gonorrhea but not for trichomoniasis, you can be re-infected with gonorrhea from the trichomoniasis which has been feeding on it. This is because the antibiotics do not kill the gonorrhea when it is inside the trichomonas. This is one of the reasons why you should always be checked again after you have been treated for an infection, to make sure that the treatment has worked.

Figure 17.5 Trichomonas vaginalis

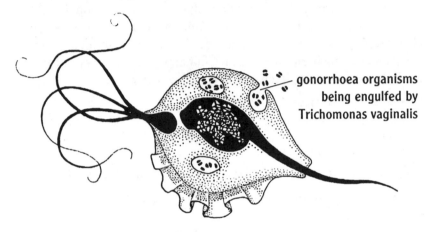

gonorrhoea organisms being engulfed by Trichomonas vaginalis

What parts of the body does trichomoniasis infect?

Trichomoniasis can infect the vagina, urethra, bladder and some of the glands that open into these areas.

What symptoms does it cause?

Up to 90% of infected men have no symptoms at all. Trichomoniasis may cause pain on passing urine, or make you feel like you want to go more often than usual. It may cause some itchiness of the urethra (the tube which carries urine through the penis) and sometimes causes swelling and pain of the epididymis (the tubes at the back of each testicle). It can sometimes cause inflammation of the prostate (see Chapter 15 *Prostatitis*). Occasionally it can cause inflammation under the foreskin which can sometimes cause an ulcer. There may be a discharge from the penis.

Women too can have trichomoniasis and show no symptoms, but this is less common than it is for men. Symptoms may include a vaginal discharge, soreness of the vagina and vulva and an unpleasant odor. The vaginal discharge, if there is one, can vary from thin and watery to thick, yellow and frothy. The infection causes inflammation so there can be patches of redness on the cervix, a condition described by doctors as a 'strawberry cervix'.

How is trichomoniasis spread?

Trichomoniasis is mainly spread by having sexual intercourse with someone who has it. It is theoretically possible to catch it by using an infected person's bath towel, or from the splash of the toilet if it wasn't flushed properly, however this is extremely unlikely. I say that you can only catch sexually transmittable diseases from toilets if you have sex on the toilet seat!

Rarely, trichomoniasis can be passed on to babies at birth.

How long will it take to find out if I have caught it?

If you have had sex with someone who has trichomoniasis you may not have caught it. If you have, it can show up as soon as four days afterwards, or it can take up to four weeks. Remember that without being tested you will not know for sure, because often there are no symptoms at all.

If there are no symptoms, why should I worry about being treated?

STDs like to travel together. You need to make sure you have not been given any other sexually transmitted disease that may cause harm. In addition the infection causes inflammation and this is not good for you. If you change sexual partners the infection may make them sick, and they might not be too pleased with you for having given them this infection.

How is the diagnosis made?

The doctor will take some fluid from the vagina or penis and place it in a drop of salt water on a slide. Mostly the slide will be sent to a laboratory for examination. If there is no laboratory close by the doctor may take a specimen to grow the organism. Even with good specimens and laboratories, the diagnosis is difficult to make and is often missed. Both partners should always be tested as trichomoniasis may be found in one but not the other.

What sort of treatment should I have?

Treatment is usually with four tablets (two grams) of either metronidazole or tinidazole, to be taken all at once. When you take the tablets you should not drink alcohol for three days: if you do you may feel very sick. Some doctors will give a longer course of tablets.

Occasionally you may feel a little nauseated or dizzy after the single dose treatment, but some people notice side effects such as nausea, an unpleasant taste in the mouth and depression from the longer treatment. The best thing about the one-off treatment is that you can be tested again in just a few days and if the infection is gone then you can have alcohol and sex again.

You should avoid sex until you have been re-tested to make sure the treatment has worked, and until you know your partner has also been tested and successfully treated.

What treatment can I have if I am pregnant?

See Chapter 20 *STDs and Pregnancy*. Metronidazole or tinidazole should not be used in the first trimester (three months) of pregnancy.

Should my partner be treated too?

Yes. Trichomoniasis is found in most men whose female partners have the infection, if they have had sex with them within the last two days. After that time the chance of finding the infection in the male falls progressively. This means that they probably have the infection, but the tests have failed to find it. If only one partner is treated the odds are they will soon catch the infection back again!

This is one of the reasons it is always best to test both (or all) partners. The combined information may be much more helpful to the doctor — and thus to the patient — than isolated tests.

Scabies

What is scabies?

The main symptom of scabies is a skin rash. Scabies is an infection caused by a tiny bug or mite called *Sarcoptes scabiei*. It has four legs and can walk quite quickly on human skin, covering 24mm (one inch) per minute looking for a spot to make its burrow. This mite burrows under the skin making a small wavy line. It lives about 30 days and lays big eggs in its burrow at the rate of two or three a day. These hatch out in 10 days.

Figure 17.6 Sarcoptes scabei

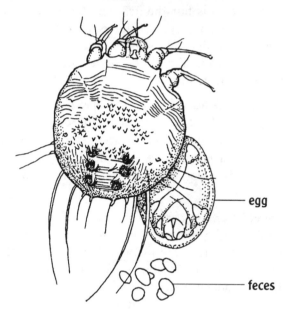

egg

feces

How is scabies caught?

You can catch scabies by your skin coming in contact with the skin of someone who has it, or by coming into contact with infected clothes that have eggs in them. In adults it is usually spread by sexual contact.

What symptoms do you get with scabies?

Usually the rash occurs on the wrists, between the fingers, in the armpits, or on the penis or thighs. The face is not often involved. The rash is very itchy especially if you have just had a warm shower or bath. It is usually the itching which makes people realize they have something wrong. You may see small lumps which are where the eggs have been laid, or tunnels. The average number of female mites on a person who has the infection is eleven.

Sometimes people scratch themselves so badly trying to relieve the itching that they tear the skin and a skin infection starts.

How long will it take to find out if I have caught scabies?

You won't like to hear this but the itch you get from scabies is due to a reaction of your body against the excrement of the mite. Yes, the little droppings it does in your skin are the places where you itch like crazy. It takes about one month after infection to become sensitive and start itching.

How does the doctor know I have scabies?

To be absolutely sure about the diagnosis the doctor needs to see the mite or its eggs or feces. Sometimes it can be seen by the naked eye, other times a microscope is needed. Often though, if the diagnosis is not certain, you may be given treatment for scabies just in case.

What sort of treatment is there for scabies?

The drug of choice in the treatment of scabies is 5% permethrin (Elimite). Alternatives include lindane (Kwell, Scabene) and crotamiton (Eurax). Permethrin should be removed by bathing after 8 to 14 hours, lindane after 8 to 12 hours and crotamiton after 48 hours. Lindane should be used according to the instructions to avoid toxic effects. Lindane should not be used by pregnant or breast feeding women.

Remember that all your clothes and bed linen and your partner's need to be washed in the hot cycle of the washing machine at the time you are treating yourself, otherwise you will become re-infected.

Some people think that because they are still itching, they still have the infection, and treat themselves more often. This is not advisable as over-treatment can cause dermatitis. Also, some of the drugs can accumulate in your body. Occasionally further treatments are needed, but most commonly continued itching is caused by the feces of the mite which have not yet been cleared from the body, even though all the mites and their eggs have been killed. This itching may last for several weeks after you have been treated.

Sometimes the itching is so bad you need a cream or tablets to stop you scratching so you can sleep at night. Your doctor will know some treatments that will help you.

Is the treatment different if I am pregnant or breast-feeding?

Yes. You should not use lindane.

Should children be treated?

Sometimes scabies is a family disease caught by everyone in a household. The whole family should be treated at the same time. Benzyl benzoate 25% is safe, but can be very uncomfortable for an infant. Sometimes in infants it is best to dilute the solution 1 part to 2 parts of water. The treatment needs to be put on for 24 hours, making sure that the hands and soles of the feet are also treated. It should not be put in the mouth or eyes. One treatment is usually enough. Occasionally the treatment needs to be repeated and this can be done after seven days. Crotamiton ointment is also safe but needs to be put on every day for seven days.

Should I be tested for other STDs?

Many people get their own treatment from the pharmacist, but I recommend you visit your doctor or STD clinic to have tests to make sure you didn't catch anything else as well. Remember many STDs will give you no symptoms, but can cause serious harm to your body.

18

ORAL SIGNS OF STD INFECTION

Can you catch sexually transmittable diseases
in your mouth? Yes. In fact, all of the diseases
listed below can occur in the mouth. This can
happen if you put your mouth to the genitals
of someone who has the sex disease or they
put their genitals in your mouth. Genital herpes
and syphilis that is present in the mouth can
be passed on by kissing.

- Syphilis (Chapter 16)
- Chlamydia trachomatis (Chapter 10)
- Gonorrhea (Chapter 12)
- Genital warts (Chapter 5)
- Genital herpes (Chapter 4)
- Infections associated with HIV (Chapter 7)
- Thrush (Chapter 9)

If you are worried about a sex disease in your
mouth you should go and see your doctor for
tests. You must tell the doctor that you have
been using your mouth for sex, otherwise only
your genitals may be tested.

This chapter concentrates on what may happen
if a sexually transmitted disease involves the
mouth. The genital manifestations of the
infection are not discussed in this chapter. For
further information on each infection refer to
the appropriate chapters.

Genital herpes

In Chapter 4 *Genital Herpes* I talked about two types of herpes infection, type I infection that involves the mouth and causes cold sores, and type II which involves the genitals but can also involve the mouth.

The type II genital herpes can cause ulcers in the mouth just like cold sores and can keep recurring, although this does not happen often. The lesions when they occur are highly infective and you must be careful not to kiss anyone when you or they have the sores in the mouth or lips. At these times you should not use your mouth for sex. If it is the first time you have had a herpes infection in your mouth you are usually quite sick with a fever, extremely sore throat, headache and sore lymph glands in the neck.

If you have the ordinary type of cold sores (type 1) in your mouth, and your partner puts his penis in your mouth you can give him the type 1 herpes on the penis. This appears as small blisters just like the type 2 infection. Then if you have sex with him a few days later when he has sores on his penis he can give you the type I infection in your vagina or rectum depending on where you have sex.

A good rule is that if you have sores you should rest and not have sex. If you do it usually ends up hurting one or both of you, as well as spreading the infection.

Acyclovir is a drug which can be given to control the infection if it is particularly bad. Unfortunately it does not eradicate the infection from the body or stop the infection from coming back again.

Genital warts

Warts in the mouth are uncommon. If they occur they may be found at the margin of the outside of the lips and skin, or inside the mouth on the inside of the cheek, the roof of the mouth or under the tongue.

People with HIV infection can get extremely severe infection with warts in the mouth, and in these cases the warts can occur on the surface of the tongue. The warts in the mouth look exactly the same as the ones that occur in the genital regions. It is extremely uncommon for people not infected with HIV to have warts on the surface of the tongue, although it is common for people to think that the normal lumps on their tongue are warts, especially the big red lumps on the back of the tongue. Warts in the mouth can be treated by having them frozen or cut out.

Infections associated with HIV

The common infections of the mouth of someone with HIV are thrush, oral hairy leukoplakia, herpes, ulcers, warts and tooth and gum infections.

Thrush in the mouth is caused by a yeast called *Candida albicans* (see Chapter 9 *Candidiasis*). When thrush occurs in the mouth you see white patches either on the insides of the cheeks, the roof of the mouth or on or under the tongue. The more severe the infection the whiter the lesions and the larger the area affected. There is good treatment for this infection either in the form of liquid to swill in the mouth or lozenges to suck, or for severe cases tablets called ketoconazole and fluconazole which treat fungal infections wherever they are in the body.

Often thrush in association with HIV infection goes down in the gullet and can cause a sore mouth, loss of appetite and difficulty swallowing.

When thrush occurs with HIV infection it is a sign that the HIV infection is quite advanced. You should see a specialist so that you can be given thrush treatment and put on antibiotics to stop you getting pneumonia.

Sometimes the thrush, instead of affecting the inside of the mouth, just seems to affect the corners of the mouth, causing little cracks or redness right at the corners. This is easily treated by your doctor. Other possible causes of sores at the mouth corners are anemia, vitamin deficiency, eating poorly and badly fitting false teeth.

Oral hairy leukoplakia is thought to be due to infection with either the human papillomavirus, Epstein-Barr virus or both. In this condition whiteness develops along the sides of the tongue. Sometimes it may be painful. It seems to only occur when the disease is advanced. Treatment with acyclovir may cause some improvement. Other drugs such as zidovudine (which encourages an increase in the body's immunity) can cause the disappearance of the lesions.

Herpes lesions in HIV (AIDS) infection should always be treated with acyclovir if they keep recurring. This is because the herpes virus activates human immunodeficiency virus and encourages it to multiply within your body. The more HIV infection you have within your body, the more likely you are to become sick.

People with HIV infection may get large painful mouth ulcers called apthous ulcers. These often do not heal readily though doctors have now found that the drug thalidomide can cause improvement in a lot of cases.

Dental abscesses and warts in the mouth occur more commonly in patients with HIV infection. Recurrent painful bleeding gums are also common. Regular visits to the dentist to have the teeth looked after is essential. A course of treatment with the antibiotic metronidazole may be helpful.

Sometimes in severe HIV infection in men who have acquired the infection through anal sex, purplish lesions called Kaposi's sarcoma may occur in the mouth. These may cause no problem, but sometimes they are painful or bleed. They may occur on other parts of the body either on the outside or inside. Unfortunately there is no really good treatment to remove these lesions. If particularly troublesome they can be treated with radiotherapy or surgically removed.

Chlamydia trachomatis

Chlamydia trachomatis can infect the throat, particularly the tonsils area. If the tonsils have been removed it is still possible to catch the infection because there is usually a small amount of remaining tissue. Some people may complain of a sore throat when they become infected but others may not have any symptoms at all. This infection is cured by a simple course of antibiotics.

Gonorrhea

You can get gonorrhea in the mouth by taking the penis of an infected person in your mouth or placing your mouth against the vagina of someone who is infected. It seems it is most easily passed on by the penis being placed inside the mouth.

The infection may cause tonsillitis or a sore throat, but over 90% of the people with the infection in the mouth have no symptoms. Occasionally the mouth can be the only site of infection. Gonorrhea of the mouth is cured by tablets or an injection.

Syphilis

What are the symptoms of syphilis of the mouth?

The first evidence of syphilis in the mouth is a dull red spot or ulcer, which is painless. It can take up to 90 days to develop into an ulcer which is called a chancre. The chancre is teeming with tiny little snake like organisms. It's highly infectious.

As the syphilis advances, symptoms include a sore throat, swollen lymph glands in the neck and small shallow ulcers in any part of the mouth, including where you swallow, and the voice box. Other parts of the body are affected as well.

Sometimes people do not realize that there is anything wrong. They just feel sick but they eventually get better so they do not bother to see a doctor.

Syphilis in its final (tertiary) stages can paralyse the face muscles as though from a stroke. If the disease is not too bad it can cause lumps called gummas. These gummas are a nuisance and besides looking ugly can ulcerate. The medical books usually show a picture of a man with a gumma in the roof of his mouth which has ulcerated and made a hole in his mouth going from the mouth to the nose. Just imagine: every time you ate, the food could come out of your nose!

Gummas can also affect the nose bones, hard palate (roof of the mouth) and the tongue, as well as other parts of the body.

How is syphilis of the mouth caught?

If someone has a syphilis sore on their lips and kisses someone or uses their lips on someone's genitals, the infection has a 60% chance of being spread to the other person. Usually to become infected there needs to be a break in the skin for the syphilis organism to get in. This could occur by cleaning your teeth, or a bite, or from having cold sores.

How is syphilis of the mouth diagnosed?

Syphilis of the mouth can only be reliably diagnosed by a blood test for antibodies, after they have had time to develop. The diagnosis made by examining the fluid from the base of the ulcer under a microscope is not reliable for a mouth ulcer, because the mouth normally contains organisms which look like the syphilis organisms. These look-alike organisms are the ones that cause infected gums.

Children and syphilis

Children who are born with syphilis usually show oral symptoms, particularly deformed teeth. See Chapter 21 *STDs and Your Baby.*

Treatment of syphilis of the mouth

The treatment for syphilis anywhere in the body is a course of penicillin injections. If you are allergic to penicillin other treatment is available. Syphilis is one of the STDs that can easily be treated and cured, but if it is not treated the consequences are very severe (see Chapter 16).

Reiter's syndrome

This is an illness that sometimes occurs after chlamydial urethral infection. The people who get this infection are usually men with a particular genetic predisposition. They develop arthritis of their body, particularly the knees and ankles, inflammation of the urethra which causes a penile discharge or pain passing urine, inflammation of the eyes and ulcers in the mouth.

People with this condition should be tested and treated for chlamydia. Their partners should also be tested. Treatment of the arthritis is with drugs that reduce the amount of inflammation in the affected joints.

19

THE ABNORMAL PAP SMEAR & CANCER OF THE CERVIX

KEY CONCEPTS

CIN   Cervical intraepithelial neoplasia or changes occurring in cells on the cervix that suggest cancer might develop.

Langerhans cell   A special cell in the skin which detects things going wrong. The number of these cells is reduced by smoking cigarettes.

PAP smear (Cervical cytology)   A test which is done to pick up abnormalities on the cervix. Ideally it is a test to detect pre-cancer rather than cancer. Regular PAP smears reduce the chance of getting cancer of the cervix.

Pre-cancer   A patch of skin which may one day become cancer. Treatment at this stage stops the cancer developing.

Transformation zone   The area on the cervix where squamous metaplasia has occurred. This zone is the area where most of the cervical cancer and pre-cancers are found.

Anatomy of the cervix

To really understand PAP smears it is helpful to learn a little about the anatomy of the cervix. You might like to refer back to the diagrams in Chapter 3.

The vagina is lined with cells which are flat and layered: these are called stratified squamous cells. These cells continue up to the outside of the cervix, which is the lower part of the uterus.

The uterus and the endocervical canal are lined by a different kind of cell called columnar epithelium. These cells are tall.

The two cell types meet on the cervix or sometimes inside the endocervical canal. Where they meet is called the squamocolumnar junction.

Figure 19.1 The cervix transformation zone

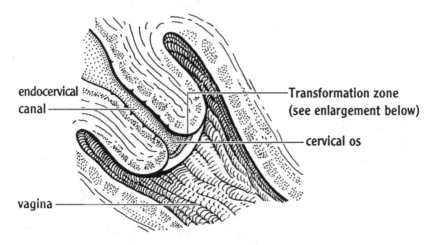

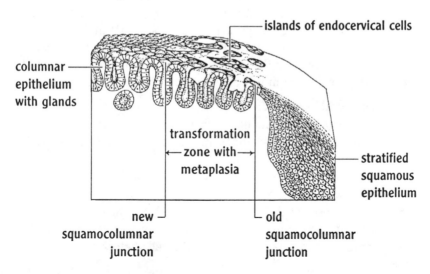

Top, the cervix. Bottom, enlargement of the transformation zone.

Columnar cells which are exposed to the acid of the vagina change in shape and they start to look like flat squamous cells. These changes are called squamous metaplasia. The cells underlying the changes multiply to create a new surface of cells called metaplastic squamous epithelium.

The area where all this is happening is called the transformation zone. See Figure 19.1.

What actually happens is quite complex, so you might like to skip ahead to the next section, though I find a lot of women really want to know.

The transformation zone lies between two junctions: the original join of the squamous and columnar cells, and the new join of metaplastic cells and columnar epithelium. See the diagram where the joins have been illustrated. In 40% of women the transformation zone lies in the endocervical canal.

At different times more columnar cells from the endocervix get pushed out onto the surface of the cervix. This pushes the original join of squamous and columnar cells further out on the cervix.

Changes at the transformation zone have been linked to the onset of cervical cancer.

The size of the transformation zone varies from person to person and changes during puberty, pregnancy, and menopause. (See Figure 19.2) When the cells are just newly changing, such as during menarche (when a girl's periods first start) and following pregnancy, they are very susceptible to things which may stimulate the start of cancer. See the section *Who is likely to get cancer of the cervix?* (further on in this chapter) for a list of these things.

What is a PAP smear?

A PAP smear is a sampling of cells on the cervix. Its major importance is to detect changes in the cells before cancer has developed.

PAP is a shortened name for George Papanicolaou, a Greek doctor who was Professor of Anatomy at Cornell University in the USA. He did most of the original work on PAP smears. When he first started doing the tests he was looking only for cancer, but he found that he could detect changes in the cells before they became cancer.

Figure 19.2 Changes in the position of the squamocolumnar junction

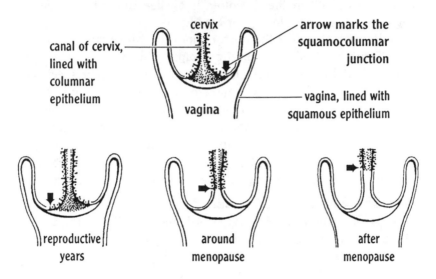

A PAP smear is made by wiping the surface cells of the cervix and cervical os (hole in the centre of the cervix) with a small wooden or plastic scraper and cotton swab or brush.

The cells are smeared onto a glass slide and sent to a specialist to examine under a microscope for any changes which may suggest that at some stage in the future you could develop cancer.

This means a PAP smear is a test to pick up pre-cancer. Women who have regular PAP smears are extremely unlikely to get cancer of the cervix because it can be detected and treated before cancer develops. A similar test is now being developed for men, to detect pre-cancer in the anus.

How is a PAP smear taken?

A PAP smear requires you to either lie on your side or on your back with your legs bent up, the position depending on the doctor's examination couch. The doctor then inserts a speculum. A speculum is an instrument which is made either of plastic or metal which is opened up in the vagina so the doctor can see the cervix and walls of the vagina through it, and do tests. This is usually a painless procedure and is made very easy if you can be totally relaxed whilst the speculum is being inserted. Occasionally the test can be uncomfortable, particularly if you are feeling very embarrassed or are tense. When the speculum is opened up you may feel a slight pressure especially if your bladder is full.

To do the PAP smear the doctor wipes the whole surface of the cervix with a wooden or plastic scraper (one type is called an Ayres spatula) to collect cells from the surface. Another specimen is taken from the hole in the middle of the cervix (the cervical os), to collect cells from the transformation zone. Sometimes if inflammation is present on the cervix, the person who interprets changes in the cells has difficulty making the report and asks for the test to be repeated. It takes four to six weeks for the cells to regrow, so it is best to wait this time before the test is repeated.

Who should have a PAP smear?

All women should start having PAP smears within one year of starting to have sexual intercourse and continue having them every two years or more often as indicated. Screening can stop at age 70 provided there have been two normal PAP smears in the last five years. If you are over 70 and have never had a PAP smear, if you think there are special reasons or if you just want to be sure, then you should have one. If someone has had their womb removed for cancer of the cervix they should continue to have smears from the top of the vagina in case cancer may develop there.

Your doctor will be able to advise you how often to have PAP smears. This depends on whether you have had one before, whether it was abnormal or not, your age, whether you smoke, whether you have genital herpes or genital wart infection, and even whether there is a history of cancer of the cervix in the family.

If you have not had a PAP smear yet, it is a simple painless test, although a little embarrassing for some women. It helps to let the doctor know you've never had a PAP smear test, and to ask them to show you what will be done in the test. Some clinics have nurses who are able to explain the procedure to you. Some women feel more comfortable with the test being done by a female doctor, but I know plenty of women who are pleased with the way their male doctor does the examination. The test is best done between menstrual periods. This is so the blood does not cover over the cells which need to be looked at.

Figure 19.3 The cervix, Ayres spatula and Cytobrush

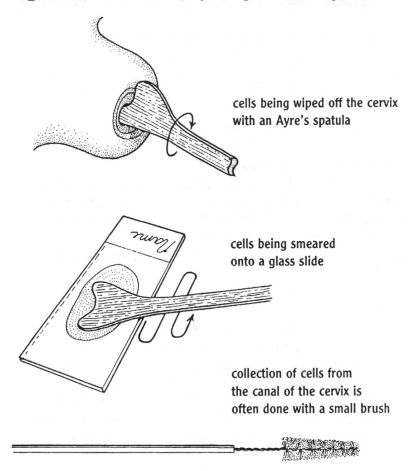

cells being wiped off the cervix with an Ayre's spatula

cells being smeared onto a glass slide

collection of cells from the canal of the cervix is often done with a small brush

Cervical intraepithelial neoplasia (CIN)

A PAP smear will detect cancer of the cervix, but the real reason for having regular PAP smears is to detect the changes that take place before cancer starts. Early treatment can prevent the onset of cancer.

Cervical intraepithelial neoplasia or CIN is the precursor of cancer which a PAP smear tests for.

There are three recognised grades of cervical intraepithelial neoplasia (CIN):

- Grade 1 mild dysplasia (CIN 1)
- Grade 2 moderate dysplasia (CIN 2)
- Grade 3 severe dysplasia (CIN 3) and CIS (carcinoma in situ)

These grades are discussed in more detail below. What is important to note is that CIN is not cancer and it may never develop into cancer. Grade 1 CIN can progress to grade 2 and then to grade 3 but so too can grade 3 return down to grade 2 and grade 1 and back to normal. This reverse process from the more severe stages is thought to be unusual. Even if the CIN advances to cancer, early detection means there are effective treatments.

Can CIN develop into cancer?

Yes, CIN can develop into cancer but, as discussed above, some people with CIN stay the same, some get better and some progress. Research to date indicates that up to 35% of CIN 3 lesions progress to cancer if they are not treated. Doctors are currently unable to say which women with CIN would go on to develop cancer if not treated.

For the vulva, penis and anorectum the cancer risk is low and the process very slow in most people.

Who is likely to get cancer of the cervix?

Until PAP smear screening became common in Western countries, cancer of the cervix was the second most common malignancy in women after breast cancer. In some countries within Africa, India, and some Asian countries it is the most common cancer in women. It is also prevalent in some parts of Latin America. Countries like Sweden, which run PAP smear programs for all the women in the country and remind the women when their next PAP smear is due, have markedly reduced both the number of women developing cancer of the cervix and the death rate from cancer of the cervix.

The initial cause of cancer of the cervix is not yet known, but several factors are known to be associated with an increased risk of developing cervical cancer. These include sex at an early age, multiple male partners, smoking cigarettes, infection with herpes simplex virus type II (see Chapter 4), papillomavirus (HPV, see Chapter 5), possibly *Trichomonas vaginalis* (see Chapter 17) and chlamydia (see Chapter 10), using oral contraceptives, and vitamin A deficiency. Many of these are discussed in greater detail below. A depressed immune system, such as in women who have kidney failure or a kidney transplant, is associated with a greater chance of developing cervical intraepithelial neoplasia (CIN), which is the precursor of cervical cancer.

Women who start to have sex at a young age are more prone to develop cervical cancer because the area of metaplastic cells on the cervix is increased when the cells are just changing over from columnar cells into metaplastic cells. The number of these cells decreases as the woman grows older.

Several things happen in women who smoke. Nicotine and cotinine, two chemicals known to cause cancer, have been found in the mucus secreted by the cervix. The numbers of a certain type of cell in the cervix called Langerhans cell are reduced. This cell acts like a guard. It detects things going wrong and sends signals to other parts of the body for healing action to occur. In smokers, because the number of these cells is less than usual, things can sneak through without the body detecting them until it is too late. Luckily if you stop smoking the number of Langerhans cells eventually returns to normal.

The herpes virus is not now considered to be a cause of cancer although many years ago people thought it was. The herpes virus is thought to act as an initiator, which means it may start the cancer process. Presumably there are other things that can do this but they are not known at the moment.

Some studies have found that the oral contraceptive pill may be associated with the development of cancer of the cervix, particularly if it has been taken for a long time. There is still dispute as to whether the contraceptive pill does encourage the development of cervical cancer.

Deficiency of vitamin A has also been associated with CIN. Vitamin A and its precursor, which is called B-carotene, are both thought to protect against the development of cervical cancer.

Studies have found that Jewish women are less likely to develop cancer of the cervix than some other women. The reason for this is not known. Some suggestions include a greater emphasis on lifelong relationships with just one partner, and that Jewish men are circumcised.

The PAP smear report

Interpreting the results

Some women automatically think the worst if their PAP smear report reveals any abnormality. They imagine their condition will quickly get worse and turn into cancer. This is not true for a very large number of women. Changes on the cervix usually happen slowly, over several years. Changes can reverse and return to normal. Even if the situation deteriorates, early detection and treatment is most often highly effective.

A PAP smear is subject to interpretation. If any changes are mild, the interpretation can vary between two people reporting on the same PAP smear. What is important is any trend established across two or more tests. You must allow time to pass until it becomes clear whether things are getting better or worse. As long as you are being seen by a doctor experienced in this area, there is hardly ever a need to rush into treatment.

It is important to realize that a PAP report which says you have CIN (cervical intraepithelial neoplasia) does not mean you have cancer. CIN can develop into cancer, but it does not always. What causes CIN to develop into cancer is not known. The causes may not be the same as those which lead to CIN in the first place.

Most PAP smears are reported as negative or normal, only about 20 per 1000 are reported as having a low grade abnormality and three per 1000 as having a high grade abnormality. Your chance of having anything found wrong is extremely low, and if you have regular checks any problems will be detected early when they can be effectively treated.

Types of report

The types of report that you might get are:
- Normal or negative
- Low grade abnormality (minimal or mild)
- High grade abnormality (mild, moderate or severe)
- Unsatisfactory

Other things your report might mention could be:
- no endocervical cells
- human papillomavirus (HPV) changes

Normal or negative

Your report may say that no significant cytological abnormality was found. Cytological is another word for cell. This report means exactly what it says: nothing wrong has been found in the cells. There is nothing to worry about with a report like this. Just remember to have your next PAP smear when recommended.

Low grade abnormalities

Low grade abnormalities may be classified as minimal or mild.

Minimal This may include HPV (human papillomavirus) changes, inflammation, atrophic changes, and borderline change. Things are not looking serious at all. These changes can be caused by lots of things such as irritation from thrush. HPV changes are due to the human papillomavirus. Often the next PAP smear is entirely normal.

There will be a recommendation for you to have another PAP at some time within the next six months. It is quite common these days to have a report like this and it is important that you follow the recommendations.

Mild This indicates Grade 1 dysplasia or CIN 1. It is mild and may be treated or just monitored with regular PAP smears and colposcopy, to see if it changes.

There is no need to panic, this is not battle stations. What changes like this mean, long term, is currently being debated, with studies producing conflicting results. One Australian study which monitored women for 18 months after a diagnosis of mild abnormality found 16% went on to high grade abnormalities, 45% got better, and in 39% the changes stayed the same.

Often human papillomavirus virus changes (see the section on HPV changes) are mistaken for CIN. Some studies have shown that women with evidence of human papillomavirus on their cervix have a 4% to 10% increased chance of developing CIN. However, more sensitive tests now show most women may have HPV on their cervix, so no one really knows yet what this means. Maybe the changes due to HPV simply indicate the presence of a greater amount of HPV.

You should however have a colposcopy at some time within the next few months. Sometimes waiting lists can be long. Don't panic. It is alright to wait with this sort of report. Remember that with waiting you may be improving and the changes disappearing.

It is not uncommon for this to happen. If your appointment is a long time off, just don't forget it when the time comes.

High grade abnormalities

High grade abnormalities are classified as moderate or severe.

Grade 2 dysplasia or CIN 2 This is a greater cause for concern. *Grade 3 dyplasia* or CIN The lesions are quite severe and have at least a 40% chance of going on to become invasive cancer, that is, cancer which grows in that area and then spreads to the rest of the body.

If you are told you have a high grade abnormality suspicious of invasive cancer you had better take things seriously. This means that the results found in the PAP smear will need to be checked quickly by colposcopy and biopsy. If you are lucky it will all turn out not to be as bad as first reported, for others it may be that you need more extensive treatment. Many women with this type of report do not actually have cancer but do have CIN 3 or pre-cancer. The important thing is not to panic, your doctor will do that for you if it is necessary! If you've had regular PAP smears whatever it is will usually be in an early stage that can be cured with proper treatment.

Unsatisfactory

PAP smear tests can be inconclusive or unsatisfactory for several reasons:

- The sample taken may have been inadequate or too scanty.
- There may be a possible high grade abnormality but due to the way cells fixed on to the slide the pathologist cannot be sure.
- There may be inflammation or atrophy (shrinkage of the cells) in the sample which makes reliable interpretation impossible.
- Sometimes if you have douched recently there may not be enough cells present.
- If a PAP smear has been repeated too soon, the cells may not have had time to regrow.
- The cells may have been smeared on too thickly.

- Menstrual blood may have interfered with the cells being seen.

'Inconclusive' means what it says: no reliable conclusion can be drawn, one way or another. These smears should be repeated soon, but allow enough time for the cells to grow back on the cervix (four to six weeks).

No endocervical cells

No endocervical cells were present. This means that the sample of cells from the inside of the cervix has either not been taken or is unsatisfactory. Sometimes this can happen if the cervical os is too small to get a sample from, or sometimes the os is so big the sampling brush does not touch the sides! Other times there are just not a lot of cells to collect on the brush unless a very firm rub is made. If endocervical cells are not present the PAP does not usually need to be repeated until it should be for other reasons. The people reporting on PAP smears prefer to see samples with endocervical cells because it indicates to them the whole of the transformation zone has been sampled by the doctor.

Human papillomavirus changes

Human papillomavirus changes are quite commonly mentioned on PAP smear reports. This can be a big surprise to women who have never been aware of having human papillomavirus previously. Whether the human papillomavirus is found on the cervix or not these days may depend on the type of test the doctor uses to look for HPV. If an ordinary microscope is used to look for HPV then up to 10% of women may be found to have changes. This figure sounds high but wait until I tell you the rest. If research techniques are used to look for HPV (the most common technique being used at the moment is one called the dot-blot technique) then 20% to 30% of women are found to have HPV. Even this is not the end of the story. There is now an even more sensitive technique being used called the PCR (polymerase chain reaction) technique. This test is so sensitive it can show up only small numbers of viruses in a cell. Some studies just now being reported are finding that most adolescents have HPV when tested by this technique. Other studies have shown up to 90% of presumably healthy women to have HPV type 16. Virgins can have HPV type 16.

What does this mean? Yes, maybe it is normal to have HPV. The studies for men are still being done, but if nearly all the women have got it, it's a good bet nearly all the men have got it as well!

So where does this leave the human papillomavirus story? I think it is important to understand that there are different stages of human papillomavirus manifestations. (See Figure 5.3 in Chapter 5.) These are:

Latent This is probably the most common sort. In this stage HPV is in the bottom layers of cells in the skin but is asleep and is not causing any problem. The only tests that might pick up this infection are the PCR or sometimes the dot-blot test.

Subclinical This stage is one where the PCR or dot-blot techniques show HPV but other tests such as biopsy (histology), PAP smear or colposcopy are not always diagnostic. That is, sometimes they show HPV and sometimes they don't. Human papillomavirus changes may get better spontaneously, they may persist, they may fluctuate (get better and worse or vice-versa), they may get worse, they may stay the same then eventually get better or they may get better then out of the blue get worse again. This is why all women should continue to have regular PAP smears even if previous

Clinical All the diagnostic methods such as colposcopy, PAP smears, biopsy (histology), the dot-blot test and in-situ hybridisation show definite presence of HPV.

To be safe, if your PAP report indicates HPV-induced cell change then the PAP should be repeated again in six months. If the changes are persisting then you will need a colposcopy.

The high risk male

The definition of 'the high risk male' is 'a male who places his female sexual partner at an increased risk of cancer of the cervix.'

Studies have shown that the typical high risk male is one who smokes cigarettes, has a job which requires him to travel away from home on a regular basis, has multiple sexual partners, and who has had infection with genital warts. The second wives of men whose previous wife died of cervical cancer have a four times higher risk of developing cervical cancer. The husbands of women with cancer of the cervix on average have had more sexual partners than the husbands of women with no cervical cancer. Women whose husbands have cancer of the penis have a higher chance of developing cervical cancer.

The protein from spermatozoa are thought to possibly be associated with the development of cancer of the cervix. The protein amount varies from man to man and maybe men who have high amounts of the basic protein place their partners at higher risk. Vasectomy may lower the risk of cervical cancer in their partners.

What do I do about my partner?

Some studies have shown that if a woman has CIN (cervical intraepithelial neoplasia) and her male partner is examined, there is a 10% to 15% chance of him having macroscopic genital warts (warts that can be seen with the naked eye) and a 50% chance of him having subclinical evidence of wart infection (seen only with the use of acetic acid and colposcopy). Even if the wart is macroscopic many men are unaware of it.

Some studies have also shown that if the woman has changes such as CIN then in 5% to 10% of cases their partners will have severe penile skin changes such as severe dysplasia or what is called PIN (penile intraepithelial neoplasia).

I recommend therefore that if you have an abnormal PAP report, particularly one that mentions HPV changes, then you should advise your partner to go for a checkup.

The sequel to this is the unanswered question, 'Will the men with these changes develop cancer of the penis?' Husbands of women with cervical cancer have a higher incidence of penile cancer. It is thought though that most affected men won't go on to develop penile cancer because it is very rare in our society. It may be that some will, but it takes a long time for this type of cancer to develop – up to 15 years.

Circumcision tends to give some protection against developing penile cancer.

The only thing that is clear about this area is that much more research needs to be done before any firm conclusions can be drawn. It is not really known how common subclinical and macroscopic genital wart infection in men is, which particular HPV types are associated and what the risk of developing cancer is. The amounts of HPV which might cause particular diseases have not yet been established.

What are the sexual implications?

People who have human papillomavirus always want to know whether they are infectious. Unfortunately, because the virus cannot be grown, no-one knows the answer to this question. Different doctors will give different answers.

I recommend if you have never had warts that you or the doctor can see with the naked eye, or feel, then you can carry on with your normal sex life. If you don't have a regular sex partner please take care not to catch a sexually transmitted disease. If however you have warts that you can see or feel or that the doctor has found, then I recommend abstinence until the warts have been treated, and then condoms for at least six months until the cycle of possible re-infection or recurrence is broken. See Chapter 5 *Genital Warts and Human Papillomavirus Infection (HPV)* for more information.

What is a colposcopy?

A colposcope is a sophisticated magnifying instrument used for examining various parts of the body, in particular the cervix, vagina, vulva and penis. It can magnify up to 25 times normal size. First the area to be examined is washed in a diluted vinegar solution (3% to 5% acetic acid). This makes it easier to detect abnormal areas.

When should I ask to be referred for colposcopy?

If your doctor can see an abnormality on your cervix, you should be referred for a colposcopy. If there are abnormalities on your PAP smear that suggest pre-cancer you should have a colposcopy. Sometimes if the PAP reports HPV changes you will be referred, although now it seems that most women in this situation do not need colposcopy. Often there are other reasons for you to be referred and you should discuss these with your doctor.

What is a cervical biopsy?

Abnormal areas often need to be biopsied, which means they are cut out. Special instruments have been made for doing this as quickly and painlessly as possible.

A small piece of skin will be taken from the cervix and sent to a laboratory for analysis. Biopsy is not painful, but you may feel slight cramps or some mild discomfort for a few seconds. There may be some vaginal spotting for two or three days afterwards. Once the bleeding has stopped it is OK to start having sex again. If the bleeding is heavier than your usual period go back and see your doctor.

What is a cone biopsy?

This is a procedure where the centre part of the cervix is cut out. If a PAP smear has revealed high grade abnormality, a cone biopsy may also be used to remove the unseen part of the transformation zone where there could be pre-cancer or cancer. Another use for cone biopsy is to remove lesions that go into the endocervical canal, and there are other uses in special circumstances. Luckily this is not very common.

What treatments are there?

The treatment given depends on many things including how severe any abnormality is and your age. Colposcopy usually allows the specialist to see exactly where any lesion is, so the treatment can be applied to that area only, and matched to your individual situation. Treatments now are less severe than they used to be.

Some of the treatments are laser, cryosurgery (freezing) and diathermy (burning the area with an electric current). For special cases a cone of tissue is removed by laser or knife-cutting. In a few instances removal of the womb may be advised.

New treatments called LEEP (loop electrocautery excision procedure) and LLETZ (large loop excision of the transformation zone) are now available in specialized centres.

Many women I have talked to have been quite frightened of the treatment, but if the affected areas are small (which they usually are if you have had regular PAP smears) it can be done as an outpatient. Most times the procedure takes only five to fifteen minutes. You can go home the same day though it is advisable to have the rest of the day off. It's nice to have a friend or relative on hand to take you home. After treatment you will be asked to return again for review.

Usually treatment does not interfere with your ability to get pregnant or to have children.

How long after treatment before I can have sex again?

Don't have sex with penetration or use tampons for four weeks after treatment of the cervix. If an IUCD was used for contraception, it will have been removed at the time of treatment and a new one will have to be put in after the cervix has healed. If you are on the oral contraceptive pill continue to take it as usual.

Cancer of the cervix

Despite lots being written about it, cancer of the cervix is not as common as you might think. Only about one in 1,000 women over the age of forty develop this cancer.

There are two types of cervical cancer. Squamous cell cancer develops in the transformation zone, while adenocarcinoma develops from the columnar cells which line the endocervix. The squamous cell cancer is the commonest and the age at which it affects women is getting lower. Adenocarcinoma is not very common but seems to be gradually increasing.

Once cancer starts growing in an area, if untreated it can spread into the parts of the body next to it and then via the veins of the blood stream and lymph channels to the rest of the body. Detection by regular PAP smears followed by removal of pre-cancer prevents cancer of the cervix developing.

The stages of cancer of the cervix:

Stage O   Cancer exists only inside some cells, called carcinoma in situ (CIS).

Stage I   Cancer involves only the cervix.

Stage II   The cancer has spread beyond the cervix but not outside the pelvis.

Stage III   The cancer has spread as far as the walls of the pelvis or down to the bottom third of the vagina.

Stage IV   The cancer has spread out of the pelvis or into the bladder or rectum.

If cancer is found, it and the areas where it has spread to may be removed. Follow up treatment can include radiotherapy (X-rays), and chemotherapy (drugs that kill cancer), depending on the type of cancer. You will have to be admitted to hospital.

Cancer of the cervix is one of the worst nightmares a woman can have. The crazy thing is that it is a preventable disease. If you have regular PAP smears, changes that might turn into cancer can be detected and treated before cancer actually develops.

How do I know if I might have cancer of the cervix?

If you haven't been having PAP smears and you do develop cervical cancer, you might notice bleeding in between periods or bleeding after sexual intercourse. The bleeding might be heavy or it might be light with just a pinkness noticed after you pass urine.

If you do have abnormal bleeding, visit your doctor for tests, but don't panic. The most common cause of abnormal vaginal bleeding in women these days is break-through bleeding from being on the oral contraceptive pill.

HPV, pregnancy and your baby

See Chapter 20 *STDs and Pregnancy* and Chapter 21 *STDs and Your Baby.*

Section Five

STDs, Pregnancy

and Babies

20

STDs & PREGNANCY

Drugs

Unborn babies are very susceptible to harm from drugs taken by the mother, especially during the first trimester (three months) of pregnancy. This is when the baby's brain and nerves, heart, digestive organs, arms, legs and muscles start to form. The risk of deformity is at its highest. Use of drugs later in pregnancy can cause some disorders of growth and function including brain damage, but not the really horrible deformities that can occur if they are given earlier. If you're pregnant, you should avoid all drugs not prescribed by your doctor.

Alcohol, nicotine and illegal drugs are obvious dangers. Some treatments you can buy without a doctor's prescription may also pose a risk. Luckily many of the drugs used to treat STDs are quite safe to use at any stage of pregnancy, but some are not.

If you are receiving treatment for an STD, it's vital you tell your doctor if you are or think you may be pregnant. If you are not sure, have a test right away. Major damage to the child is possible from the third to the tenth week of pregnancy. Often people do not know they are pregnant until after this stage. Take precautions to make sure you do not become pregnant while you are being treated.

A few STDs are best left untreated while you are pregnant. This may inconvenience you, but it will benefit your baby. Many STDs must be treated to prevent harm to your baby, as well as to you. Some risks and dangers are unavoidable: modern medicine does not have the answer to everything.

The rest of this chapter reviews the impact on pregnancy of treatments for common STDs. I have noted what is known about the safety of various drugs for use during pregnancy, but this knowledge is not complete.

Prevention is . . .

What I have said about STDs and their effects on babies will worry a lot of people, and rightly so. A trip to the doctor may not be enough to make it all right. So the responsibility falls on you to reduce the risks you impose on your baby.

The most responsible thing you can do is have a full STD checkup including the HIV or AIDS test before you become pregnant. Once you have decided to go ahead, you should take extra care to guard against STD infection throughout your pregnancy.

Herpes

What happens if I get genital herpes for the first time while I am pregnant?

If you get genital herpes for the first time when you are pregnant, there is a chance you may miscarry. If the baby is infected during the first trimester you will most probably miscarry.

If your first genital infection occurs during the second trimester there is an increased chance the baby will be born earlier than normal. Infection across the placenta during the second trimester is possible but it has not been proved to occur, so it is most likely that the baby will be born normal and without infection.

Infection with genital herpes during the third trimester of pregnancy poses the greatest risk of infection to a baby at birth, particularly if you do not know you have the infection.

What happens if I get a genital herpes recurrence during pregnancy?

If you have had genital herpes in the past and get an outbreak during pregnancy it is unlikely the baby will be infected unless there is an outbreak at the time of delivery. Even then the chance the baby will be infected is very low. The baby seems to get some immunity from the mother which protects it from becoming infected.

In the past doctors used to test women with herpes prior to the time of delivery, to see if they were infective. More recently it has been found that tests done weeks beforehand don't predict whether the mother will be infective at the time of delivery, which is when it really counts. What is now recommended is that if either partner has had genital herpes, the doctor or midwife looks very carefully for any symptoms or signs of infection, at the time of delivery. If there are no symptoms or signs then a normal delivery can be made. If there are symptoms then a caesarean delivery will be performed.

Doctors may take cultures for herpes from the birth canal at the time of delivery, but these results take up to a week to come back so they are only useful if the baby becomes ill.

Can my baby be delivered normally?

Your baby can be delivered normally provided you do not have your first infection with genital herpes after 36 weeks of pregnancy. There is no evidence to suggest that delivering the baby normally is bad for you or increases the baby's chance of being infected. The people who are present at the delivery will need to take special precautions that they do not become infected by your secretions (blood, amniotic fluid, and vaginal secretions). Even the secretion in the babies mouth when it is born can carry infection, and the staff have to be very careful when handling the baby.

Can I use acyclovir in pregnancy?

Acyclovir is not recommended for pregnant women.

Genital Warts and HPV

Genital warts should be treated during pregnancy if this is possible, or they may grow quite a lot bigger. Occasionally they can grow so big they block the vagina, and the baby needs to be delivered by a caesarean operation. Sometimes treatment is too difficult so it is best to wait until after the baby has been born.

Podophyllin cannot be used at any stage of pregnancy because it can harm the baby. Podophyllin is thought to cause abnormalities including skin tags in front of the ears and on the cheek, one skin crease only in the palms of the hands (called a simian crease), inflammation of multiple nerves in the body (polyneuritis) and abnormal development of the arms, legs and heart. Death of a baby in the womb has also been reported.

Treatments that can be used during pregnancy include trichloroacetic acid, silver nitrate, freezing, or burning with a diathermy machine or laser.

Hepatitis B and pregnancy

If you are a hepatitis B carrier, there is a 70% to 90% chance you will pass the infection on to your baby at the time of birth or afterwards. The risk of your baby being infected is much higher if you have already got one child who is infected. The risk is also very high if you catch hepatitis B during pregnancy and are infectious during the second or third trimester or within two months of delivery. The baby can be infected in the womb, but usually the infection occurs around the time of childbirth with the baby swallowing some of the infected mother's secretions or some of the mother's blood leaking into the baby's blood. Most babies infected around birth become carriers of the hepatitis virus if they are not treated immediately.

Fortunately the babies of hepatitis B carrier mothers can be given treatment at birth to stop them becoming chronic carriers and going on to develop the illness later in life. Many hospitals now routinely check pregnant women for hepatitis B, but be sure to tell your doctor if you know you are a carrier.

HIV (AIDS) infection

If you become pregnant or want to become pregnant and you have been infected with HIV, you must face some difficult questions.

The chance of the virus being passed on to the baby seems to be in the 15% to 30% range. This can happen as early as the first trimester of pregnancy, but may not occur until the time of delivery. It appears that having a caesarean delivery does not reduce the chance of the baby being infected, as infection with the mother's blood is still probable.

Mothers who have more advanced infection appear more likely to pass it on. Measurement of your immune status by your specialist will tell you how much the HIV infection has affected your body.

Mothers with HIV are more likely to have their babies early (premature), but there is no convincing evidence that HIV infection causes deformity of the baby during pregnancy (congenital malformation).

A significant proportion of HIV infected babies die before their second birthday. Just as in adults, the longer a baby has the infection the more likely they are to become sick.

The toughest question you must face is, 'Should I continue with this pregnancy?'

There is no easy answer. I suggest you talk to your partner and to your doctor, and try to do what feels right for you and the baby. Read Chapter 7 *HIV (Human Immunodeficiency Virus or AIDS)* to find out what happens to babies who are infected with HIV.

If you choose not to continue with the pregnancy, your decision should be made no later than 12 weeks, and even that is leaving it a little late.

If you choose to go ahead, there are other questions to be faced.

'What happens to the baby if I get sick and am to ill too look after it?'

'Is my partner going to be able to look after the baby or is it likely that he will also be sick or have died?'

'Am I able to bring up the child without a father, or with a father who is sick and needs to be looked after as well as the baby?'

In the short term there may seem to be easy answers to these questions, but remember that the longer you have the infection the more likely it is you are going to become unwell. Who is going to be around to look after your child as they grow up?

No-one can tell you what you must do. It is a decision that you eventually must make for yourself and for your unborn baby. Remember though, there are a lot of places that offer counselling to help you arrive at the answer that is right for you.

What if I want to become pregnant?

Perhaps you or your partner are infected and you want to have a child.

You might think it worth postponing becoming pregnant in the hope a new treatment will become available. HIV is a chronic disease that is proving quite difficult to conquer, but it is just a disease. Many researchers are working hard to find a vaccine or a cure, but this goal may not be achieved within the next five to ten years.

What if you are not infected but your partner is HIV positive and you want to become pregnant? Some people in this situation only have unprotected sex at the time they are likely to fall pregnant but this puts you at an extremely high risk of becoming infected yourself. You should consider artificial insemination from an HIV negative donor.

Is becoming pregnant when I am HIV positive likely to make my infection worse?

So far the research is not definite, but early indications are not encouraging.

Sometimes being pregnant can delay the diagnosis of illness due to HIV infection. For example the tiredness due to HIV infection may be put down to the pregnancy instead.

Being pregnant may mean that you can't start taking treatment for your HIV, because the drugs are a risk to your baby. Your infection will go unchecked for longer.

Early evidence suggests that becoming pregnant hurries up the growth of the virus inside your body, so that you get sick sooner than you might have done. Also, if you catch some viral infection you may get sicker and find it harder to recover than if you were not pregnant.

HIV is associated with the infections cytomegalovirus and toxoplasmosis, which can cause severe birth abnormalities. Toxoplasmosis can cause the baby to be stillborn or to be born with severe eye infection, a small brain and pneumonia. Cytomegalovirus may make the baby mentally retarded. If you are pregnant then baseline tests for these infections should be done, so they can be checked on throughout your pregnancy.

Advanced HIV infection and pregnancy

People with advanced HIV infection will probably be taking several drugs.

Sulfamethoxazole and trimethoprim are two antibiotics given for *Pneumocystis carinii* lung infection. They can cause a baby to be born yellow and occasionally the baby may be born with abnormalities, though this is not common.

Sulfadiazine, used to treat an infection called toxoplasmosis, can also cause a baby to be born yellow. There is a small chance of other abnormalities occurring. The yellow color disappears as the baby gets a little older.

Zidovudine is a drug which stops the HIV virus multiplying. The risks of taking it during pregnancy are not known, nor is it known if zidovudine reduces the risk of transmission of HIV infection to the baby.

Taking care of yourself

If you are HIV infected and pregnant you must really start taking care of yourself, to give yourself and your baby the best chance possible.

Try and avoid stress to your body. Stress may increase the rate at which the virus grows inside you. Equally important is to avoid catching infections, such as other sexually transmittable diseases, or hepatitis B. Give yourself as much sleep and rest as your body asks for.

Read Chapter 22 *Building Good Health.*

Are there any special precautions for health care workers who become pregnant?

Pregnant women are advised not to work in health care settings where they could become infected with HIV. They should consider working in other areas with less risk.

The reason for this is two-fold. Firstly if you sustain a needlestick injury or are exposed to HIV infected blood on a sore, eczema, or in the eye or mouth, it is not known whether you should be given zidovudine, the normal treatment for HIV exposure. Secondly if you are nursing HIV patients you will be exposed to infection with toxoplasma and cytomegalovirus. Each of these infections cause severe deformities of babies during pregnancy. It may be that you have had these infections previously and you can be tested for this, but if not it is advisable you do not work with these patients while you are pregnant.

Bacterial vaginosis

Some medical studies have shown that women who have bacterial vaginosis in pregnancy may have premature rupture of the membranes, which means the waters break early and the baby is born early. There is some doubt about the interpretation of this research. Medical studies can be very difficult to understand. Sometimes the wrong conclusions can be reached because there is another cause for the findings that hasn't been discovered yet. Such is life for medical researchers.

If you are pregnant and are found to have bacterial vaginosis discuss with your doctor whether you should be treated. It may not be an easy decision for either of you to make.

Metronidazole cannot be used in the first trimester of pregnancy and its safety in the rest of pregnancy is not known. Amoxycillin, cephalexin or clindamycin can be used if you and your doctor decide you should be treated.

Candidiasis

It is quite common to get an outbreak of thrush during pregnancy. The body's hormone levels are different and the acid balance in the vagina is changed, making it easier for an overgrowth of the yeast organism to occur. In addition sugar may appear in the urine during pregnancy in some women.

The usual treatment is with nystatin pessaries and cream. Nystatin is not absorbed into the body. This treatment has been shown to do no harm to the growing baby.

Miconazole is another, more effective treatment which so far appears to cause no harm to the growing baby. Miconazole is however absorbed from the vagina, so there is a risk there may be harm to the baby even though no studies have shown this yet.

Ketoconazole is a treatment for extremely severe cases of thrush. It poses no known risks during pregnancy, however it has not yet been proven safe for general use.

Chlamydia

Infection with *Chlamydia trachomatis* which reaches the fallopian tubes can cause scarring of the tubes and consequently an increased risk of ectopic pregnancy, which is a pregnancy that develops in the fallopian tubes instead of the womb. This is a very serious condition. The tube can burst causing severe bleeding, enough to cause death in a matter of hours. In these circumstances you need to be rushed to hospital for emergency surgery. Chlamydia is a cause of prolonged bleeding after delivery of the baby.

It is not known for sure whether chlamydia causes premature delivery or abortion. It is possible that chlamydia causes babies to be born smaller than they should be. More research is being carried out.

If you have untreated chlamydia at the time of child birth the chance that your baby will be infected is from 44% to 67%. Of those who are born infected, 35% to 50% develop inflammation of the eyes and 11% to 20% get pneumonia.

Women with chlamydia can develop infection of the uterus and of the fallopian tubes (salpingitis) after giving birth. Chlamydia is easily treated during any stage of pregnancy with the antibiotic erythromycin.

Gonorrhea

If you are pregnant and have gonorrhea which is not treated there is an increased chance that you will miscarry if the infection has spread to the uterus. There is also the risk that the gonorrhea infection may spread into the baby's blood stream. Inflammation of the fallopian tubes can occur although after the fourth month of pregnancy the cervical os gets blocked off by the growing baby and it is exceedingly difficult for germs to get into the uterine cavity. Sometimes the baby may be born premature (early), or there may be inflammation of the fluid and membranes surrounding the baby in the womb. Occasionally the labour can be longer than normal because of the gonorrhea infection.

Treatment to stop these complications occurring is with amoxycillin and probenecid, or an injection of ceftriaxone.

PID

Most women who have had PID and been treated are still able to have a normal pregnancy. There is a risk of developing an ectopic pregnancy, where the fetus develops in the fallopian tube instead of in the uterus, so you should see a doctor as soon as you become pregnant. You must take special precautions to avoid having any more episodes of PID. See Chapter 14 *PID (Pelvic Inflammatory Disease)*.

Also, take precautions against becoming pregnant accidentally. A PID infection may have reduced your chances of becoming pregnant, but not eliminated them. If you become pregnant unintentionally an abortion may further reduce your chances of becoming pregnant when you really want to.

Syphilis

The syphilis organism can pass through the placenta to the baby at almost any stage of pregnancy. The organisms in the blood of the mother reach the baby's blood by the small blood vessels in the placenta. Unlike adult infection, where the organisms burrow into the skin from the outside, in the fetus the infection is spread directly by the blood stream.

The reaction by the fetus against the infection does not start until it is at least four to five months old. It can cause miscarriage, stillbirth, or premature delivery. The placenta is large and heavy in some cases but can look completely normal.

Commonly women do not know they have syphilis until later in the disease, so they could be infecting their baby without realising it. Consequently most doctors will test women in early pregnancy to make sure they are not infected. Syphilis can cause severe harm to the fetus.

If you have either primary or secondary syphilis in pregnancy and are not treated, it is almost certain the baby will be infected and be born with abnormalities. The chances of stillbirth or premature delivery is also very high. If you have latent infection (the third stage of syphilis) there is still a high chance that you will pass the infection on to the baby during pregnancy.

The abnormalities which result from syphilis can be so severe the baby may need to be cared for in an institution for the rest of its life. Sometimes a baby can be born with the infection but show no signs until it is older and the bones and teeth grow abnormally. See Chapter 21 *STDs and Your Baby* to find out more.

Treatment early in pregnancy (before 16 weeks) will stop the baby developing complications of the infection and the baby will be born normal. The baby is usually treated with penicillin at birth, to make doubly sure, and should be followed up with blood tests to make sure the treatments worked.

Testing for syphilis should always be done during pregnancy.

Group B streptococcus

Group B streptococcus is a normal organism in about 5% to 25% of women but can sometimes be associated with premature rupture of the membranes so that ineffective labour occurs. At the moment there is no clear reason to be treated for this germ unless it is thought to be causing you problems.

Pediculosis pubis

Pediculosis pubis is commonly treated with lindane cream applied over the body. This should not be used if you are pregnant. The cream has been shown to accumulate in fat and there is the possibility of congenital damage to your baby if you use this treatment.

Treatment that can be used in pregnancy is crotamiton 10% cream or lotion that is put on for two nights in a row.

Scabies

This is another STD that is commonly treated with lindane, a definite no-no if you are pregnant. Benzyl benzoate 25% can be used, it should be applied to the whole body from the neck down, paying particular attention to the skin of the hands and soles of the feet, and left on for 24 hours. Crotamiton 10% can be used, applied to the whole body from the neck down for two nights in a row, and washed off 24 hours after the second application. Crotamiton is particularly good if persistent itch is a problem. Clothing and bed clothes should be washed in the hot cycle of the washing machine at the time the treatment is started. Make sure your partner is treated as well, and their clothes washed. Sometimes the itching can last for three weeks after you have been treated. Very occasionally additional treatment is necessary.

Trichomoniasis

The usual treatment for trichomoniasis is with the drugs metronidazole or tinidazole, but you should not take these during the first trimester of pregnancy.

If you are given metronidazole or tinidazole it is imperative you do not drink alcohol. These two drugs stop alcohol from being broken down in the body. If you are pregnant the alcohol may cause developmental damage to your baby.

Povidone-iodine douches should not be used because they can stop the baby's thyroid gland developing normally.

Clotrimazole vaginal pessaries used nightly for six days are an alternative therapy.

21

STDs & YOUR BABY

Sexually transmittable diseases can be passed on to your baby while it is growing inside you, at the time of delivery and sometimes after birth. If your baby is found to have one of these infections you and your partner should be tested too, for the full range of STDs.

Herpes

Herpes is common in adults, but it is extremely rare in babies. This is fortunate, because herpes is a very serious illness for a baby. The infection in the baby may be mild, just involving part of its body, or it may be severe and spread throughout the inside and outside of the baby. If the infection is only affecting one small part of the body and not the eyes, there are not likely to be any long term problems.

In severe infection the baby may develop small blisters on its skin at any part of the body, and the infection may involve the inside parts of the body including the brain. When this happens the baby may be very sleepy or even impossible to wake up. The baby may not suck properly, may be extremely irritable, have diarrhea and breathing problems and may have epileptic fits. Other parts of the body that can be affected are the eyes, liver and spleen. Babies with widespread herpes infection may die or be left with long term brain or eye damage. Even though the death is a tragedy it is probably a kind way of nature preventing the baby from suffering long term problems.

Fortunately even if a mother has genital herpes it is extremely uncommon for her baby to be born infected or to develop herpes shortly after birth. If this does happen the baby will need to be nursed in an isolation unit in hospital. The drug acyclovir will be given, to stop the virus multiplying and reduce the damage done. The baby cannot go home until it is better and is no longer infectious. Babies who survive the infection with herpes may have recurrences during childhood. Luckily the outbreaks are localised and, provided care is taken to cover the lesions, it does not spread to other parts of the body.

Genital warts

A mother who has the human papillomavirus (which causes genital warts) can pass it on to her baby either during pregnancy or at delivery. Nothing can be done to prevent this. As infection can occur in the womb, having a caesarean delivery is no safeguard. Luckily though, it is extremely rare for babies to develop problems due to human papillomavirus infection.

In very rare cases infection in a baby can cause warts of the vocal cords, the medical name of which is laryngeal papillomatosis. Lumps grow very quickly on the vocal cords and epiglottis. Occasionally the windpipe and lungs are involved. Mostly it appears between two and five years of age. Even more rarely the lumps may develop in the teens, causing hoarseness, changes in the voice, stridor (which is a harsh noise on breathing) and later difficulty breathing because the air has trouble moving in and out. In most cases the lumps will go away by themselves, though sometimes they return. They can be cut out but may recur. They can also be treated with radiotherapy, but this is associated with a later risk of developing cancer.

Genital warts can occur in children and may be acquired from the mother at the time of birth, or sometimes from family members. Some cases are due to sexual abuse. The warts can appear on the vulva, penis or anus.

If a baby or young child has genital warts it is important to keep an open mind about how they could have got them. Do not jump to the conclusion that your child has been sexually abused. The child should however be examined for evidence of sexual abuse and tested for other STDs such as gonorrhea, chlamydia, trichomoniasi s and syphilis. If one of these other infections is found, then it is a near certainty that your child has been sexually abused. This must be reported to the appropriate authorities.

Hepatitis B and babies

Babies can catch hepatitis B from their mothers during pregnancy, at birth or from breast feeding. Babies are prone to being infected because it takes quite a while for their body's immune systems to develop.

Eighty five to 90% of the babies who catch hepatitis B from their mothers become chronic carriers, unless they are vaccinated at birth. More than 25% of the babies who become chronic carriers later die from cirrhosis of the liver or liver cancer (hepatoma). The risk is much greater if they are male.

Hepatitis B in babies is often asymptomatic, which means it is mild or not noticeable. Other times the baby may feed poorly, vomit and fail to gain weight normally. It may have yellow eyes and dark urine. Sometimes its liver and spleen may be enlarged and it may bruise and bleed easily. Occasionally severe hepatitis may cause death. If the baby is sick it will most probably have to be looked after in hospital.

Most babies can be saved from becoming chronic carriers or getting sick from hepatitis B by being given immunoglobulin and hepatitis B vaccination. The injections must be given at birth or soon after so they can start working and eradicate any infection. Immunoglobulin must be given within two days of birth to be effective. Use of these treatments reduces the chance of the baby becoming a carrier by 85% to 95%. Using only one treatment reduces the chances by about 75%. Further vaccination with the hepatitis B vaccine should be given at one and six months, and the baby should be tested for immunity at nine months.

HIV (AIDS) infection

HIV infection can be passed on during pregnancy, at the time of childbirth, or afterwards during breast feeding.

A significant proportion of HIV infected babies die before their second birthday. Just as in adults, the longer a baby has the infection the more likely they are to become sick.

Should I breast feed my baby?

A baby can be given HIV infection through breast milk from an infected mother. If a baby is infected HIV infection can be passed on to an uninfected mother by breast feeding. This has happened in Russia and Romania where large numbers of babies were infected in hospitals and some passed the infection on to their mothers.

If your partner has HIV infection but you don't and you have just had a baby with him, then it is wise to bottle feed the baby to avoid any chance of it becoming infected.

This recommendation has been made in Western countries because there are good replacement substitutes for breast milk. In other countries or remote regions this is not so and in these situations it is thought best to feed the baby breast milk. The nutrition in the breast milk keeps the baby healthy and stops it from getting sick and dying from other infections. In underdeveloped countries the risk of the baby dying from malnutrition or other disease is greater than the small chance of the HIV infection being passed on if the baby does not already have it.

In some communities mothers allow their babies to be breastfed by other women who are also breast feeding. This is no longer a safe practice. A baby who is not infected can be given the infection through breast milk, and a baby who is infected can pass the infection on to any mother who breast feeds it.

Is there treatment for HIV infected babies?

The treatment for babies is pretty much the same as for adults except that they are given much smaller doses. Doctors think it is useful to give antibiotics to stop the baby getting pneumonia and that zidovudine, a drug which slows down the growth of HIV, is a useful treatment. Special feeding formulas may need to be given, to help the baby put on weight.

When HIV babies are sick they cannot learn some of the things other babies of their age can. It is important to give them time to sleep and rest, and to try and give them as normal an environment as possible.

If there are other children in the family they may need counselling to help them understand the problem with the new baby. This is particularly so when the general community is not accustomed to living with people with HIV.

What sort of illnesses does the baby get?

There are two patterns of illness which may affect babies with HIV. The first pattern starts soon after birth. The baby may have severe brain damage from the virus directly infecting the brain. The baby's immune system will be badly affected so they cannot easily fight infection. Some of the illnesses they may get are thrush in the mouth, failure to put on weight or grow as normal, frequent throat and chest infections, enlarged lymph glands, an enlarged liver, recurrent diarrhea, ear infections, recurring fevers, low blood counts, septic infections and enlargement of the salivary glands. Only half of these babies live as long as three years. It is thought that these babies were infected early in pregnancy.

The other pattern of disease is more common. It affects older babies who take longer to get sick. Their immune system is not so badly affected, but they can still have brain damage and may develop any of the illnesses listed for the first pattern, especially pneumonia, heart and kidney problems. Most of the babies with this form of the disease are still alive at three years.

How do I know if my baby is infected?

Diagnosis is by blood tests. Sometimes it is difficult to know whether a baby is infected or not. Occasionally it takes up to 18 months to be sure. Improved tests are now available, for example the polymerase chain reaction test which can multiply a small number of viruses to the point where they can be detected, but it takes time before doctors can be sure how accurate a new test is.

If you are infected with HIV your doctors will probably do follow up tests on your baby for many years.

Should the baby be vaccinated?

In Australia it is recommended the babies are vaccinated with the usual vaccines, except that instead of vaccination with the live polio vaccine, which is taken orally, they should be vaccinated with another type which is made from a killed virus, given intramuscularly. Your doctor will take your baby's immune status into consideration before giving the definite go ahead for vaccinations.

Candidiasis

Candidiasis or thrush infection in babies is very common. It affects at least 5% of babies. It is not a serious infection but does sometimes make the baby irritable. Most commonly the infection occurs in the mouth affecting the tongue and inner cheeks. It appears as white patches. Sometimes the infection can affect the surface skin appearing as a pimply rash over any part of the body including the face.

It seems babies pick up candidiasis from their mothers at birth, although it is possible for the infection to be picked up from the hands of hospital staff if the baby has to be nursed in hospital.

Treatment for mouth infection is with nystatin . Infection on the skin often gets better by itself, but topical antifungal creams help.

Chlamydia

A baby has a high chance of catching chlamydia from its infected mother at the time of birth. The infection can cause severe inflammation of the eyes, pneumonia of the lungs and inflammation of the ear canal. Infection in the eyes usually starts about two weeks after birth. Luckily, despite the appearance of the eyes, blindness is unlikely to occur. However if the chlamydia is not treated it will become a chronic disease and will keep recurring, eventually causing scarring.

Pneumonia usually shows up at about six weeks. Symptoms are a cough and much faster breathing, though often the baby's temperature is normal. If the coughing is bad, it can stop the baby feeding properly and the baby will not put on weight or grow as fast as other children. Treatment is with the antibiotic erythromycin .

Gonorrhea

If gonorrhea is not treated in the mother before the baby is born, the baby may catch the infection at the time of delivery.

Infection occurs mainly in the eyes, but it may also appear in other parts of the body such as the throat. It usually shows in the first month, most commonly in the first week. The baby will develop very sticky eyes. Initially the eyes may just water excessively but soon the discharge becomes creamy and sticky. The eyelids swell and the baby may be unable to open its eyes. If the eyes are not treated the baby can become blind due to ulceration and scarring of the cornea.

Figure 21.1 Gonorrhea affecting the eye of a newborn baby

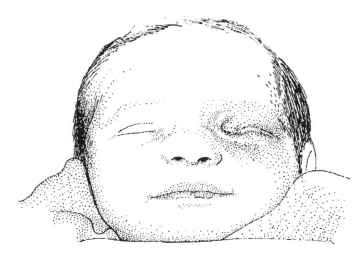

Sometimes a baby will be infected with both gonorrhea and chlamydia. This is usually the result of the baby coming in contact with infected secretions from the cervix at the time of birth. Rarely the infection can spread into the blood stream.

Treatment is given in the hospital with antibiotics for the gonorrhea and eye washes to clear the eyes. In some places where gonorrhea is very common, all the babies born are routinely treated with silver nitrate eye washes to stop the infection. This does not stop it in all cases and does not stop the infection due to chlamydia.

Syphilis

If the mother is not treated during pregnancy it is extremely likely the baby will be infected in some way. Tests taken from the baby at birth may indicate syphilis infection, but it can take some time after birth for the blood test to confirm infection.

Syphilis infection in a baby is called congenital syphilis. There are two forms, an early form in which the infant develops signs in the first two years of life, and a late form in which illness occurs later on in childhood or adolescence.

In the early form the baby may be born normal but within two weeks develops trouble breathing, a runny nose and 'snuffles'. There may be a rash on the skin which can be flat, raised or blister-like. If it is severe the skin may peel off. Sometimes the blistered areas can be as big as three centimetres (over an inch) wide. The rash may also involve the corners of the mouth. When the area around the mouth heals, fine scarring results which lasts into adult life. The child may have trouble gaining weight, and may suffer recurrent infections and anemia. There may be enlargement of the lymph nodes. The liver and the spleen may be swollen causing the belly to stick out, and there may be involvement of the brain, eyes and spinal cord. Brain involvement can cause neck stiffness and brain damage. In addition the baby may suffer from pain and swelling of the bones, particularly the lower part of the arm and leg near the knee.

In the late form of congenital syphilis there may be no signs until the child is over five years old. Then there may be lumps which grow on the skin, bones and inside the nose and mouth, and other parts of the body. Involvement of the bridge of the nose can create a hole in the cartilage inside the nose resulting in a nasal voice, and food going into the nose when trying to swallow. Bowing of the shin bones can occur giving a condition called 'sabre tibia'. The brain can be involved.

Late congenital syphilis may be suspected because of poor grades at school, difficulty walking, continued wetting in late childhood and paralysis of an arm or leg or side of the body. Hearing difficulties and paralysis of some of the nerves which affect areas on and around the head may occur. The eyes may be involved resulting in excessive watering, pain and blindness. In this late stage of the disease the child needs a thorough evaluation by a specialist to see what parts of the body are affected.

Untreated syphilis organisms will stop the baby's teeth from growing properly. The incisor teeth (the teeth at the very front) will have a notch in the middle of them and grow smaller than usual. The enamel coat on the teeth is not as good. These are called 'Hutchinson's teeth' after the man who first described them.

Other teeth may also be affected such as the those next to the front, called the lateral incisors. The molar teeth (which are at the sides and back of the mouth) also grow abnormally, looking like a string purse or mulberry. These teeth are called 'Moon's mulberry molars' after Henry Moon, who first described the appearance.

Figure 21.2 Tooth deformities due to congenital syphilis

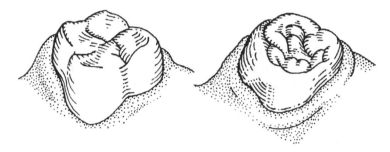

A normal molar tooth (left) compared with a Moon's mulberry molar (right)

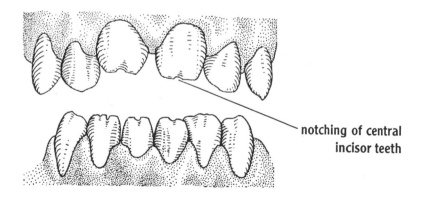

notching of central incisor teeth

Hutchinson's incisors are mishapen with a central notch

Treatment of congenital syphilis

Treatment for the baby is with 10 days of penicillin given either intravenously or intramuscularly. Most doctors, if they think a baby might be infected, will treat it just in case. The earlier treatment is commenced, the less permanent damage the baby is likely to suffer.

Unfortunately this terrible list of disfigurements caused by syphilis is not yet complete. Other possibilities include disfigurement of the face with collapse of the bridge of the nose due to destruction of the nose cartilage, resulting in what is called a saddle nose. The bottom jaw bone may not grow as large as it should, this is called 'bulldog facies'. There can be scarring at the angles of the mouth.

Children affected in these ways have the abnormalities for the rest of their lives. Just by looking at them you can tell they were born with syphilis, and that their mother and possibly father also had syphilis.

Figure 21.3 Saddle nose deformity due to congenital syphilis

In saddle nose deformity the bridge of the nose is flattened

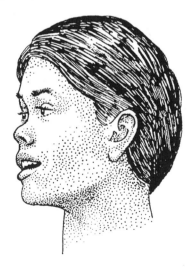

Group B streptococcus

A high percentage of babies born to mothers with group B streptococcal infection end up having the germ as part of the bugs normally living inside their body. Rarely they become sick from this bug. They can develop pneumonia, inflammation of the lining of the brain, infection in the blood stream, inflammation and swelling of the skin, or infection in the bones or joints. Half of the babies who get this severe problem recover with treatment but the other half die.

Even if the mother is treated during pregnancy the organisms usually return. Some people say that all babies should be treated just in case, but since the vast majority of babies don't have a problem this means they are being treated with antibiotics for nothing. Scientists are trying to work out a way they can predict which babies or mothers should be treated so that only those who need treatment are given it.

Group B streptococcal infection is not common, but it can be a devastating infection for babies. Care should be taken during pregnancy and at the time of birth to avoid transmission to the infant.

Cytomegalovirus infection (CMV)

Cytomegalovirus (CMV) is a common viral infection. The older a person is the more likely they are to have had it at some time. It is passed on by close contact and sexual intercourse. Most people who get the infection do not even know when they got it.

There are times when people are most likely to come in contact with this virus. These are early childhood and then later when they become sexually active, in the teenage years and young adulthood. During active infection the virus is found in saliva, urine, milk and ejaculate. The virus can be found in these fluids for many months after infection.

Once established cytomegalovirus stays in the body for the rest of the person's life, and during periods of reduced immunity the person can become infectious again.

A small number of babies born to mothers with active cytomegalovirus are infected, either during pregnancy, at the time of delivery or afterwards, by breast feeding. Most of the time the mother's immunity seems to protect the baby.

Of those who do become infected, 85% to 95% do not suffer any long term side effects. The chance of a baby becoming infected and developing severe disease is highest if the mother has her first infection during pregnancy.

Some of those who are born with the infection but show no signs of the disease may later develop learning and hearing problems. It may take many years to attribute the cause to CMV infection.

A mildly affected baby may develop deafness which becomes more noticeable as it grows older. More severe infection results in failure to grow to the proper size during pregnancy, and enlargement of the liver and spleen.

In very severe infection additional symptoms include a small head, anemia, blindness, heart defects and pneumonia. These babies may grow to become mentally retarded, have cerebral palsy (spasticity), fits and trouble with their eyesight.

Diagnosis of cytomegalovirus can take some time because single blood tests are not conclusive. Multiple blood tests over a period of time are needed to make the diagnosis.

There is a vaccine being developed to prevent cytomegalovirus, but it is not yet available for widespread use.

Cytomegalovirus and HIV

CMV infection is very common in people who also have human immunodeficiency virus. Nurses looking after HIV patients should have their immune status checked if they are pregnant or thinking of becoming pregnant. If they don't have CMV then they probably should not nurse HIV patients.

Trichomonas vaginalis

Very rarely babies can catch *Trichomonas vaginalis* from their mothers at birth. It may cause a vaginal discharge or irritation of the vulva in the baby. It is treated with metronidazole.

Section Six

Building Good Health

22

BUILDING GOOD HEALTH

This chapter will be valuable for anyone who wants to live a healthy lifestyle, stay young for longer and reduce their chances of becoming ill.

It will be of particular benefit to people with recurrent genital herpes infection, recurrent candidiasis, recurrent bacterial vaginosis, recurrent genital wart infection, persistent NSU and infection with HIV (AIDS).

Doctors, by themselves, can't give you good health. Wonder drugs, by themselves, won't cure you of serious illness. Health is a state of mind as well as a state of body.

To keep your immune system working optimally you should avoid doing things that stress or damage your body. Examples are not eating properly, using certain drugs, smoking and not getting enough sleep. When your body is struggling to get well, your positive actions can add to the benefits of medicines such as antibiotics, so that together they help you get better quickly and reduce long term damage.

Alcohol

People often ask if drinking alcohol will impair their body's immunity. Well, we know that drinking large amounts of alcohol makes the body much more prone to illness.

What about small amounts? Some doctors say a small amount of alcohol is good for you. We do know that alcohol is a depressant, which means it reduces the brain's capacity to function. Three drinks in an hour will impair your capacity to drive a motor car. Your mind is the master conductor for your fight against disease, so things which impair your mind's ability to function will impair your body's ability to become healthy or remain at optimal health.

I once asked a professor at a scientific meeting what alcohol did to the special white cells in the body called macrophages. These run around the body gobbling up infection as well as performing more specialized functions. I received my answer from someone at the back of the room who told me that alcohol is used by scientists as a fixative. Fixative means that it kills cells and preserves them so they don't decay. I was quite amazed to realize that alcohol does this to such an important part of our body, yet so many people drink it. Maybe when you are healthy and have lots of these cells it is something the body can recover from quite easily, however if your body's cells are not working too well, or you are striving for maximal health, then it seems to me that even a small amount of alcohol may cause you harm.

Lifestyle decisions

In making lifestyle decisions about whether to drink alcohol or not you also have to think about what it does for you. If you enjoy drinking with your friends, and stopping drinking alcohol will mean you lose the enjoyment from that part of your life, then you are probably better off to do what you enjoy. Maybe you could switch to lower alcohol drinks or have fewer drinks.

Being healthy should be a gradual process where you take steps that make you feel better, so you want to take more steps – not an ordeal where you stop doing things because you think you should. To be healthy is not a matter of denial but a subtle process of learning to respect the feeling of wellness in your body. It is a choice for lasting good feelings, not a rejection of pleasure. This understanding comes gradually but it is one of the best gifts you can give your body.

As you learn to respect your body you will learn that certain things make you feel unwell. In time you will prefer not to do these things. This is a process of respect and understanding, not a process of force and denial.

Smoking

Smoking cigarettes greatly impairs the body's immune system, in many ways. For example, smoking reduces the number of Langerhans cells. These cells act like a watch dog cell in the skin, detecting foreign substances and signalling the body to take action against infection. Having fewer of these cells means it is easier for infection to get through. Someone with genital warts who smokes has fewer of these cells to detect a newly developing wart and stop it from growing. The link between smoking and cancer of the cervix is thought to be that there are fewer Langerhans cells to detect the early form of the cancer. Luckily the number of these cells returns to normal when you stop smoking.

This is just one example of how smoking reduces the body's immune response. The damage caused by cigarette smoking is now very well documented: if you choose to ignore the evidence, then there is no value in my repeating it here. If you are concerned about your health you won't smoke.

Drugs

I'm not going to talk much about the other drugs in our society either. Some, including marijuana, are known to greatly impair the body's immune system. Though the specific long term effects of some illegal drugs are not known, many are known to impair memory and other thought processes. People using illegal drugs are putting thier mind and body at risk.

You could wait for the scientists to go through the laborious process of doing all the research, but I think you can answer the question for yourself using common sense. Do you think that drug use can possibly be good for your health and your immune system?

Physical exercise

Regular physical exercise acts as an antidepressant and improves your body's immunity. It also helps to relieve stress and tension. With regular exercise you develop a sense of well being.

It is important when exercising not to overdo it. You are not trying to punish yourself or to prove anything, you just want to tone up your body. Exercise that makes you feel tired or gives you sore muscles (at least after the first week or two) is overdoing it, stressing your body and reducing your immune system. Top athletes know that after severe exercise their bodies are more susceptible to illness, despite them being in exceptional physical condition.

If you overdo it, your body will have to clean up the excess products of overuse and make good the damage to injured tissues. In other words, by exercising too hard you are giving your immune system extra work to do. This will not help you achieve healing. If it's healing you want, focus just on healing.

If the exercise is regular and gentle you will be able to integrate it as part of your lifestyle much more easily than if it makes you feel tired or stiff. Anyone can find 20 minutes three times a week if they really want to, but if you set yourself a goal of exercising for hours on end it is going to be hard to keep finding the time, year after year. A healthy exercise program is one that fits into your schedule easily and is a regular part of your lifestyle, from now right into old age.

If you exercise regularly you will be able to gradually increase the amount of exercise you do without overstressing your body, but be gentle with yourself. Your body has to last for a long while yet.

All sorts of exercise are good for you, but the best are cardiovascular exercises: those which improve heart and lung fitness. Brisk walking will do this. Cycling, swimming and jogging are also popular. The best exercise is the one you enjoy doing.

Aim for overall fitness. Don't use only one type of activity that only exercises certain parts of your body, aim for a balance of exercise that works all the parts of your body.

The best way to achieve this is with variety. Do different things on different days, perhaps cycling one day and swimming the next. Work out for yourself what feels right for you. Everyone is different and what feels right for you will probably be very different from what feels right to your best friend.

An important part of exercising that most people forget is stretching. You should stretch before and after exercise to avoid injury. Another way to enjoy stretching is to do it first thing in the morning when you get out of bed. The muscles are quite tight then and they really welcome 15 minutes of slow stretching before they start their work of the day carrying you around. You will find that, with regular morning stretching, a lot of your aches and pains will miraculously disappear.

Caring for your body takes time and dedication. Try and remember the feeling of healthiness you get from your body when you look after it so that when you forget your goals and priorities you can dream of those nice feelings, and remember the more refreshing and contented sleep you enjoyed then. This will encourage you to think again about nurturing and caring for your body.

The better you look after your body the more it will do for you and the more you will be able to get out of life.

Nutrition

You are what you eat, claims the old saying. Have you ever stopped to ponder what this means? How do you eat to achieve maximal health?

Medicine does not know the answers to this yet.

We do know that food that is washed and clean is better for you than food which is contaminated by disease. So hygiene and cleanliness of your food are very important.

Organisms grow in food if it has been left around for a while or if it has been heated and left to cool out of the fridge. So a good general principle is the fresher the food the better it is for you.

Everyone should eat a well balanced diet that contains adequate amounts of protein, carbohydrate, fats, vitamins and minerals. Eating a wide variety of foods can help achieve this. A book on nutrition can be helpful to teach you about the different foods.

People these days are talking a lot about chemicals in our foods and saying these can affect the body. Medicine has not yet worked out ways to detect any very subtle changes in the body that might result from all these chemicals. It may be that they interfere with the body's functioning, or maybe they don't. No-one knows the full truth yet. All you can go on is what feels right for you. If you think that biodynamically or organically grown produce is what you should be eating then eat it. If you don't think it matters then don't bother about it and eat what you feel like.

Eat what you feel like does not mean eat whatever is conveniently placed in front of you. We live in a society that is always trying to sell us things and we often get tempted to buy foods that we know don't make us feel well after we have eaten them. Do you remember a sickly feeling inside that lasted for hours when you pigged out on that yummy cake and ice cream, or the indigestion you suffered for a whole day after that fantastic meal where you had appetizers, followed by entree, main course, sweets, then chocolates with coffee? These are the results of eating not what your body wants for health but what you are encouraged to want.

By eat what you want I mean you should assess carefully how you feel after eating various kinds of food. Stick with those foods that leave you feeling good and avoid those foods that leave you feeling not so good. The taste sensation in the mouth lasts only a few seconds but the results of what you swallow last for hours and become an integral part of the body you live in.

This is all simply part of the process of learning to respect the feelings inside your body. Gradually you will be guided to eat only foods that make you healthy. This will become a process of respect and care. You'll feel less and less like you're missing out on some amazing taste sensation. You won't want to feel heavy, bloated and lethargic when you know the foods your body prefers will leave you feeling light, clear and alive.

These changes take time, patience and the discipline of respecting the feelings that your body gives you. Once you are tuned in to your body you will be delighted at its response and the changes it has from day to day. No two days for your body's needs are ever the same, and you will be forever trying out new recipes and combinations of foods.

Relaxation

Relaxation is particularly important in our very busy modern lives. We need to achieve a balance of work and relaxation in order to be really healthy.

We're all familiar with the stereotype of the hard working, heart attack prone executive. If this type of person could lead a properly balanced life including a focus on a sense of peace and calmness inside their body, they would be able to do their work and stay healthy. One piece of research in the United States has shown that the most successful executives are different from other executives in that they all allow themselves a certain amount of time each day where they are inaccessible to everybody. They use the time to relax, with no external stimuli.

Rest

When I talk about rest I mean not only rest of the physical body but also rest of the mind. How do you rest your mind? Resting the body is easy, you can just plonk it on the bed or a comfortable sofa, but the mind?

Meditation is one way of resting the mind. Another is to think of pleasant things, perhaps anticipating future pleasures or reliving past pleasures. Other ways are to become attuned with nature. You might like to watch sunsets, or experience the rain or wind on your body. Another way is to listen to music, but it has to be very special music which is quiet and relaxing. Rock, jazz, pop and a lot of classical music can make you feel agitated or jumpy inside — that may even be what the composer or musicians intended. The more in tune with your body you are, the more you will experience the feelings that music has inside your body. The special type of music to make you rest your mind has to make you feel warm, peaceful and quiet inside.

Strangely, many of us look after our cars better than we look after our bodies. We use the right fuels and oils. We make sure our cars are maintained, to protect our investment in them and keep them reliable. When they are broken we don't keep driving them around because we know that will cause more damage. We might even cause a major accident. If only we looked after our bodies the same way!

Sleep

Sleep is extremely important for health. It is during sleep that your body has its major chance to heal any illness and repair the wear and tear you have given it. If you are unwell you have to allow your body the amount of sleep it asks for. Don't fight it. If you need ten hours of sleep a night give it to yourself. Sometimes you will need more sleep than others.

Another function of sleep is dreaming. The dreams you have allow healing to occur by discharging or processing pent up emotions and feelings. If these charged up feelings are not released it makes it harder for you to become really well.

Stress reduction

The most important step towards reducing your stress level is to realize that you are stressed. Stress has become so much a part of our daily lives that many people think it is normal to be stressed, or that to get things done you have to be stressed. I don't agree. In fact I find that when people are relaxed and calm more work gets done because they have time to be creative and are able to think of more efficient ways of doing things.

To recognise whether you are stressed or not it is useful to identify certain feelings in your body. You need to be able to remember how you felt on your last holiday where you didn't have to do anything except lie around, eat and sleep and do whatever you felt like doing. Then you need to remember how you felt when you last had to take an exam. Each person has their own feelings inside that they identify with. To learn to avoid being stressed you have to go on your feelings. Avoid the things that make you feel like you are taking an exam, or arrange your day so that if you have a lot of those type of feelings you also have times when you can relax.

Having to meet deadlines and having to be at lots of meetings can be very stressful. The only way you can change this is to say you don't want to keep working this way and spend five to ten minutes planning your day. Remember to include relaxation breaks, at least one in the middle of the day and maybe more if you are highly stressed. Relaxation during the day actually makes you more effective and more efficient in the work that you do.

To take time out to plan your day and to relax takes discipline. Once you start doing it you will find that your life will become less stressed and you will have more energy to do everything you have to.

Positive thinking

If you have tried to unlock the secrets of life, you may have realized that the key to remaining well is to understand your mind and the power within it. Your thoughts and attitudes affect your susceptibility to disease. If you do get an infection, they influence how badly you suffer from it. A positive mental attitude might not cure you of some disease (maybe the infection can only be killed by certain drugs) but a negative attitude will certainly make the effects of the disease worse and slow the recovery medicine might bring.

I think it is also true that to do anything well means to concentrate on only one thing at a time. So to become well or stay well you have to focus on what it is you really want to achieve and then order your life accordingly.

It is often difficult to do this by yourself, particularly when you are feeling sick and miserable, so it can be helpful to visit a counsellor or go to courses which provide you with time out to spend looking at your life and what you want out of it. Just as good or even better can be to sit down with a trusted friend and talk. Often just talking to someone will clarify issues in your mind, and a friend will usually have useful ideas to help you set your goals.

The most important thing, after you have focused on your goals, is to start watching the way your mind thinks and learn to think positively. In other words, step back and look at what you are thinking about. If your thoughts are all about hopelessness, loss and death, you are not going to help yourself get better. You can't ignore reality, and you should think about these things when you have to come to terms with them, but to brood constantly without reaching any resolution is self destructive. If you really want to improve your health you have to catch yourself when you slip into such negative thoughts and instead force yourself to think about something positive.

Taking control of your thoughts can be really hard when you're slipping into depression, especially if you have no training in mental techniques. Use the times when you are feeling OK to prepare yourself, by developing good things to think about later when negative thoughts strike.

The best things to think about are the things you are going to do when you are healthy and the dreams you would like to fulfil. Imagine yourself strong and healthy, living out your dream and feeling great. Concentrate on really picturing the scene in as much detail as possible. Make up a story that you can play out like a film in your head. This is really good mental exercise but it is also hard work, so work out a few easy daydreams or fantasies as well. Even listing the things you would do if you won lotto is better than thinking about how sick you are or might be.

Some people find training in meditation or yoga or even a martial arts discipline to be a great help.

Don't get upset with yourself when you first start doing this and realize how many bad things you think about yourself and others. Most people let their minds run riot, not understanding the power of their own thoughts and how we program ourselves to be the people we are. How can you be cross with yourself if no-one told you any better?

Some people will reject all this as hocus pocus. If you are sceptical but you do want to get well, just suspend your disbelief for a while and try it.

You need to understand that to change yourself and the way you think means you have to reprogram your unconscious. This takes a variable amount of time depending on what it is you are reprogramming and the amount of insight you already have into who you are. This chapter will deal with some of the ways you can reprogram your life to be healthy and happy. You will be successful if you choose to focus on your goals. Each person, depending on their belief system, takes a different amount of time until they have manifested their wishes. The more you believe in yourself and understand your own thought pattern, the quicker you will change your life and be successful in your aims.

Affirmations

An affirmation is a very powerful way of reprogramming your unconscious mental processes. An affirmation is a positive thought you either think repeatedly or write down and read to yourself often. Eventually the affirmation, instead of being external to the way you think, becomes part of your unconscious and conscious thought processes.

At first when you start doing affirmations (particularly ones that are quite different to the way you currently think) there will be a little voice or feeling inside you that says or feels that the affirmation is not true, or it is not possible for you to become the way you are describing. This is a normal reaction that nearly everyone experiences. Don't despair. Usually if you practice the affirmations two or three times a day for two weeks your thoughts and feelings will become aligned with the affirmation. I like people to write down their affirmations and read them back to themselves because I find that the reading process is an exceptionally powerful way of directly reprogramming the unconscious thought process. It is more powerful than just thinking the affirmations.

Here are some sample affirmations. You should make up your own as well.

· I have self healing powers.
· I love myself.
· I am willing to change.
· I like change.

- Whatever the result of the medical test, my future will be better than the past.
- I release my past and am now free to go forward in life.
- I am in peace and harmony with life.
- My body and mind are working together towards complete health. My body wants to be whole and healthy. I will cooperate to become healthy, whole and complete.
- I release the need to blame anyone including myself. I allow love to flow from me and to me.
- I am centred and balanced, and have as much time as I need to do the things I want to do.
- I accept the masculine and feminine parts within me and allow them to be balanced within me. I am at peace with myself.
- I am calm and happy, flowing with life as it comes to me.
- I am relaxed and at peace with myself.
- My body is strengthening itself day by day.
- My body is healthy and full of vitality, with an endless supply of healing energy.
- The more I love myself the more love I have to share with others and the healthier I become.
- My thought patterns are becoming more and more positive.
- I lovingly forgive myself.

Visualizations

This is another very useful technique for reprogramming your unconscious thought pattern. Research has shown that this technique can help patients with cancer, so it is well established. Many people have found it works in other situations too.

Again, because the unconscious mind takes time to be reprogrammed, it is a process that needs to be repeated. I recommend that you do a visualisation twice a day for two weeks. You should spend about five minutes doing the visualisation you choose from the examples below or others you have made up for yourself.

When you are first learning to do affirmations or visualizations it helps to use some that other people have done. Be very careful with the initial ones you do yourself by making sure they do not contain negative input or limitations on yourself, otherwise that will be another piece of deprogramming you will have to do later on.

Here are some examples of visualizations.

- Imagine a very powerful army fighting against the disease and eradicating it.
- Imagine that you are being filled with total love. Feel its warmth, peace, calmness and healing, and see the infected cells in your body being filled, nourished, transformed and healed by the love; see the disease going away because it cannot live any more in your body.
- Imagine the disease just floating out of your body and your body being filled with health.
- See yourself sending love to the person you hate the most. Surround them with love and goodness. (This is a good visualisation to do with past lovers or family members you can't talk to about your sexual identity).

Drawing

A third technique for reprogramming your unconscious thought process is drawing. You draw the situation you would like to deal with, say for example a medical illness, and how it is affecting your body and the people around you. Use lots of different colors and shapes and sizes. You do not have to be an artist, stick figures will do. In the drawing represent the healing force of life making you better. With this method you do not have to acknowledge that you alone have to do the healing, instead show the force of life which causes growth, healing and regeneration doing the work for you. Then each day do another drawing of the same problem but with a little improvement. Do it each day for at least a week. Always draw in the life force energy helping with the healing. Be consciously aware as you do each drawing that healing is occurring. You will be surprised at the pictures you draw, especially if you allow yourself to be imaginative with color, sizes and shapes. This is a process which uses your eyes to get through to the unconscious.

Often people think the exercises through in their mind rather than actually getting out the pen and paper. I find that until you are really in tune with yourself, you have to do the physical process of writing or drawing to make the reprogramming work.

Meditation

Scientists say we normally use only 10% to 15% of our brain. Meditation is a process which through practice starts to open up some of the other 85% to 90%. This is where you can really start to tap into your own healing powers.

The late Dr Ainslie Meares, who was a psychiatrist at the Austin Hospital in Melbourne, was aware of the healing power of the mind. He used to run successful meditation groups for cancer patients. Once he was able to meditate to have an operation without a general anaesthetic. This seems to be a rather remarkable achievement, but similarly amazing feats are not all that uncommon for well trained minds. Dr Meares has written several books on the subject, that you might like to read.

Another doctor who is aware of the healing power of the mind is Dr Bernie Siegel. He has written a recent best selling book called *Love, Medicine and Miracles.*

The benefits of meditation have led many practitioners to recommend it for stress reduction. Meditation however offers much more than stress reduction. We are only just starting to know some of the other benefits meditation offers: my expectation is that future research will validate some claims that are currently regarded as fanciful.

To experience the benefits of meditation, like any other lifestyle measure, you need discipline to do it on a regular basis and make it an habitual part of your daily living.

Preparing to meditate

I recommend 15 minutes of meditation twice a day, once in the morning as soon as you get up out of bed and again in the evening.

It is best to meditate when there is quiet around you and you can be sure of not being interrupted. Choose a special place. Make yourself comfortable on a chair or cushion. It is best to meditate sitting up because if you lie down you can often fall asleep. Lying down can also prevent you from experiencing the soft, gentle movements that happen in the body at different times during meditation.

Types of meditation

There are different types of meditation. There is a prayer meditation where you sit in your special spot and pray for what you want. Some people have described this sort of meditation as making a telephone call to God.

Another sort of meditation is what I call an open meditation where you open yourself to whatever the universe wants to give you. This is the most important sort of meditation to do if you want to expand the power of the mind. Sometimes you will experience special things during the time you are sitting, but most of the time you may not be consciously aware of what is happening. However you will notice on the days you do meditate that there is a subtle change in the way your life runs. There is less stress, things seem to flow, you feel calmer and stronger inside and there is an improvement in the state of your well-being.

For open meditation it is a good idea to make not only the place where you are meditating free from interruption and noise, but also to give yourself some protection. When you start the meditation ask that you be protected by a shield of white light that allows only goodness and love to enter within. Imagine this shield. Do this each time you meditate.

Another type of meditation is a focused meditation. This is where you focus on a particular subject such as healing a part of your body, world peace, or healing the planet. If you are doing this sort of meditation it is helpful to do the other open meditation on a daily basis because they work in different ways. The results of the focused meditation can then be far greater than you will even have hoped for.

Here is a healing meditation that can be used for people who have never meditated or who have done only a little meditation.

Seat yourself in your chosen meditation seat with your back upright and make yourself comfortable. Close your eyes and take four deep breaths counting to seven on each in and out breath: in through the nose and out through the mouth. As you breathe out release all the negativity and anger you have stored in your body.

Ask for a shield of divine white light to surround you and allow only love and goodness to enter within you. Then focus on the part of the body you want healed. If you have HIV infection focus on a cell in your body that is infected with HIV. The body can be regarded as a hologram in meditation, so focusing on one cell like this can bring healing to the whole body. Fill that part of your body or cell with crystal green light that enters through the top of your head and goes to where you direct it. The green is antiseptic, it cleans and disinfects. Allow this process to occur for two to three minutes. The green color can leave your body however you choose but you may find it leaving through the hands and feet.

Now change the color to a crystal clear vibrant blue. This is a healing color and kills or transforms the disease or infection. Allow the whole part of the body involved or the whole cell to be bathed in a continuous, endless stream of this light for another two to three minutes. Next bring in a crystal clear pink-mauve color. This color restores your ill body or the cell back to what it was before you became ill.

Finally bring in a translucent white light tinged with gold. This light brings perfection to your body and transforms it to perfection, filling it with vitality and new life.

While you are doing this meditation try and experience the feelings that happen when you use the different colors and the changes that actually occur in your body whilst you are doing the meditation. It may take some time for you to experience these feelings, for others the appreciation will be instantaneous. Remember though, that if you haven't used your mind like this before, it takes regular practice to do it well.

If you already meditate regularly you may by now be starting to use other parts of your mind. You may be able to experience your electromagnetic field and thus tap into other dimensions of consciousness to work on healing yourself.

Meditation or healing power: science or fantasy?

Some people will regard most of this chapter, and especially the sections on meditation, as fanciful mumbo-jumbo. Maybe you're happy reading what a doctor and STD researcher has to say about viruses and vaccines, but hearing her opinions on meditation and affirmation makes you uncomfortable. I can understand that.

Western culture is traditionally suspicious of phenomena it cannot see and measure. Anything which is intangible is regarded as somehow not real. One of the attractions of Eastern cultures to some people is their greater emphasis on spiritual and mental matters. The Western emphasis on scientifically demonstrable reality and the Eastern emphasis on spiritual experience often seem to conflict.

Increasingly though the battlegrounds are giving way to areas of agreement. The physical benefits of meditation for instance are now being scientifically documented. Acupuncture has become an accepted part of mainstream medical practice, and doctors are becoming interested in other 'alternative' approaches to healing.

The simple fact is that there is a lot goes on in the body and especially the mind that we have scarcely begun to understand.

Another simple fact is that meditation works. It is scientifically proven that it reduces stress. Why it works may be open to debate. Perhaps there is some underlying scientific factor that has not yet been realized. Perhaps in the future this factor will be distilled into a convenient tablet you can take with your morning coffee. Perhaps.

For the moment, I am content to observe that meditation and visualising and drawing and affirmations all help the healing process, just as do exercise and rest and antibiotics and vaccinations.

My aim as a doctor is to heal, and I will use whatever techniques work best in achieving that, regardless of whether they fit preconceived Western or 'alternative' notions.

My aim as a doctor writing this book is to give you the information you need to best look after your own sexual health. Whether you like it or not, I would be remiss if I didn't tell you that there is increasing evidence that a whole range of non-medical techniques are very important elements in the campaign for personal healing and health. If you want to do the most to improve your health, which is what this chapter is about, then you will use all the techniques available to you.

Fortunately it does not seem to matter whether you 'believe' in meditation or not: if you just do it, regularly and with full concentration, you will get the rewards. What else is there in life that will reward you even if you don't believe it? At least try it.

Altered lifestyle

To maintain health or become healthy most of us have to alter our current lifestyle to a less frenzied pace that allows us to rest, to exercise regularly and to eat, consistently, food that is good for us. Our lives need to balance work, play and rest.

Lifestyle changes like this are always difficult to achieve and to maintain. You have to work at them. You need discipline and determination. Sometimes you will slide back and have to pull yourself up again. I can't offer you any easy fix for this: it is going to be hard work.

Only you can do it. Whether you choose to do it or not will depend on how much you want to be healthy.

FURTHER READING

Sexually Transmitted Diseases Holmes K K, Mardh P, Sparling P F, Wiesner P J, Cates W, Lemon S M, Stamm W E. 2nd Edition McGraw -Hill Information Services Company 1990. ISBN 0-7-029677-4.

Venereal Diseases King A, Nicol C, Rodin P, Bailliere Tindall. 1980, ISBN 0 7020 0816 8

Venereological Medicine Willcox R R, Willcox J R, Grant McIntyre Ltd, 1982, ISBN 0 86286 001 6

Sexually Transmitted Diseases A Textbook of Genitourinary Medicine GW Csonka & JK Oates, Bailliere Tindall 1990. ISBN 0-7020-1258-0

Fundamentals of Obstetrics and Gynaecology Volume 2 D. Llewellyn-Jones. 4th edition Faber and Faber 1986

The Clinician's Guide to Sexually Transmitted Diseases Levin et al, Year Book Medical Publishers Inc, 1987

Tropical Venereology Arya OP, Osoba AO, Bennett EI. Churchill Livingstone 1988.

1989 Sexually Transmitted Diseases Treatment Guidelines MMWR 1989; 38 S.

Genital Tract Infection in Women Ed M J Hare. Churchill Livingstone 1988 ISBN 0 443 03485 0

Handbook on sexually transmitted diseases National Health and Medical Research Council Australian Government Printing Service Canberra 1990 ISBN 0 644 10566 6

Getting Well Again Carl and Stephanie Simonton

Goodbye to Guilt Gerald Jampolski, Bantam, ISBN 0 553 34574 5

Love, Medicine and Miracles Bernie Siegel, Arrow, ISBN 0 09 963270 5

The Wealth Within Ainslie Meares, Hill of Content, ISBN 0 85572 086 7

Creative Visualisation Shakti Gawain, Bantam, ISBN 0 553 27044 3

Being Happy Andrew Matthews, Media Masters Singapore, 1990, ISBN 981 00 0664 0

You Can Heal Your Life Louise L Hay, Hayhouse, ISBN 0 937611 01 8

Do You Want To Meditate? Eric Harrison, Lamb Printers Pty Ltd, ISBN 0 646 04232 7

Peace of Mind Ian Gawler, Hill of Content, ISBN 0 85572 167 7

The Fine Arts of Relaxation, Concentration and Mediatation Joel Levey, Wisdom, ISBN 0 89171 040 1

GLOSSARY

(A separate glossary of slang terms follows this glossary.)

A

abstinence To go without sexual activity of any sort. To abstain from sex.

abortion Expulsion of the fetus either by natural events or induced before 28 weeks of pregnancy.

abscess A collection of pus in a localised area.

acanthosis Overgrowth of a special layer of cells in the skin.

Accu-Jac A sophisticated male masturbation device. It has a vacuum pump that connects to a sleeve that is put over the penis and allows a sucking movement.

acute In the context of disease means of sudden onset.

acyclovir A drug which stops the herpes simplex virus multiplying and which is used to treat some people with genital herpes.

adenocarcinoma A cancer of glandular tissue.

AIDS Acquired Immune Deficiency Syndrome. The final stages of infection with HIV where the body's immune system has been severely damaged.

anemia A condition of the blood which alters the red blood cells to commonly make either less of them, or the cells to be an abnormal shape.

anaerobic Able to grow without oxygen.

anal canal The part of the rectum (back passage) that is closest to the anal sphincter.

anal intercourse/anal coitus Sexual intercourse where a penis is inserted into the anus.

anal sphincter A circular muscle that closes the anal canal.

aneurysm A swelling, a little like a balloon, on a blood vessel.

angina Pain in the heart due to lack of oxygen. This is commonly due to narrowing of the blood vessels by cholesterol and fat deposits.

antibody Protein produced by the body in response to toxins or foreign organisms.

aorta The blood vessel that carries oxygenated blood from the heart to the rest of the body.

aortic regurgitation Inadequacy of the aortic valve that allows blood that has been pumped out of the heart to leak back.

antibiotic Drug that kills bacterial infections.

antibiotic resistance Normal antibiotics no longer work and new antibiotics have to be used. Often when antibiotic resistance occurs, resistance to more than one antibiotic occurs.

antibody A protein made by the body to fight against something the body thinks should not be there.

anus The opening on the surface of the body of the last part of the digestive system (rectum or anal canal).

arthritis Inflammation of a joint.

asymptomatic infection Infection which causes no symptoms so that the person is unaware they have the infection. The disease is still there, it can cause damage to the infected person and they may pass it on.

atrophic cellular changes Distortion of the cells due to dryness and hormonal changes. This may happen in women after menopause (when the periods have ceased) and there are low levels of the female hormone oestrogen.

autopsy A procedure where a body is examined after death to find out why the person died.

B

Bacillus of Döderlein The most common bacteria in a healthy vagina in a woman who is old enough to have children. It turns the glycogen in vaginal cells into lactic acid.

bacteria A microscopic organism which can cause infection. It is usually round or cigar shaped. On average 500 would stretch across a pinhead. Bacteria are living cells which can divide to reproduce themselves. Whether or not they actually cause infection depends on the type of organism, where in the body they are living, and the immune defence system of the person. See also *virus*.

bacterial prostatitis Bacterial infection of the prostate gland causing inflammation.

bacterial vaginosis An overgrowth of certain bacteria within the vagina which can cause disease.

balanitis Inflammation of the head of the penis.

balanoposthitis Inflammation of the head of the penis and the part of the penis under the foreskin or just below the head.

Bartholin's glands Glands which make a lubricant for sexual intercourse at the opening of a woman's vagina.

basal cells The name of the bottom layer of cells in the skin.

biopsy An operation to cut out a part of the body usually to find out what the problem is. This can be a big thing to have done or a very small thing.

birth canal Another name for vagina.

bisexual A term which means a person who gets sexual pleasure from both men and women. Both men and women can be bisexual.

bladder A distensible sac. Usually the term refers to the part of the body that stores urine before it is ready to be released from the body.

Bowenoid papulosis A skin condition that occurs on the genitals of men and women.

C

caesarean section (delivery) An operation to deliver the baby via the abdomen.

Calymmatobacterium granulomatis The bacterium which causes the disease donovanosis (granuloma inguinale).

Candida albicans A yeast-like fungus which causes candidiasis.

carunculae myrtiformes The remains of the hymen.

CD₄ cells A type of T-cell called helper cells.

celibacy/chastity Total avoidance of any form of sexual activity with another person.

cerebral palsy Spasticity of the body due to brain damage at birth.

cervicitis Inflammation of the cervix.

cervix Neck of the uterus (womb).

cervical canal A tube in the cervix which joins the vagina to the uterus cavity.

cervical ectopy An increased number of cells from the cervical canal on the outside of the cervix. This can be seen by doctors when they look at the cervix though a speculum.

cervical os The opening of the cervical canal on the surface of the cervix.

chancre The ulcer which occurs in the first stage of syphilis.

chancroid An infectious sexually transmitted disease that causes ulcers.

chemotherapy Treatment of the body with powerful drugs. When used to treat cancer these drugs often kill some sensitive parts of the body that then have to grow back again after treatment.

chlamydia The disease due to *Chlamydia trachomatis* or other members of this organism's family.

Chlamydia trachomatis The organism which causes genital chlamydia infection.

cholecystitis Inflammation of the gall-bladder.

chronic Continued for a long time.

cilia Something that looks like a tiny hair on the surface of a cell. These hairs are able to make movements.

CIN Cervical intraepithelial neoplasia. Changes within cells that suggest that cancer may possibly develop.

circumcision An operation to remove the foreskin or prepuce of the penis.

cirrhosis Scarred liver due to long term damage.

CIS Carcinoma-in-situ. Cancer in cells that has not spread beyond the cells.

clap   Slang word for gonorrhea.

clitoris   Part of the female sex organs that is extremely sensitive and swells up like the penis during sexual stimulation. It lies just below the part where the two labia minora join.

clue cells   Vaginal wall cells coated with bacteria which give the cells a particular appearance under the microscope.

cofactors   Events which facilitate something happening.

colposcope   A magnifying instrument with a light in it which is used mainly to examine the cervix and other parts of women's sex organs. The procedure is totally painless and is done with the woman awake. A speculum is used so the cervix can be seen.

colposcopy   The procedure of looking through a colposcope.

columnar epithelium   Tall cells which line many of the internal surfaces of the body.

condom   A sheath usually of rubber which is worn over the erect penis during sexual intercourse either to reduce the chance of infection, or to catch the sperm to prevent pregnancy occurring. The failure rate can be as high as 15%. Reasons for failure can be forgetting to put one on, tearing, slipping or bursting.

condylomata   A lump or tissue outgrowth you can see or feel.

condylomata accuminata   Genital warts.

condylomata lata   Warts due to syphilis.

cone biopsy   A biopsy of the cervix that takes out the centre part including the endocervical canal.

congenital malformation   An abnormality that exists before or at birth.

congenital syphilis   The infection which babies are born with if their mothers have syphilis which is untreated during pregnancy.

contagious   Infectious.

coronal papillae   Glands that grow around the edge of the head of the penis (corona glandis) and which are commonly mistaken for warts.

coronal sulcus   The furrow that occurs just below the head of the penis underneath the coronal papillae.

corpora cavernosa   The parts inside the penis that fill up with blood when an erection occurs.

cotinine A substance found in cigarette smoke.

Cowper's glands Special glands in men that open into the urethra of the penis.

crab louse The small organism called Phthirus pubis that causes crabs and causes the medical illness called pediculosis pubis. The infection is most commonly spread through sex.

crotch The part of the sexual anatomy in either men or women that is between the top of the legs.

cryosurgery Treatment by freezing.

cunnilingus A form of oral sex where the vulva, clitoris and vagina are stimulated by the tongue or mouth.

cystoscope A special instrument with a light that is used for looking inside the urinary bladder.

cytomegalovirus A virus that belongs to the herpes family. It is a very common infection commonly occurring in people who are unaware they are infected.

D

dermis The supporting layer for the skin.

dermatitis Inflammation of the skin.

diabetes This is usually taken to mean diabetes mellitus which is a disease in which blood sugar levels in the body are too high.

diathermy A medical treatment that uses electricity to burn the part of the body which needs to be removed.

dilatation and curettage An operation which dilates the cervical os so that an instrument can be passed through the endocervical canal. This instrument is then used to scrape off the lining of the uterus.

disseminated infection Infection which is widespread throughout the body.

donovanosis (granuloma inguinale) A sexually transmitted disease caused by the bacterium *Calymmatobacterium granulomatis*.

douche Fluid placed inside a body cavity by a bag or tube. Usually the term is used to refer to douching of the vagina which in effect means rinsing out the vagina.

ductus deferens Vas deferens. An excretory duct of the testis and an extension of the epididymis.

dysmenorrhea Pain and or cramps in the back or lower abdomen during menstruation.

dyspareunia Pain in women caused during sexual intercourse. This can be superficial due to problems at the opening of the vagina, or deep where it can be due to PID or the position of sexual intercourse.

dysplasia A cell with an abnormal nucleus (computer control part of the cell) surrounded by normally developed cell parts. Normally all parts of a cell grow together, but in dysplasia the nucleus and surrounding part of the cell grow at different rates.

E

ectopic pregnancy A pregnancy which occurs outside of the normal place which is in the uterus. Ectopic pregnancies commonly occur in the fallopian tubes.

ejaculate The fluid which is ejected from the penis during sex. Also, the act of ejaculating this fluid, which is usually associated with orgasm in the man.

EMLA 1:1 oil/water emulsion of lignocaine and prilocaine 5%. This is a cream that anaesthetises the skin without an injection having to be used.

endocervical canal The tube which links the vagina to the uterus through the cervix.

endocervix The lining of the endocervical canal.

endometritis Inflammation of the uterus.

epidemiological treatment Treatment given to the sex partner of someone who has tested positive for a sexually transmitted disease, just in case they have the infection too.

epididymis A sausage shaped structure made of convoluted tubules which is attached usually to the back of the testis and goes to the vas deferens.

epididymitis Inflammation of the epididymis.

epithelial Of the epithelium (skin).

epithelium Closely layered sheets of cells which make up the skin which covers the whole of the body.

epiglottitis Inflammation of the epiglottis which is found at the back of the tongue and stops swallowed food from going into the wind-pipe.

F

feces Excrement.

fallopian tubes Part of the female sexual anatomy. These are two tubes about 4 inches long which go from the front sides of the uterus near the top to the ovary on each side.

fellatio A form of oral sexual intercourse in which the penis is stimulated by either the tongue, lips or being placed in the mouth.

Fitz-Hugh-Curtis syndrome An illness caused by *Chlamydia trachomatis* or *Neisseria gonorrheae* that causes inflammation of the lining of the liver and mimics gallstones.

fomites Inert objects such as clothes or instruments which are able to pass on infection.

Fordyce's spots White spots found on the penis just below the head of the penis. Sometimes they can be more widespread.

foreskin The prepuce. A fold of thin skin which covers the neck and head of the penis.

fossa navicularis The end part of the urethra in the penis.

fourchette The part of the female sexual anatomy where the labia minora (inner lips of the vulva) join at the bottom.

frenulum A fold of skin or mucous membrane. The frenulum of the prepuce is on the underside of the penis and runs from the head of the penis to the prepuce.

fundus The bottom of an organ. Often used to refer to the rounded widest part of the uterus, but the term can be used for other parts of the body such as the stomach.

fungus A plant without chlorophyll.

G

Gardnerella vaginalis A normal organism in the vagina of many women. Some people use this term to mean the disease bacterial vaginosis.

general paresis An advanced stage of syphilis called neurosyphilis where the patient has delusions and has other forms of nerve damage.

genetic Inherited. Other meanings are to do with birth, reproduction, or congenital abnormalities.

genital anatomy The sex organs of the male or female that are used for sexual activity.

genital wart A wart that has a predilection for the genitals.

gland A collection of cells that make fluids called secretions.

glandular fever An infection due to the Epstein-Barr virus which is a herpes virus and commonly affects young adults, causing fever, swollen lymph nodes and a sore throat. Also called infectious mononucleosis or kissing disease.

glans penis The last part of the penis commonly called the head of the penis.

glycogen Animal starch. Iodine on cells full of glycogen makes them go a deep red-brown color.

gram negative diplococci The appearance of certain bacteria including the gonorrhea organism under the microscope when a special stain called a gram stain has been used.

granuloma An excessive growth made of granulation tissue. Granulation tissue is made by the body to repair cuts and ulcers.

granuloma inguinale (donovanosis) A sexually transmitted infection due to the bacteria *Calymmatobacterium granulomatis*.

groin The groove where the upper thigh turns into the lower part of the abdomen.

Group B streptococcal infection A bacterial infection with group B streptococcus. This is a normal organism in some women.

gumma Growths in the late stage of syphilis called gummatous syphilis. These can occur anywhere in the body, but commonly occur in the skin or bones.

H

head of the penis Glans penis. The mushroom shaped end of the penis.

hepatitis Inflammation of the liver.

hepatitis B carrier Someone who has been infectious with hepatitis B for at least six months.

hepatitis B vaccination A series of injections to build your body's immunity to prevent you from becoming infected with hepatitis B.

hepatoma Cancer caused by long term infection with hepatitis B.

herpes Infection with the herpes simplex virus either type I or type II.

herpes simplex type I (HSV-I) Infection with one of the herpes family viruses called herpes simplex type I.

herpes simplex type II (HSV-II) Infection with one of the herpes family viruses called herpes simplex type II.

herpes virus A group of DNA viruses which are all related. These are herpes simplex virus, Epstein-Barr virus, cytomegalovirus, varicella zoster, and the newly discovered human herpes virus type 6.

heterosexual Sexual attraction to a person of the other sex.

histology The branch of science associated with the microscopic study of the body tissues.

HIV Human immunodeficiency virus, the infection that eventually progresses to group IV disease called AIDS.

homosexual Sexual attraction to a person of the same sex.

hormone A chemical substance made by one part of the body which travels to another part of the body to exert its effect.

HPV Human papillomavirus. The virus associated with wart infection.

hydrocele A collection of fluid around the testis.

hyfrecation A surgical process which involves burning the skin with a needle heated by an electric current, if high voltages are used, or destruction of tissue like a laser by evaporation of intracellular water, if low voltages are used.

hygiene The science of health.

hymen A membrane that stretches over the opening of the vagina, partially closing it.

hysteroscopy A procedure in which an instrument with a light at one end is inserted into the cavity of the uterus.

I

immune system The body's defences against illness which includes special cells and proteins called antibodies.

immunodeficiency A defect in the ability of the body to fight infection.

impotence Inability of the male to achieve or hold an erection to have sexual intercourse.

incubation The length of time it takes for illness to be diagnosed or cause symptoms once it has entered the body.

infectious When it refers to a person with an infection, it means they are able to pass that infection on to someone else. An infectious organism is one which is able to invade and spread in the host.

infertility Inability to have children. This can be due to either problems with the man or woman.

inflammation The reaction produced by the body in response to damage or infection.

inguinal The groin region.

intercourse A term which commonly means sexual intercourse where the penis is placed inside a part of the body.

introitus The opening of a cavity within the body such as the vagina. Vaginal introitus means vaginal opening.

IUD Intrauterine contraceptive device.

J

Jarisch-Herxheimer reaction A reaction that can occur when syphilis is treated. There may be a temperature, headache or general feeling of being unwell. It rarely lasts longer than two days and is due to the spirochaetes (organism which causes syphilis) being killed.

K

Kama Sutra A Hindu book on love and sex. It describes a large number of sexual intercourse positions.

Kaposi's sarcoma A growth of the cells which line blood vessels. There are several types, one of which is thought to be due to a sexually transmitted organism that has not been discovered yet.

keratin A protein made by skin cells that makes the skin waterproof.

keratosis Thickening of the skin and abnormal maturation of cells in the skin. There are many causes of this skin condition.

kissing disease Infectious mononucleosis which is also known as glandular fever.

koilocytes Special changes in skin cells due to wart virus. The cell nucleus is pushed to one side and there is an appearance of a halo around the nucleus.

L

labia majora The two outside lips of the vulva.

labia minora The two inside lips of the vulva.

Langerhans cell A special cell in the skin which detects things going wrong. The number of these cells is reduced by smoking cigarettes.

laryngeal papillomatosis A growth on the vocal cords caused by a certain type of human papilloma virus.

laparoscope A tube-like instrument with a light at one end used for looking inside the abdomen. The hole made in the abdomen to let the instrument through is quite small.

leucoplakia White plaques. This can be due to infection with *Candida albicans* Sometimes it is due to thickening of skin cells in which case there is a chance of developing cancer if it is not treated.

leukorrhoea White discharge from the vagina.

LEEP Loop electrocautery excision procedure.

lesbian A female homosexual. A woman who is sexually attracted to another woman.

lesion An abnormality of the body such as an infection, area of injury or a growth such as cancer.

LLETZ Large loop excision of the transformation zone.

lubricant Something which makes things smooth and slippery.

lymph A special fluid made by the body carried in lymphatic vessels. These vessels eventually empty into the blood stream after the fluid has been filtered through lymph nodes.

lymph nodes (glands) Bean shaped lumps that occur at intervals on the lymphatic vessels. They often occur in groups.

lymphadenopathy Enlargement of the lymph glands.

lymphatic vessels The channels in the body that carry the lymph.

lymphocyte A white blood cell found in lymph glands and the blood.

lymphogranuloma venereum A sexually transmitted disease caused by a special serotype of *Chlamydia trachomatis.*

M

macroscopic infection An infection you can see.

malformation Abnormal development.

malignancy Cancer.

masturbation Stimulation of the sexual organs, usually either the penis or clitoris, causing sexual arousal of oneself.

menarche The time when a girl starts menstruating.

meningovascular To do with the blood vessels of the lining of the brain.

menopause The time in a woman's life when menstruation ceases.

metaplasia The changes that occur in cells as they change from squamous (flat) cells to columnar (tall) cells. The changes are brought about by the effect of the acid in the vaginal secretions on the endocervical columnar cells as they bulge out onto the cervix during pregnancy, puberty and at other times.

miscarriage Loss of pregnancy before 28 weeks.

molluscum contagiosum A skin infection usually sexually transmitted in adults caused by a virus called the pox virus. The lesions are white and waxy looking.

mons pubis The mound of fat that covers the top of the front part of the pubic bones where both sides meet.

mucus A secretion made by the body which has a protective action.

N

Neisseria gonorrheae The organism which causes gonorrhea.

neurosyphilis Syphilis involving the brain and nerves.

nicotine A substance found in cigarette smoke.

nonoxynol-9 A spermicide that also has activity against the human immunodeficiency virus.   Its effect against HIV will depend on many things including how much HIV it comes in contact with.

nonspecific urethritis (NSU) Inflammation of the urethra in men for which the cause is not known at the time the diagnosis is made.

O

opportunistic infection Infection by an organism that is normally within the body and causes no harm, but becomes a severe problem when the body's immune system is no longer working properly.

oral hairy leukoplakia An infection of the mouth in people with AIDS that is thought to be caused by the Epstein-Barr and human papilloma virus.

oral sex Sex using the mouth, lips, tongue or throat. This can be kissing, licking, sucking, nibbling, biting, fellatio or cunnilingus.

organism A single living entity either animal or plant.

orgasm The peak of sexual excitement culminating in ejaculation in men and vaginal contractions in the female.

orifice Opening.

ovary A female sex organ near the uterus that produces eggs, from menarche to menopause, and also makes the female hormones oestrogen and progesterone.

P

PAP smear A test performed on the cervix to examine the cells on the cervix.

papillae Multiple small fine growths from a surface on or in the body.

papilloma A growth that occurs on a stalk on a surface of the body either inside or out.

parakeratosis Changes in the cells in the top layer of the skin, associated with wart virus.

PCR Polymerase chain reaction. A very sensitive technique that amplifies a protein so that it can be detected. Performed properly it can pick up one viruses in ten million cells. The technique needs to be done in special laboratories and there are still some problems with false positive results.

pediculosis pubis The sexually transmitted disease due to the crab louse called phthirus pubis.

pelvic inflammatory disease (PID) Inflammation of the fallopian tubes which may result in scarring of the tubes and consequent sterility.

pelvis The basin shaped ring of bone at the bottom of the trunk of the body. It also refers to the area bounded by the hip bones, sacrum and tail-bone at the back and pubic area at the front.

penetrative sexual intercourse Sexual intercourse in which one of the body's orifices is penetrated, usually by the penis.

penis The male sex organ that is cylindrical in shape and enlarges and becomes erect because of filling of spaces within it with blood.

perinatal Around the time of birth.

perineum The area between the vagina and anus in a female or the scrotum and anus in a male.

peritonitis Inflammation of the lining of the abdomen.

phallus Penis.

pharynx The back part of the mouth where both air and food go in. The pharynx extends above to the nose and below to the larynx.

PID Pelvic inflammatory disease.

PIN Penile intraepithelial neoplasia.

ping-pong infection A descriptive term which refers to a sexually transmitted disease being passed backwards and forwards between sex partners.

placenta The organ that is formed in pregnancy. It is attached to the wall of the uterus and forms into the umbilical cord that is connected to the fetus.

Pneumocystitis carnii An infection by a protozoa that causes pneumonia in people who are infected with HIV.

pneumonia Inflammation of the lung.

podophyllin A drug used to treat genital warts.

predisposing conditions Conditions which make it more likely for a person to develop a condition for example candidiasis.

pre-cancer The changes in cells that occur before cancer occurs. These changes are not cancer.

premature Early. Done before the due or proper time.

prepuce. Foreskin

primary There are several ways this word can be used: either to mean the first in a series or the most important.

primary syphilis The early stages of infection with syphilis.

prodrome The early symptoms that signal an infection. Often the symptoms will be different to that of the disease.

prophylactic Preventing disease.

prostate gland A gland in the male located around the neck of the bladder.

prostatitis Inflammation of the prostate.

protozoa A unicellular microscopic organism of the animal kingdom.

puberty The time at which the sex organs in boys and girls mature and become active.

pyosalpinx A collection of pus in a fallopian tube.

R

radiotherapy Treatment with ionising radiation.

rectum The end part of the intestines between the colon and anal canal.

recurrent infection More outbreaks of the infection after it has first occurred.

Reiter's disease An uncommon disease which affects both males and females and causes arthritis, eye problems and urethritis.

retrovirus A virus that contains an enzyme called reverse transcriptase. This enables it to make a DNA copy of its RNA.

risk The chance of damage or infection that can result in harm.

S

safer sex Sexual activity that reduces the risk of acquiring a sexually transmitted disease.

salpingitis Inflammation of the fallopian tubes.

Sarcoptes scabiei The organism which causes scabies.

scabies An infectious disease of the skin caused by the mite Sarcoptes scabiei.

scrotum or scrotal sac A bag of skin that contains the testes, epididymis and the lower parts of the spermatic cords. It is located at the root of the penis near the perineum.

sebaceous glands Glands that produce the fatty secretion called sebum.

secondary Taking second place. Sometimes it can be used to mean a spread of cancer to another place in the body.

secondary syphilis Further active infection with syphilis which happens after the first stage and before the infection becomes quiet.

seminal vesicles A pair of hollow tube like structures located near the prostate gland that make seminal fluid and empty into the vas to form the ejaculatory duct.

seroconversion time The length of time it takes for detectable antibodies to be made in the body once the infection has occurred.

seropositive Antibodies against the infection which can be found by special tests on the blood.

sex The characteristics that distinguish between men and women. The term can also mean the act of having intercourse.

sexual intercourse A term which means coitus, or sexual activity that usually involves penetration of the body by the penis.

sexually transmittable disease (STD) An infection that is caught by sexual activity. Intercourse does not need to occur for some infections to be passed on.

smegma The sebaceous secretion produced by glands around the head and neck of the penis.

spasticity Stiffness of the muscles due to damage in the brain or spinal cord.

speculum An instrument which is used to look inside a tube in the body. Usually it means the instrument which is used to look in the vagina, called a vaginal speculum.

sperm Spermatozoa. The male seed.

spirochete A tiny snake like micro-organism.

squamocolumnar junction The join of columnar cells and squamous cells. This happens when outside skin changes to inside skin, or where the cells of some other parts of the body meet, such as in the anal canal, oesophagus and cervix.

squamous cell A plate-like or flat looking cell that lines body surfaces, in particular the skin.

squamous cell carcinoma Cancer of squamous cells.

squamous metaplasia Normal changes in cells of the cervix in the change over area of squamous to columnar cells.

STD Sexually transmitted disease.

STD examination The examination and tests done by a health worker to see if you have a sexually transmittable disease.

sterility Inability to fertilise the ovum to cause pregnancy.

stratum corneum The outer layer of the epidermis (skin) which is made of dead, scaly cells.

stratum granulosum The skin layer second from the top.

stratum spinosum The skin layer second from the bottom.

stratified squamous epithelium Flat cells occurring in many layers.

subclinical infection An infection you can't see with the naked eye.

superinfection Infection with one organism which then becomes superinfected with other disease-causing organisms.

symptom Awareness of a disturbance in a bodily function.

syphilis A sexually transmitted disease caused by the organism *Treponema pallidum*.

T

tabes dorsalis A form of neurosyphilis (late stage syphilis) which damages the brain, spinal column and nerves.

T cell A type of white blood cell in the immune system.

tertiary The third in a series.

testicle Testis.

testis The male sex organ which is suspended in the scrotum by the spermatic cord. The left testis usually hangs lower. Spermatozoa are made in the testis.

testes Plural of testis.

tertiary syphilis The last stages of syphilis where it may affect the skin and bones, heart and brain.

threads Strings of protein formed in the urethra when there is urethritis.

thrush (candidiasis) Infection with the yeast *Candida albicans*.

tonsils A collection of lymph tissue on each side of the pharynx (back of the mouth).

tonsillitis Inflammation of the tonsils.

transition zone The area on the cervix where cancer is most likely to arise due to exposure to the acid in the vagina.

Treponema pallidum The organism which causes syphilis.

Trichomonas vaginalis A protozoa which causes the infection called trichomonas. The organisms when they are seen are sometimes called trichomonads.

trichomoniasis The sexually transmitted infection due to the organism *Trichomonas vaginalis*.

tubal infertility Inability to become pregnant because of malfunction of the fallopian tubes.

tubal ligation A surgical operation to cause sterility by blocking the fallopian tubes by tying or cutting them.

Tyson's glands Glands on the head of the penis.

U

urethra The tube through which urine passes from the bladder.

urethritis Inflammation of the urethra.

urethroscope An instrument with a light at the end used for looking inside the urethra of the penis.

urinary tract infection Infection of the bladder, urethra or kidneys. Usually the term means infection of the bladder.

uterus Hollow, thick-walled muscular organ in a woman where the baby grows. If the woman is not pregnant the lining of the uterus is shed each month causing menstruation.

V

vagina The tube in a woman that goes from the vaginal opening (introitus) to the uterus. The cells which line the vagina are multiple layers of squamous epithelial cells.

vaginal acidity The vagina normally is acid with a pH of less than 4.5.

vaginal ecosystem The normal balance of organisms and pH that occurs in health.

vaginitis Inflammation of the vagina.

vas deferens Ductus deferens. The tube that carries the sperm from the epididymis to the area near the prostate. It joins the seminal vesicles to form the ejaculatory duct.

vasectomy An operation on the male to make him infertile. The ductus deferens is tied or cut. Often this is done under local anaesthetic.

venereal disease (VD) Diseases transmitted by sexual intercourse.

venereal warts Genital warts.

VD Venereal disease.

viruses The smallest of the disease causing organisms, viruses live inside the cells of a person's body. They cannot live outside of cells. Whether or not they actually cause infection depends on the type of organism, where in the body they are living, and the immune defence system of the person. See also *bacteria*.

vulva The part of the female sex organs which consists of the labia majora and minora, clitoris, mons pubis, and vaginal introitus.

W

wart An overgrowth of skin cells causing a lump that can be either seen or felt.

womb Uterus.

Y

yaws A skin and bone infection caused by a spirochete called Treponema pertenue that looks exactly like the one which causes syphilis. The changes in the blood with yaws are exactly the same as the changes in blood that happen with syphilis.

Z

zidovudine A drug available to stop the human immunodeficiency virus multiplying.

GLOSSARY OF SLANG TERMS

There are slang terms for just about everything to do with sex. Shakespeare used 1,500 words or phrases with sexual meanings. Some slang terms are simply euphemisms, coined to avoid the embarrassment of using the proper word. Others are intentionally derogatory, intended to insult women, some neighbouring race, or people with atypical sexual habits. The use of slang often indicates ignorance of the correct terms and often ignorance of the anatomy and functions referred to. Most slang terms are regarded in varying degrees as at least impolite and sometimes obscene, but these judgements differ from group to group and can change over time. Slang also has its fun side, and sometimes it shows great inventiveness.

Whether it is approved of or not, slang will continue to be used in just about any context where sex is discussed. Here is a brief listing of some of the more common words you might encounter. I've grouped them rather than defining each term. Slang words are often imprecise in their meanings. Interpretations will differ from group to group and sometimes be very different.

The word *fanny*, for example, refers to the buttocks in the US, but to the vulva in Australia. A *'pat on the fanny'* will be interpreted rather differently in the two cultures.

anal intercourse active, ass-fuck, break and enter, buttfuck, bumfuck, chocolate speedway, enter from behind, force fuck, German vice, Greek (the Greek way), gut fuck, Italian culture, insertee, inserter, 99 (ninety-nine), Oscarize, passive, ram job, round eye (to get some round eye), sexual analism, 66 (sixty-six), take it from behind, Turkish culture.

anilingus ass-blow, ass licking, brown job, rimming, ringing, ream.

anus/buttocks a-hole, ass, asshole, backdoor, back passage, brown eye, bum, buns, exhaust pipe, eye, fanny (US only), freckle, khyber, manhole, nates, ring, round eye, tail, the big A, tush, wrong door.

bisexual AC-DC, bi, bi-gaited, bilingual, fence sitter, gate swinger, half and half, simulsex, swing both ways.

clitoris bud, button, clit, clitty, sensitive spot.

condom balloon, con, durex, franger, Frenchie, French letter, gumboot, Italian letter, loveglove, parachute, prophylactic, raincoat, rubber, safe, sheath, sleeping bag, mouse's sleeping bag, Wellington boot, wetcheck.

cunnilingus box lunch, dive, eat, eat a beaver, eat a furburger, eat at the Y, eat hair pie, eat hairburger, eat out, French, a French job, give head, go down on, go south, lick, mouth music, muff dive, oral coitus, oral sex, 69 (sixty nine), skin dive, vice versa (cunnilingus between two women).

erection blue vein, blue veined junket pumper, bone, boner, crack a fat, hard-on, lead in the pencil, stiff.

fellatio blow, blow job, cock-eating, cock sucking, deep throat, eat French, a French job, give head, go down on, go south, head, head job, mouth music, oral coitus, oral sex, play the flute, 69 (sixty nine), suck, ultimate kiss.

female sexual anatomy (general) affair, beaver, down under, downstairs, fanny (Australia), private parts, privates, snatch.

glans penis acorn, draw the blinds (draw the foreskin back over the glans penis).

heterosexual breeder, civilian, commoner, straight.

homosexual bent, bull dyke, bum bandit, butch, camp, daisy, dyke, diesel, faggot, fairy, friend of Dorothy's, fruit, gay, he-she, homo, in between, intermediate sex, nancy, Oscar (after Oscar Wilde), poof, poofter, queen, queer, she-male, shirtlifter, third sex.

male sexual anatomy (general) Adam's arsenal, affair, privates.

masturbation bat, bat off, finger, finger fucking, finger pie, frig, go it alone, hand job, jack off, jerk off, jill off, keep the census down, meet Mrs Palmer and her five daughters, play solitaire, play with yourself, pocket billiards, relieve yourself, self abuse, self pleasuring, self stimulation, toss off, the hand sisters, wank.

orgasm big O, climax, come, die, dump a load, go all the way, go over the top, little death, make it, get off, get your nuts off, get your rocks off, go off, O, shoot, shoot your load, spend, squirt.

penis Aaron's rod, banana, big brother, blow stick, cock, dick, dipstick, dong, donger, doodle, eye opener, hanger, jimmy, John Thomas, joint, joystick, ladies' delight, little brother, love pump, male member, male organ, meat, muscle, nob, pecker, percy, plonker, pills, pistol, pizzle, poker, population stick, prick, one eyed trouser snake, one eyed monster, organ, rod, schlong, schmuck, shaft, slug, solicitor general, the old-fella, tool, walloper, wand, weapon, wedding tackle, willie, winkle.

scrotum bag, sack.

semen cream, cum, spoof, sprog, spunk.

sexual intercourse act (the act), action, ball, bang, blow, boff, bonk, carnal knowledge, coit, coitus, congress, dip the wick, do it, drill, feed the pussy, frig, fuck, get a leg over, get inside someone's pants, get it on, get it together, get some, get laid, get your end in or away, get your oats, go all the way, go to bed with, how's-your-father, hump, indoor sports, intimacy, be intimate with, it, jive, last favour, lay, lie with, love making, make feet for children's stockings (or shoes), make love, make out, make it, mate, mating, nookie, number three, on the job, plonk, poke, poontang, put it to (someone), quickie, ram, roger, rut, score, scrape, screw, shaft, shag, stick (stick it to or in), two backed beast, to make the beast with two backs, sleep together, sleep with, tail (get some tail), the other.

sexually transmittable disease (STD) clap, dose (cop a dose), forget-me-not, full house (simultaneous gonorrhea and syphilis), pox, pizzle rot (balanitis), social disease.

testicles balls, ballocks, bollocks, cobblers, family jewels, goolies, knackers, marbles, nuts, rocks.

vagina bull's eye, centre of bliss, cockpit, cunt, dead end street, eye, fanny (Australia), fish, front door, front passage, front window, futz, garden of Eden, hair burger, hair pie, honey pot, main avenue, nookie, plum, pussy, real thing, tush, twat, twot.

vulva black forrest, bush, crack, crotch, crutch, flaps, fur, furburger, gash, lips, muff, pubes, pussy, sacred triangle, slice, slit.

INDEX

C

D

E

M

S

z